The
Chesapeake Bay
Cookbook

The Chesapeake Bay Cookbook

Rediscovering the Pleasures of a Great Regional Cuisine

John Shields
Photography by Jed Kirschbaum

Aris Books

Addison-Wesley Publishing Company, Inc.
*Reading, Massachusetts   Menlo Park, California   New York
Don Mills, Ontario   Wokingham, England   Amsterdam   Bonn
Sydney   Singapore   Tokyo   Madrid   San Juan*

Aris Books Editorial Offices and Test Kitchen
1621 Fifth Street
Berkeley, CA 94710
(415) 527-5171

Many of the designations used by manufacturers and sellers to dis-
tinguish their products are claimed as trademarks. Where those designations appear in this book and Addison-Wesley was aware of a
trademark claim, the designations have been printed in initial capital
letters (e.g., Old Bay seasoning, Tabasco sauce).

Library of Congress Cataloging-in-Publication Data

Shields. John (John Edward)
   The Chesapeake Bay cookbook : rediscovering the pleasures of a
great regional cuisine / by John Shields ; photography by Jed
Kirschbaum.
      p.   cm.
   "Aris books."
   ISBN 0-201-51808-2
      1. Cookery—Chesapeake Bay Region (Md. and Va.)   2. Cookery
(Seafood)   I. Title.
TX715.S5519   1990
641.59755'18—dc20   89-38687
                                                            CIP

Jacket design by Copenhaver Cumpston
Jacket photography by Jed Kirschbaum
Text design by Janis Capone Owens
Interior photography by Jed Kirschbaum
Technical illustrations by Pamela Manley
Illustrated map by Deborah Young
Set in 10 point Berkeley Old Style by NK Graphics, Keene, NH

ABCDEFGHIJ-VB-9543210
First printing, March 1990

*This book is dedicated in loving memory
to my grandmother Gertie Cleary, my teacher and friend.*

Photographs

· Contents ·

· Acknowledgments ·

The Chesapeake Bay Foundation is a group dedicated to preserving the ecology of the Bay and its tributaries. Its membership is 70,000 strong and growing all the time. For twenty-three years they have been involved in environmental education, environmental defense, and wetland conservation. Here, at a benefit for the foundation at Harrison's Chesapeake House on Tilghman Island, members demonstrate their musical talents by serenading the bluefish and "rocking" the Bay.

My sincere thanks to family, friends, and all the wonderful people of the Chesapeake Bay who so graciously opened their homes, hearts, and recipe collections to me.

A special tribute must be paid to the Chesapeake Bay Foundation and similar grass-roots organizations dedicated to the protection and preservation of this glorious national treasure, the Chesapeake Bay.

Additional thanks are in order to the many people who gave me their time, energy, and support during this undertaking. Words cannot express my gratitude to my sister Kathleen Komber, for her moral and word-processing support. I am indebted to my Chesapeake friend and guide Glenn Jordan, and to my other *Chesapeake Bay Cookbook* mentors Bernie Curtis, Denny Beattie, Donald Au Coin, Linda Gerson, the Aris/Addison-Wesley crew, and the whole gang "over to" PC Micros.

And finally, my love to all of the members of the Baltimore and San Francisco Bay fellowships, without whose encouragement and support this book would not have been possible.

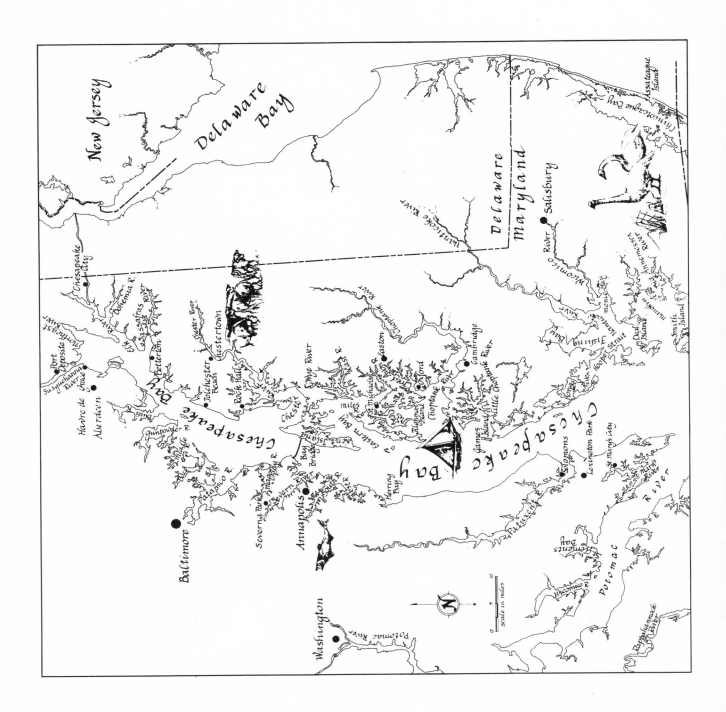

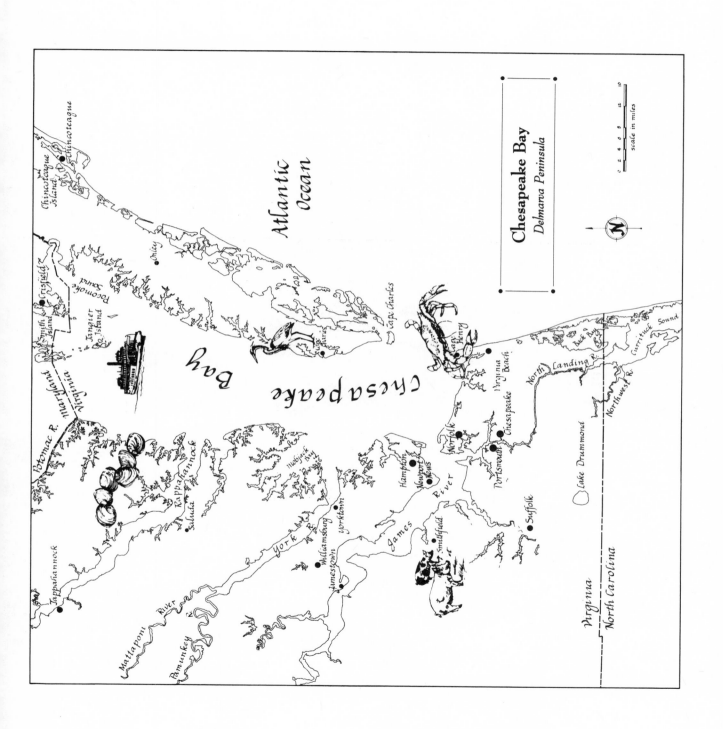

Chincoteague

Chincoteague Island

Crisfield

Onley

Pocomoke Sound

Smith Island

Tangier Id. Island

Maryland

Virginia

Potomac R.

Atlantic Ocean

Chesapeake Bay

Cape Charles

Cape Henry

Virginia Beach

Back Bay

North Landing R.

Currituck Sound

Northwest R.

Chesapeake

Lake Drummond

Norfolk

Portsmouth

Suffolk

Hampton

Newport News

Mobjack Bay

Rappahannock

Saluda

Urbanna

York River

Williamsburg

Yorktown

James River

Smithfield

Jamestown

Tappahannock

Mattaponi River

Pamunkey

Virginia

North Carolina

Chesapeake Bay
Delmarva Peninsula

N

0 2 4 6 8 10
scale in miles

· Introduction ·

The skipjack is the workhorse of the Chesapeake Bay oyster indus-try. These majestic two-sail, shallow-bottomed craft dredge and seed the Chesapeake oyster beds and are part of the only sail-powered commercial fishing fleet in the country. They first ap-peared on the Bay over a hundred years ago, and their design has changed little since. The main ports of the skipjack fleet are Tilghman Island, Deal Island, Cambridge, and Wingate.

Welcome to the Chesapeake Bay. Or in the words of my beloved Aunt Minnie, "Greetings, greetings, greetings!" You are invited to come over and visit with me and my friends for a spell while we guide you on a tour of our Bay region and its gastronomic wonders.

Story has it that when Captain John Smith guided his ship into the mouth of the Chesapeake Bay in 1608, he had no idea what was in store for him. From his writings, however, it's clear that it did not take him long to discover that he and his crew had happened upon a veritable Garden of Eden. "The fish were so thick, we attempted to catch them with frying pans," wrote Captain John.

In a sense, John Smith's exploration was the initial step in the development of today's Chesapeake Bay cuisine. Now by no means was Captain Smith's sportfishing party the first to discover the biologically rich Bay, thick with crabs, oysters, and clams. The first Keepers of the Waters were various Indian tribes, and they called it as they saw it: *Chesapeake,* in Indian dialect "Great Shellfish Bay." Judging from the amount of oyster shells found amassed at former Indian village sites, it seems these early Chesapeake inhabitants had quite a taste for shellfish.

After John Smith's exploration of the Bay, the neighborhood would never again be the same. The colonists came and began to build towns and ports along the banks of the Chesapeake. It was the first U.S. Interstate—a water highway—the only convenient way to travel between Annapolis, Baltimore, Washington, Norfolk, Williamsburg, and Richmond. Great ports blossomed along its shore, and it was soon teeming with ships bringing goods from Europe and carrying away the newly found riches, such as tobacco and spices. During all these grand goings-on, the new residents of the Chesapeake were developing a cooking style that remains with us today. Thank God!

Well, enough talk about history. What exactly is Chesapeake Bay cooking? Crabs, of course crabs, and

The Great Escape! A feisty blue crab (Callinectes sapidus) *makes its way back to the Bay. These small, aggressive, quick-moving crustaceans are the trademark of the Chesapeake Bay. The saltwater marshes and shoals of the Chesapeake offer the perfect habitat for this celebrated seafood commodity. Crabbing season is in full swing from May to October. More crabs have been harvested from the Chesapeake Bay than from any other body of water in the world.*

oysters and clams and all manner of fin fish, terrapins, ducks, geese, wild turkeys, pheasants, rabbits, chickens, deer, muskrats, squirrels, cattle, hogs, lamb. And, of course, crabs. If a visitor is asked what the Chesapeake

Bay is all about, the likely reply will be the Chesapeake Bay blue crab. To be sure, these beautiful swimmers are the hallmark of Chesapeake Bay cookery, and the locals do have a culinary love affair going with the feisty crustaceans. But to sum up Chesapeake Bay cooking as simply crabs does a great injustice to this varied regional cuisine.

To best illustrate the special qualities and flavors of the Bay, I have divided its Eastern and Western shores into six geographic regions, each with its own distinct culinary attributes. Following a brief profile of each area are recipes, from appetizers to desserts, that highlight the local fare. As a toast to each region, I end the recipe section with a beverage or libation typical of the area.

The densely populated Western Shore features Baltimore, Annapolis, and St. Mary's County, all in the state of Maryland. Along the Chesapeake's legendary Eastern Shore are Chestertown and the Tilghman Island Peninsula—both in Maryland—and the Mouth of the Bay, which includes Crisfield, Maryland, and Tangier Island and Norfolk, both in Virginia.

Each area contributes its own personality to a broader, but still distinct, Chesapeake Bay cuisine. There are the European-inspired dishes of Baltimore's ethnic enclaves, with such Mediterranean-inspired creations as Packets of Veal Stuffed with Crabmeat and Mozzarella. The plantation flavors of the southern counties are fashioned into the famous St. Mary's County Stuffed Ham. On the Eastern Shore, where you "catch the fish in frying pans," cooking is quick and simple—just the ticket for delectable Fried Soft-shell Crabs and Stuffed Rockfish. When thinking of Bay cooking, one must remember, too, just where the Chesapeake lays; it is south of the Mason-Dixon Line, and the flavors and methods of the Old South are ingrained in its culinary heritage.

Chesapeake cookery is one of the oldest and simplest of North America's regional cuisines. It has certain traits that shape its preparation, flavor, and presentation. The Bay's abundant shellfish are prepared in ways that preserve their delicate flavors. The classic crab cake calls for lumps of blue crabmeat, lightly bound and spiced, to produce a scrumptious mound of crab that can be lightly fried or broiled. Chesapeake oysters are served *au naturel*

on the half shell, or are bathed in hot milk and enriched with butter in a sublimely elegant stew. Pots of *manninose,* or soft-shell clams, are carefully cooked until the fragile shells open and release their briny juices, producing a delicious dipping broth. In Chesapeake kitchens ancestral crab pots hold steaming baskets of lively jumbo blue crabs for boisterous family crab feasts. All manner of local fish, fowl, and game are featured in a tremendous number of one-pot meals.

Early Chesapeake Bay kitchen duty was not an easy task. The hardships produced a provincial cooking style in which a primary pot contains all the ingredients for the meal. This necessitated the development of excellent timing skills: Each ingredient must be added at just the right moment so that one meal emerges from the pot, yet each food must retain its individual characteristics. Respect for the integrity of fish, fowl, meat, and the harvest of the field is a fundamental element of Chesapeake Bay cooking.

I was born and bred on the Bay, and I have always carried with me a love for the tastes and flavors of the region, even when I have lived far from my childhood home. I spent years away from my birthplace, preparing crab cakes, imperial crab, and shucking more Chincoteagues than I dare count for people unfamiliar with the riches of the Bay. Much of this took place at Gertie's Chesapeake Bay Cafe, the restaurant I opened in Berkeley, California, in 1983. For years, I was like an unofficial ambassador for Chesapeake Bay cuisine in the very heart of California's gastronomic capital. Then, in 1987, I sold Gertie's. I felt it was time to come home, to rediscover what it is that makes Bay cuisine unique and pleasurable, to reconnect myself with this body of water the Indians called Chesapeake. Now, back again at Gertie's as the

Executive Chef, with book in hand, I am once again a culinary ambassador.

I have tried to introduce the recipes of the Chesapeake through the words and images of the people who live around the Bay. The finest examples of Chesapeake cuisine are found in the kitchens of watermen, farmers, and the proprietors of small back-road inns and taverns. At the end of each regional section I have showcased a local personality who has created a menu that highlights the bounty and cooking style of the area.

The people of the Chesapeake are fun-loving, warm, welcoming, and even zany at times. They respect the ways and forces of nature and its impact on the Bay and their lives, and they live with a hopeful trust for the future. They accept life on life's terms. When they meet you, the important question is not what you do, but rather, who you are. This simplicity and honesty spills over into the cuisine, and an intense pride in the quality of the food is felt by everyone.

I remember as a small boy in Baltimore my grandmother Gertie's excitement with each approaching season and the treasures it promised for the table. We would marvel at the first asparagus of spring, breathe in the sweet fragrance of ripe Eastern Shore melons, and laugh at the antics of blue crabs as they escaped from overflowing bushel baskets. When my grandmother prepared the food, be it vine-ripened tomatoes or fresh-from-the-Bay rockfish, I was always aware of the quiet reverence she felt for these prized gifts.

This reverence is still felt by those of us who know the Chesapeake as a source of culinary abundance and pleasure. Now, however, we must be even more careful with how we treat this precious resource. It is a national treasure; we must not take it for granted. It is our treasure, and we have been entrusted with keeping its waters life-giving.

You are now invited to join the Chesapeake folk, to hear a few tall tales and sample recipes of friends and family. Some are fancy recipes and some are "just the way God intended it to be cooked."

Welcome to what we natives call the "land of pleasant living."

A Chesapeake waterman hand tongs for oysters in the cold, dark, morning hours of the Bay. The tongs are scissor-like rakes that collect the oysters from their beds. This traditional method of harvesting oysters requires long, hard hours of work often in the harsh winter. The life of a Chesapeake waterman is physically demanding and financially precarious, but this time-honored profession continues to be handed down from generation to generation.

· *Part I* ·
Tastes of the Bay

• A Feast of Crab •

*A Chesapeake icon, the blue crab finds its way not only onto dining
tables, but onto every conceivable manner of cup, glass, tee shirt,
sign, and billboard in the region.*

Blue crab is perhaps the most famous denizen of the Bay. To seafood lovers around the world, the Chesapeake is synonymous with these delectable crustaceans.

The Latin name for blue crab is *Callinectes sapidus,* which translates to "savory beautiful swimmer." And that they are! These crabs are a hallmark of Chesapeake Bay cuisine. They are also feisty little scrappers, so handle with care. I've seen many a bitten finger. Blue crabs are primarily available from May to October. During the winter months they burrow into the sandy bottom and the only way to reach them is by dredging. These winter crabs are poor quality, expensive, and full of sand. Let them sleep!

Blue crabs are referred to by several names, depending upon sex or stage of development. Male crabs are called jimmies and female crabs are sooks. Peelers are blue crabs about to begin the molting process, when they discard their old shells and then grow new ones.

From the time the old shells are discarded until the new ones have hardened, the crabs are called soft-shells, and they are a highly prized commodity. Seasoned crabbers can tell by markings on the hard shell when the crabs are about to molt. The crabs are placed in "floats," or holding pens, where they can be observed until their shells peel.

It takes approximately seventy-two hours for a new shell to form and harden. During this period the crabs are removed from the floats and sold live for immediate consumption or frozen for later use. Soft-shells are divided into grades according to size, from small to large: hotel, medium, prime, jumbo, and whale.

Hard-shell blue crabs are sold live or steamed. The majority are sent to "picking houses" on Maryland's Eastern Shore. The crabmeat is picked from the shells and the meat is graded.

LUMP is the very best meat money can buy: clean, big pieces with absolutely no shell or cartilage—*all* crab.

BACKFIN is the meat from the backside of the crab only. They are large pieces with low shell content.

SPECIAL identifies meat from the entire body of the crab, which includes both lump and flaky pieces. Higher in shell content, this type requires careful picking.

REGULAR meat comes from the entire body of the crab, but does not include lump meat. This is a flaky product that also requires careful picking.

CLAW is the dark, sweet meat. Excellent for soups and chowders, it also makes a very good, lower-cost crab cake.

The best crabmeat, of course, is that which is picked and sold fresh. High-quality frozen and pasteurized crabmeat (which has an extremely good shelf life) is available year-round, however.

Cooks use different types or combinations of types of crabmeat, depending upon the recipe. In general, lump and backfin are the most widely used for crab cakes or imperial-style dishes. To stretch the yield and lower the cost of the dish, some cooks will use half lump or backfin to half special or regular. The special and regular grades are excellent for dips, casseroles, fritters, and soups.

· A Chesapeake Bay Crab Feast ·

At Gunning's Crab House in Baltimore, crab pickers attending the
Baltimore Sun's Safe Driving Awards Crab Feast are poised, mal-
lets in hand, to attack a mountain of spicy, steamed crabs.

"Eh, hon. Wanna go out and eat some crabs tonight? I gotta cravin' for 'em like you can't believe. I bet ya I can eat a bushel myself!"

And with similar prodding going on all around the Bay, the masses make their summer pilgrimages to the Chesapeake's notoriously famous crab houses.

A few of these crab "hackeries" are fancy dinner spots, but nine out of ten have a club-basement motif, moved one floor up. They are lined with tables covered with heavy brown paper or out-of-date newspapers.

These crab joints are teeming with boisterous patrons, ready to party. They are staffed with a tribe of professional "girls," hair piled high, wing-tipped glasses, flying to the tables in orthopedic shoes. The waitresses,

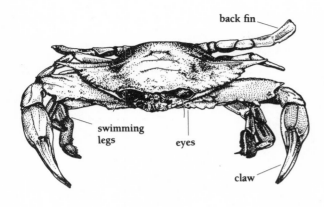

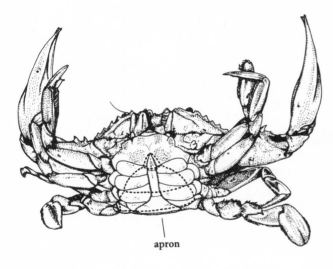

The shape of the apron on the underside of the crab, which is the first part of the crab shell that is removed in the picking process, distinguishes a male from a female. We have shown the shape of a female crab's apron with a dotted line superimposed over a male's apron.

their daughters, and their mothers have all been slinging crabs since the dawn of crustacean creation. The girls mean business and can handle the roughest, rowdiest customers by simply sliding their glasses to the ends of their noses and staring the troublemakers down. They also provide lightning-fast, table-side, crab-picking demonstrations for overwhelmed novices.

But crab houses are not the only spots for crab feasts. For most Chesapeake Bay families, the backyard crab feast is as much a tradition as Thanksgiving or Christmas dinner.

To an outsider these affairs often seem like an all-hell-has-broken-loose occasion. Several generations gather: Aunts, uncles, cousins, brothers, sisters, in-laws, outlaws, all jump madly about while bushel baskets of live crabs are loaded into the family crab pot. Children run, screaming, down lawns, pursued by renegade crabs that have escaped from overflowing baskets.

Out-of-towners complain to me that these feasts are too much work for too little crabmeat. Developing crab-picking skills does take time, and even after one learns how to pick a crab clean (see page 7), quantity of crabmeat is not the point. The crab feast is a Chesapeake social ritual. It is performed for the pleasure and bonding of family and friends. Talking and spinning tales are the main ingredients of a successful feast.

One favorite subject of conversation is former crab feasts. Tales of heroism and adventure. "Back in '48 all the crabs were at least ten inches across and heavy as horses. . . . Your Uncle Elmer could pick a crab clean as a whistle with one hand, while drinking down a mug of beer with the other without taking a breath. . . . 'Member that time when that crab got hold of Sis's toe, and she ran round the backyard, crab clamped onto the toe, like a bat outta hell?"

I was always particularly intrigued by Aunt Marg's tale of dearly departed Aunt Seal.

"Now, your Aunt Seal loved a good crab feast almost as much as she loved her pink Catawba wine.

"That last crab feast over Uncle Elmer's, she was a laughing and singing, 'I'm Gonna Wash That Man Right

Outta My Hair.' In fact, Elmer had to get her down off the table.

"Anyhow, I seen her polish off at least two dozen crabs and two bottles of pink Catawba. And she said that was just for starters. Thing that always got me was how she'd pile black pepper on the crabs and then suck it off her fingers. She just kept a-going, eating 'bout two, three more dozen crabs, piled with black pepper and two more bottles of pink Catawba.

"Round then Seal said she needed to run inside and take off her girdle. She didn't come back for quite some time, so Aunt Treasie went looking for her. Next thing I know, I heard Treasie screaming like a banshee. She found that poor dear Seal, stone-cold dead, sitting on the toilet. I thought my heart would break!"

The next hour would always bring the great family debate over what killed Aunt Seal: the black pepper or the pink Catawba.

Wherever you decide to hold your crab feast, you will need crab mallets, for cracking the shell of the legs; a paring or crab knife, for digging and cutting into hard-to-get-at spaces; plenty of cold beer; and ginger ale for the kids and beer abstainers.

If you're new at this, sit next to a pro and let the feast begin!

Steamed Blue Crabs

Serves 3 or 4

This is my family's recipe for steaming crabs. You'll need a large pot with a tight-fitting lid and a raised rack on the bottom, so that the crabs do not sit in the steaming liquid.

When choosing crabs for steaming, make sure they're alive and kicking. Jimmies (male crabs), at least five inches across, are preferable for feasts. When faced with a choice, always take a smaller, heavier crab, as opposed to a larger, lighter one. Allow six to eight crabs per person to start.

2 bottles (12 ounces each) beer, allowed to go flat
2 cups distilled white vinegar

2 dozen live blue crabs
½ cup Old Bay seasoning
6 tablespoons salt

Pour the beer and vinegar into the bottom of a large pot with rack in place. Bring to a boil.

Arrange the crabs on rack in layers, coating each layer with Old Bay and salt. Cover tightly and steam 20 to 25 minutes, or until crabs turn bright red.

No platters are necessary for serving. Just dump the crabs unceremoniously on a newspaper-covered table and "go-to-town-Miss Murphy!"

PICKING AND CLEANING CRAB

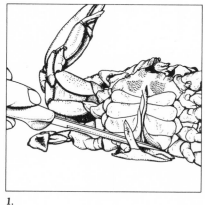

1.

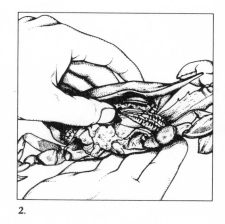

2.

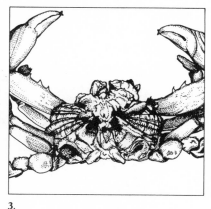

3.

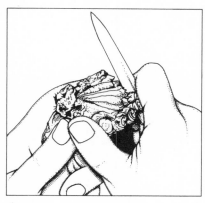

4.

5.

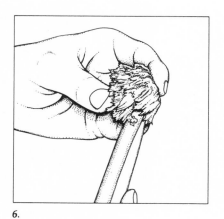

6.

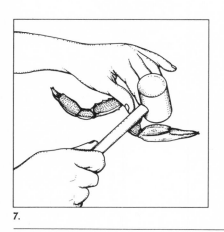

7.

1. With knife tip or finger remove apron.

2. Remove top shell with thumb or tip of crab knife or paring knife.

3. Pull off claws and set aside for eating later. Remove swimming legs and back fins. Cut away eyes and remove gills. Scrape out greenish matter (the devil), running through center of crab, but leave yellow "mustard."

4. With crab knife or paring knife, cut away edges around circumference of crab's body. Holding crab in two hands, break in half down the center.

5. Cut each half again horizontally to expose the chamber of crabmeat.

6. With tip of crab knife or paring knife, pick out lumps of crabmeat and enjoy.

7. With a mallet or handle of heavy table knife, crack claws and pick out meat. (Some folks like to use a crab knife during this process. Knife is placed across claw and driven into shell by mallet to crack it.)

• Seafood from the Bay •

*A bushel of Chesapeake Bay hard-shell clams harvested from the
waters surrounding Tangier Island. These mollusks are the basis
for many a hearty pot of stew or chowder. Although not as identi-
fied with the Bay as crabs or oysters, hard- and soft-shell clams are
an important component of the Bay's seafood bounty.*

The Chesapeake is the largest inland body of water on the Atlantic coast and its wealth is legendary. From its 4,600 miles of tidewater shoreline, watermen and sport fishermen set sail in search of shell-fish and fin fish. Previous generations spun tales of crabs with shell spans two feet across and of inlets so laden with rockfish a grown man could walk from one shore to another atop the fish.

Alas, urban encroachment has taken a toll that can be counted in the decrease in population of many fish, shellfish, and waterfowl varieties. The once seemingly limitless regenerative powers of the Bay have been put in jeopardy by industrial and waste pollution, the loss of acreage and deterioration of wetlands, and the overharvesting of many species. These and other factors have contributed to an ecological imbalance that, if allowed to go unchecked, could spell disaster for the Bay.

Fortunately, there has been an outcry from the residents of the Chesapeake and its tributaries to stop the madness. The result has been the founding of grass-roots community organizations and government agencies devoted to the restoration of the Bay. The Chesapeake Bay Foundation has been a shining example of the ability of dedicated people to come together and work for a common goal. The foundation has been instrumental in the creation and direction of a challenging conservation process that endeavors not only to reverse the damage already inflicted on the Bay, but also to initiate ecological guidelines to preserve the Chesapeake for future generations.

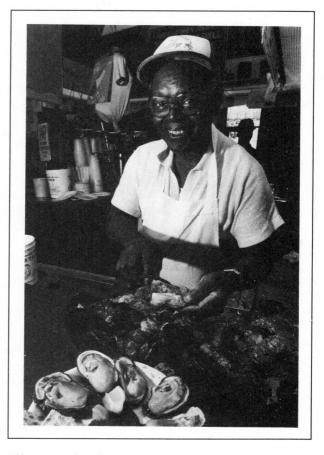

Eddie Tarver of Faidley's Seafood at the world famous Lexington Market is busy shucking a pile of Chesapeake oysters. Lexington Market houses dozens of stalls teeming with seafood, produce, meats, and dairy products. The market has changed over the years since its 19th Century beginnings, but surprisingly, many of the original family stalls still thrive in this Baltimore shoppers' wonderland.

CHESAPEAKE OYSTERS are hard to beat for delectable succulence! In the fall, when the crab pots are put away for the winter months, the oyster industry is gearing up for what many believe to be the "hardest, coldest job to be had."

Chesapeake Bay oysters are eagerly sought after by seafood distributors around the world. A hundred years ago there were countless varieties, including Choptank, Lynnhaven, Rappahannock; the list went on and on and on. True oyster connoisseurs could tell where an oyster had been harvested simply by its taste and texture. Today the natural beds are gone, seeding and transplanting having intermingled the varieties.

SHUCKING OYSTERS

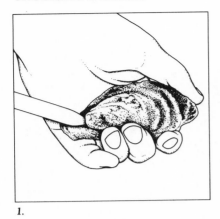

1.

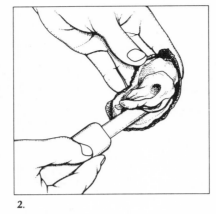

2.

1. This technique of shucking an oyster is known as the hinge method. The oyster is held in the left hand (for right-handers), and some people wrap a towel around the hand in case of a slip. The oyster knife is then pressed into the black mass between the upper and lower shell at the back of the oyster (the hinge). Twist the knife to completely open the shell.

2. Once the top shell has been removed, the oyster knife is used to dislodge the oyster from the bottom shell.

SHUCKING CLAMS

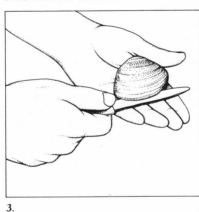

3.

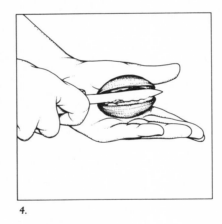

4.

3. To shuck a hard-shell clam, hold the clam in the palm of your hand with the hinge facing into the palm. Place the blade of a clam knife into the mouth of the clam and, using your fingertips, press the blade into the clam.

4. When the knife has entered the clam, twist the knife up and down (as shown) to fully open the shell. Dislodge the clam from the bottom shell with the clam knife.

The best-known Bay oysters are the Tangiers and Chincoteaques. These are almost always eaten raw—on the half shell with a squeeze of lemon—because of their wonderfully unique briny flavor.

The oyster season runs primarily from October to April. People used to believe that you couldn't eat oysters in months that did not include the letter *r*. That's not so. Oysters harvested during the winter are of a higher quality, however. In the warmer months the oysters are spawning, producing a dryer, slimmer meat.

On the Bay, oysters are enjoyed fried, steamed, roasted, or in stews and chowders. But real oyster lovers contend that the only proper way to feast on these tasty bivalves is raw.

BAY CLAMS come in a wide variety, but the locals keep it simple. They refer to them as either soft-shell clams (manninose or manos) or hard-shell clams; the latter group includes anything that's not a soft-shell.

Soft-shell clams, which are also called steamers, have

thin shells and an elongated body. They are readily identifiable by their protruding "snouts." Traditionally Chesapeake residents have not ranked them as good enough to eat, relegating them to the bait box. New Englanders vehemently disagree. For generations they have been importing vast quantities of the Bay's soft-shell clams for their clambakes and fried clams.

Chesapeake hard-shell clams include the popular cherrystone, Littleneck, and surf clam varieties. They are enjoyed raw on the half shell, steamed, fried, and in chowders and stews.

BLUEFISH, a Bay staple, is a strong-tasting, oily fish. Available year-round, it is most commonly grilled or baked. It does not freeze well and should be purchased only when very fresh. Its high fat content makes bluefish a good candidate for smoking.

CATFISH is ugly, but oh so good! Most catfish come from the tributaries and slow-moving creeks emptying into the Bay. Prime availability is during the summer months, although farm-raised catfish can now be found throughout the year. Frying is regarded by many cooks as the best way to prepare catfish, but baked or braised catfish is also good. Catfish can be substituted in recipes calling for perch and lake trout.

CHESAPEAKE CROAKERS, or hardheads, are fished mostly from Virginia waters. The tender fish is similar to that of a sea trout and is best fried or broiled.

The name croaker comes from an air-bladder condition that causes the fish to break wind, as it were, and make a sort of croaking sound. Croakers also have a stonelike knot on the top of their heads, thus the name hardheads.

EEL is the second-largest commercial fin fish in Maryland. They are not tremendously popular with local diners, however. Most of the catch is exported to Europe, where these oily-fleshed fish are highly prized. Locally, eels are used for crab bait. They are especially good smoked, but are also tasty when fried or braised.

FLOUNDER, of various types, are also fished from the Bay and are generally sold the year round. Mild-tasting, fine-textured flounder can be broiled or fried whole or filleted. It is an excellent stand-in for sole.

HERRING run up the Bay and into the tributaries in the spring. They are rather oily fish, and the most popular methods of preparation are smoked, salted, and pickled. Herring roe is eaten fried or baked.

LAKE TROUT, or whiting, have just one bone up the back, which make them easy to prepare. Locals refer to this mild-flavored fish as lake trout. It is favored for fish and chips and for neighborhood fish frys. Flounder, perch, or catfish fillets serve well in place of lake trout.

LARGEMOUTH BLACK BASS is available year-round, and is used as a substitute for rockfish in many local recipes. The flaky white meat lends itself well to fish stews and chowders.

NORFOLK SPOT is a small croaker with tender, delicate, mild-tasting flesh. Available in the summer months, the Norfolk spot tastes best when fried or broiled.

PERCH come in two varieties, yellow and white. They are fished in Bay estuaries the year around. The perch is an extremely popular local fish, with a sweet-tasting meat. It is generally panfried, baked, or broiled. Perch roe is a highly regarded delicacy. The sacks of roe are much smaller than those of shad, but can be prepared in the same manner.

ROCKFISH take their name from a local legend. Folks recall that these fish were once so plentiful in the waters of Rock Hall, Maryland, that they were virtually "jumping into the boats." Overfishing has resulted in the current ban on taking rockfish, traditionally the most popular Chesapeake fin fish, from Maryland waters. Also known as striped bass, the fish has slightly oily, white, flaky flesh with a marvelous taste. Rockfish are commonly baked whole and are sometimes stuffed. Largemouth black bass is an outstanding replacement while the rockfish population is replenishing itself.

SEA TROUT, or weakfish, is another tender, delicate, fine-tasting Bay fish. Small in size, it is usually sold whole and is most commonly fished near Crisfield, Maryland. Locals generally like it baked or broiled whole. Filleted sea trout panfries splendidly, however.

SHAD are perhaps the most sought-after fish of the Bay. They have a short-lived availability because they run only in the spring, primarily in March. Shad tend to be quite bony, but the locals have come up with a method of baking them for eight hours in lemon juice, during which time the bones miraculously disappear!

The legendary shad roe is the object of fanatical demand each spring and is a true Bay specialty. It is best when sautéed or broiled. Just don't overcook!

SHRIMP are enjoyed with much enthusiasm around the Chesapeake, but are not native to the region. Most of the shrimp used for Bay recipes are the medium to jumbo sizes fished from farther south in the Atlantic or in the Gulf of Mexico.

DIAMONDBACK TERRAPINS are small turtles that inhabit the Bay tributaries. They were quite abundant at one time. In recent years availability has drastically declined, however. The terrapin is one of the premiere delicacies of the Chesapeake. It has a strong flavor that one either dotes on or finds abhorrent.

· A Church Hall Fish Fry ·

*At St. Ann's Church Hall Fish Fry, Julia March of Baltimore serves
up a platter of fried fish with all the trimmings.*

As I walk in the front door of the old rectory at St. Ann's Church on Baltimore's Greenmount Avenue, beehivelike buzzing sounds are rising from the dark hallway ahead. Moving closer, my nostrils are greeted by the smells of fresh lake trout a-frying and pots of ham-scented greens a-percolating.

Reaching the kitchen, the only appropriate words that come to mind are Fats Waller's rambunctious lyrics, "this joint is jumping!" The girls, turned out in their colorful Sunday cooking aprons, are flying around the narrow kitchen, dipping trout in seasoned flour and laying them side by side in time-worn cast-iron skillets filled with bubbling hot oil. Plates, passed from one church-hall volunteer to another, are being piled high with mounds of spicy macaroni and cheese, potato salad, country green beans, and those melt-in-your-mouth greens—all of which the girls say are "surefire preventatives against pernicious anemia." And who can argue with that kind of medicine?

Peeking around the corner into the dining hall, I

see lines forming to stake out choice seats for this mildly spiritual culinary repast. These habitual fish-fry goers know from experience to come early in the day before the greens and beans run out. They go fast. Lips are smacking on the fine array of edibles; jaws are flapping out all the latest gossip on who's running with whom, and the physical deterioration and or improvement of grandmothers, fathers, nieces, nephews, aunts, and uncles. For what more could one ask? A friendly place to sit down and get a bellyful, plus the "411" on neighbors and friends.

In the far corner of the room, on a round, dark oak table topped with lace, are plates of all shapes and sizes bearing sweets: cakes, big and little, coconut topped and strawberry ladened; sweet potato pies; and pecan pies. Parishioners and friends make their way to these sweet treats, deciding on which of their favorites to choose. "Honey, I know I really shouldn't, but I'll just throw caution to the wind and maybe just loosen up my girdle a bit." That is the philosophy of the day.

Everyone is here to raise money for the church and the Lord—and perhaps to raise a few pounds on the scale. A small price to pay to be part of a good old-fashioned, fund-raising fish fry, the likes of which have been adding to the tills of churches and community organizations along the Bay for generations.

Come on over and join in. If you have too much ironing to catch up on, don't worry. They deliver!

Panfried Lake Trout

Miss Silvia's Potato Salad

Macaroni and Cheese

Fresh Greens and Ham

Southern Green Beans

Sweet Potato Pie

Pecan Pie

Strawberry Pound Cake with Strawberry Icing

Panfried Lake Trout

Serves 6 to 8

3 pounds lake trout fillets (see Note)
Milk, as needed
1½ cups yellow cornmeal
1½ cups flour
Salt, black pepper, and Old Bay sea-
    soning to taste

Vegetable oil, for frying
Lemon wedges and Tabasco sauce,
    vinegar, or Tartar Sauce (recipe
    follows), for accompaniment

In a shallow dish soak the trout fillets in milk to cover for one hour.

In a second dish, mix the cornmeal and flour together. Season with salt, pepper, and Old Bay.

Remove the fish from the milk one fillet at a time, letting the excess milk drip back into the dish. Coat well with the cornmeal mixture.

In a frying pan pour in oil to a depth of ½ inch and place over medium heat. When oil is hot add as many fillets as the pan will allow. Fry about 4 to 5 minutes on each side, or until golden brown. Remove the fish from the pan and drain well on paper towels.

Serve with lemon wedges, Tabasco sauce, and tartar sauce on the side.

NOTE: Catfish, Norfolk spot, or perch fillets may be substituted for the trout fillets.

Tartar Sauce

Makes 1½ cups

1 cup mayonnaise
½ cup dill pickle, finely chopped
¼ cup onion, minced

2 tablespoons chopped fresh parsley
1 tablespoon dill pickle juice

Mix all ingredients together in a bowl. Chill at least one hour before serving.

Miss Silvia's Potato Salad

Serves 6

6 medium potatoes, boiled and
  peeled
1 onion, finely chopped
3 stalks celery, finely chopped
¼ cup sweet pickle relish
2 tablespoons dry mustard

¾ to 1 cup mayonnaise
3 hard-cooked eggs, chopped
½ cup chopped fresh parsley
Salt and black pepper to taste
Paprika, for garnish

Cut potatoes in desired-sized pieces for salad and place in a bowl.

In a small bowl mix together the onion, celery, relish, mustard, and mayonnaise. Fold in the eggs and parsley. Pour over potatoes and mix well. Season with salt and pepper.

Just before serving, garnish with paprika.

Macaroni and Cheese

Serves 8 to 10

1 pound elbow macaroni
Salted water
6 tablespoons butter
6 tablespoons flour
3 cups milk
1½ teaspoons salt

½ teaspoon cayenne pepper
2 teaspoons dry mustard
Few dashes Tabasco sauce
2 cups grated sharp Cheddar cheese
2 eggs, beaten
Dried bread crumbs, for topping

Preheat oven to 375°F.

Bring a large pot filled with salted water to a boil. Add macaroni and cook until just tender. Drain and set aside.

In a saucepan melt the butter and whisk in flour. Cook a few minutes, taking care not to brown the flour.

Off the heat stir in the milk, salt, cayenne pepper, mustard, and Tabasco. Bring to a boil, stirring constantly. When the sauce thickens, simmer several minutes longer.

Off the heat stir in the cheese. When the sauce has cooled slightly, add the eggs and mix well.

Layer half of the macaroni in a buttered baking dish. Top with half of the sauce. Repeat layers. Sprinkle top with bread crumbs and bake 30 minutes, or until the top is brown and sauce is hot.

Fresh Greens and Ham

Serves 8

3 bunches collard, mustard, or turnip
  greens (about 3 pounds)
About 2 cups water
1 large onion, chopped

½ pound country ham, cut in 1-inch
  pieces, or 1½ pounds ham hocks
Salt and black pepper to taste
Few dashes Tabasco sauce

Remove stems and wash the greens well. Put into a large pot and add the water.

Add all remaining ingredients. Simmer very slowly until greens and meat are tender, 1½ to 2 hours.

If ham hocks have been used, pick off meat from bones and add back to greens before serving.

NOTE: The long cooking time for this dish and the green beans below is traditional, but you can alter cooking times to suit your taste.

Southern Green Beans

Serves 8

1 large onion, chopped
½ pound country ham, cut in 1-inch
  pieces

2 pounds green beans, trimmed
Salt and black pepper to taste
Dash red wine vinegar

Fill a pot with enough water to cover the beans. Add the onions and ham and bring to a boil.

Add the beans and cook slowly until tender, about 2 hours.

Pour off most of the water and season the beans with salt, pepper, and vinegar.

Sweet Potato Pie

Makes one 9-inch pie,
serves 6 to 8

Pastry Dough for single-crust 9-inch
  pie (see page 31)
2 cups mashed cooked sweet potatoes
½ cup granulated sugar
½ cup firmly packed brown sugar
2 eggs, beaten

1 cup milk or light cream
2 tablespoons butter, melted and
  cooled
1 teaspoon ground cinnamon
½ teaspoon ground ginger
½ teaspoon ground mace

Prepare pastry dough and line a 9-inch pie plate. Preheat oven to 425°F.

In a large bowl mix the sweet potatoes well with the sugars. Beat in all remaining ingredients.

Pour into the pie shell and bake 10 minutes. Reduce heat to 350°F and bake 30 to 35 minutes, or until the custard is set.

Pecan Pie

Makes one 9-inch pie,
serves 6 to 8

Pastry Dough for single-crust 9-inch
  pie (see page 31)
3 tablespoons butter, softened
1 cup sugar
4 eggs, beaten
2 tablespoons flour
⅛ teaspoon salt

1 cup dark corn syrup
1 teaspoon vanilla extract
1 cup pecan halves, broken into
  pieces
Sweetened whipped cream, for accompaniment

Prepare pastry dough and line a 9-inch pie pan. Preheat oven to 425°F.

In a mixing bowl cream together the butter and sugar. Add the eggs, flour, salt, corn syrup, and vanilla. Mix well. Stir in the pecan halves.

Pour into the pie shell and bake 10 minutes. Reduce heat to 350°F and bake an additional 40 to 45 minutes, or until set.

Serve warm or cold, topped with whipped cream.

Strawberry Pound Cake with Strawberry Icing

Serves 8

1 cup (½ pound) butter, softened
1⅔ cups sugar
5 eggs
¼ teaspoon salt
2 cups flour

1 teaspoon vanilla extract
½ cup chopped strawberries, plus
    halved strawberries for garnish
Strawberry Icing (following)

In a mixing bowl cream together the butter and sugar until pale and fluffy.

Beat in the eggs, one at a time. Once all the eggs are added, beat until creamy.

In a small bowl mix together salt and flour. Fold into the batter. Stir in the vanilla and fold in the strawberries.

Butter and flour a 9- by 5- by 3-inch loaf pan. Pour batter into pan and bake about 1 hour, or until a toothpick inserted in the center comes out clean. Remove from oven, cool on wire rack, and turn out of pan.

While cake is cooling prepare icing. Frost cake and decorate with halved strawberries.

Strawberry Icing

½ cup solid vegetable shortening
1¾ cups confectioners' sugar, or as
    needed

3 tablespoons heavy cream
½ cup mashed ripe strawberries

In a bowl cream together the shortening and sugar. Beat in the cream and mashed strawberries. If the icing is too thin, add more confectioners' sugar.

Flavors of the Chesapeake Region

A can of the Chesapeake's ubiquitous seasoning mix sprouts legs and makes its way through Sandy Point State Park. Next to the salt and pepper in every Chesapeake kitchen will be found a can of this spice.

COUNTRY HAMS were smoked in Early America by hanging them in chimneys. With the arrival of certain spices to the New World, other smoking and curing techniques came into use. Every self-respecting plantation or manor house was equipped with its own smokehouse. From these structures, distinctive regional flavors emerged.

In the Chesapeake Bay area, Maryland's country ham and Virginia's Smithfield ham predominate. They have become synonymous with fine dining throughout the nation.

Maryland country hams are aged from two to three years and possess a rich, smoky flavor. They complement the Bay's seafood, and the two have been paired to create numerous dishes. Southern Maryland is famous for its stuffed ham, which is not only a feast, but also a culinary feat!

Smithfield, Virginia, produces an aged, highly salted ham that enjoys worldwide acclaim. Chefs often favorably compare Smithfield ham to the prosciutto ham of Parma, Italy, the Bayonne ham of the Basque region of Spain, and the Ardennes ham of Belgium.

The Chesapeake region's country hams are not only served up on their own as entrées, but the bones, skin, and meat are used as the primary flavorings in vegetables, soups, stews, and many one-pot dishes.

The flavor imparted by country hams to other foods is a major element of the unique Chesapeake Bay taste.

HORSERADISH permeates Baltimore, which is known as one of the horseradish centers of the country. This is not entirely due to per capita consumption. It is also because of the number of local companies that prepare and bottle the pungent root. Around the Bay it is used to jazz up cocktail sauces, oysters, seafood sauces, and all manner of edibles, plain and fancy.

MACE is not a Bay crowd controller but a crowd pleaser. It is widely used in Chesapeake cooking to season everything from seafoods, stews, meats, fowl, and game to desserts. Mace, available ground, is made from the outer covering of the nutmeg seed and is milder in taste than nutmeg.

MOLASSES is a by-product of the refining of cane sugar. At each stage of the refining process, different types of molasses are formed. The final and darkest stage produces what is known as blackstrap molasses, which was widely used in Early American recipes and today is added to many Chesapeake desserts and breads.

OLD BAY lives up to its motto: "Entice with Spice." Talk about a spice being associated with a place! Old Bay is almost synonymous with crabs. Can't have one without the other. Not around the Chesapeake anyway.

For years I have been a "spice courier," traveling back and forth across the country delivering this concoction to homesick Chesapeake Bay natives. There are many crab seasonings on the market, but the favored original—Old Bay—was created by Gustav Brunn and his son Ralph. It is distributed by the Baltimore Spice Company, which is reputed to be one of the world's largest spice dealers.

The actual recipe is top secret, but Mr. Brunn's ingredients list includes salt, pepper, mustard, pimiento, cloves, bay leaves, mace, cardamom, ginger, cassia, and paprika.

Speaking from years of personal experience, I have found Old Bay to be positively addictive. Along the Chesapeake it is used in dishes from soup to nuts and even in a few drinks (a bloody Mary is great with a dash of Old Bay). When in doubt as to what seasoning to add to a Bay recipe, throw in a touch of Old Bay and you can't go wrong. (Well, leave it out of your dessert, thanks.)

OYSTER LIQUOR is the name given to the juices surrounding the oyster meat inside the shell. When shucking oysters, always save this liquid. If the oysters are purchased already shucked, pour the oysters and their liquor into a sieve or strainer over a bowl to catch the precious juices. This reserved liquor, with its concentrated briny taste, is invaluable for use in oyster or seafood soups, stews, and casseroles.

SMOKED COUNTRY BACON is not only a Bay breakfast staple, but is also a primary seasoning in all styles of soups, stews, and casseroles, and is used for larding meats and seafoods. It is often cut in pieces and added raw to foods that require long cooking, such as greens, soups, and stews. Its by-product, bacon grease, is used for sautéing vegetables, frying meats and seafoods, and in corn bread and muffin batters.

TABASCO SAUCE is made from hot red chiles that have been ground and aged with salt in oak barrels for three years, then mixed with vinegar. It is used in many Chesapeake sauces and is often drizzled on raw oysters on the half shell just before devouring. Go easy with it. It is hot!

WORCESTERSHIRE SAUCE, judging from the amount of it used in Bay cooking, would appear to have been invented and manufactured on the shores of the Chesapeake. This is not the case, however. It originally hails from England, and is made from vinegar, molasses, garlic, anchovies, and other spices. The locals use it liberally in soups, crab cakes, sauces, meat loaf, and various casserole recipes.

There are many other important flavors and ingredients of the Bay, such as garlic, green tomatoes, paprika, black pepper, chiles, and many dried and fresh herbs. You will no doubt discover flavors of your own as you incorporate the pleasures of the Bay into your cooking repertoire.

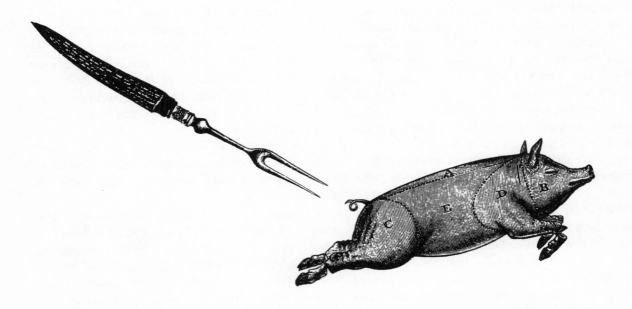

· Part II ·
A Cook's Tour of the Chesapeake

• Baltimore •

Ruth Cumberland is a dedicated patron of Baltimore's Cross Street Market. She and other regulars make their way daily to this shopping hub for provisions and the latest neighborhood news. Strolling the aisles of the Cross Street Market is like taking a walk into a bygone era.

Welcome to Charm City, aka the Monumental City, the Hairdo Capital of the World, and my hometown. We're the city of neighborhoods, white marble steps, screen paintings, farmers' markets, crab houses, and beehive coifs.

Baltimore is also known as a renaissance city. A victim of urban blight several decades ago, it has now blossomed into what *Life* magazine deemed "the most liveable city in America." Home to Edgar Allan Poe, Babe Ruth, Billie Holiday, H. L. Mencken, and Wallace Simpson, to name just a few illustrious residents, it is a city proud of its cultural heritage.

The legislature in colonial Annapolis chartered Baltimore Town to serve as a port for the growing number of farmers looking for a means to ship their goods. Over the years the Baltimore harbor, which opens onto the Patapsco River, has emerged as one of the major ports in the country, with ships from all nations anchoring there.

Baltimorians love their food and don't hesitate to let anyone know. It is the melting pot of the Chesapeake Bay. Ethnic communities still thrive here, each adapting the region's natural resources into their traditional cuisines.

Oddly enough, the blue crab has become the common denominator uniting these various groups. They all steam the crabs, dump them on newspapers spread on backyard tables, and whack them with mallets in the same manner as generations of Baltimore crab pickers have before them. Children of all backgrounds grow up eating soft-shell crab sandwiches, the little crab legs dangling from the edges of white bread.

Every neighborhood block has a tavern or two where locals meet to debate the merits of the Baltimore Orioles ball club and to have a few "cold ones" with a plateful of oysters on the half shell or of steamed shrimp with cocktail sauce. This is the city where crab cakes are king. The spicy crab mounds reign over the menu of virtually every tavern and restaurant in town.

By the way, we have our own language to boot! Wanna hear? Well hon, com on down and give us a listen. Or, meet ya over to the table to eat some crab, and we'll show yous all how to live!

Charm City Eggs

Serves 4

A Baltimore variation on eggs Benedict. The peppy hollandaise sauce, which is easily made in a blender, is the perfect topping for this charming city's number one Sunday brunch choice.

Gertie's Crab Cakes mixture (see page 38)
Vegetable oil, for frying
4 English muffins, split, lightly toasted, and buttered
8 eggs, poached
Old Bay Hollandaise Sauce (recipe follows)

Prepare crab cakes mixture and gently form 8 crab cakes to fit on the muffin halves. They will be flatter and thinner than regular crab cakes. In a skillet fry the crab cakes until golden brown on both sides. (Alternatively, slip under a preheated broiler and cook until browned, turning once.)

Place the cakes on the buttered muffin halves and top with eggs. Spoon warm hollandaise sauce over the top.

Old Bay Hollandaise Sauce

Makes about 2 cups

8 egg yolks
½ teaspoon Old Bay seasoning
2 dashes Tabasco sauce
2 dashes Worcestershire sauce
Juice of 1 lemon
1 cup (½ pound) unsalted butter, melted and kept warm
Hot water, if needed

Place all ingredients except butter and water in a blender. Blend until well mixed. With motor running, pour in the hot butter in a fine, steady stream, blending until thick. If sauce is too thick, thin with a little hot water.

Crabmeat Omelet Filling

Makes filling for 4 to 6 omelets

A rich stuffing for a puffy brunch omelet.

6 tablespoons butter
1 tablespoon minced shallots
1 cup sliced fresh mushrooms
2 tablespoons dry sherry
3 tablespoons flour
1 cup Fish Stock (see page 35) or
　bottled clam juice
1¼ cups heavy cream

½ cup grated Swiss cheese
Salt, black pepper, and freshly grated
　nutmeg to taste
½ pound backfin crabmeat, picked
　over for shells
2 tablespoons minced fresh parsley
　or chives

Melt 3 tablespoons of the butter in a heavy-bottomed saucepan. Add the shallots and cook over medium heat 1 to 2 minutes. Add the mushrooms and continue cooking until they are soft. Increase the heat and add the sherry; deglaze the pan, scraping up any crusty bits on pan bottom. Turn off the heat and remove the mushrooms with a slotted spoon. Set aside.

Return the saucepan to the stove and melt the remaining 3 tablespoons butter. Stir in the flour and cook 1 minute, stirring constantly. Off the heat whisk in the stock, stirring until completely smooth. Add the cream, return to the heat, and stir well until mixture comes to a boil. Remove from the heat and stir in the grated cheese. Season with salt, pepper, and nutmeg. Gently fold in the crabmeat and stir in the parsley or chives.

Seafood Hash

Serves 4 or 5

Hash dishes were created to use up those ever-present leftovers. Usually prepared with meats or vegetables, this version is a novel approach for large fish trimmings or leftover fillets. According to my Aunt Minnie: "Fry it up in a cast-iron skillet with some bacon drippings and you'll have the cats a-howling and your guests grinning from ear to ear." Serve the hash as is, or with poached eggs nesting on top.

2 cups diced, cooked potatoes
2 cups flaked, cooked fish
1 cup (½ pound) butter
¼ pound smoked salmon or trout,
　chopped in small pieces
1 small yellow onion, diced
2 green onions, minced
1 tablespoon chopped garlic

1 teaspoon Tabasco sauce
Salt and black pepper to taste
2 tablespoons chopped fresh parsley
1 tablespoon chopped fresh dill or
　basil
Bacon drippings or vegetable oil, for
　frying

In a mixing bowl combine the potatoes and fish, mix well. Melt the butter in a skillet and sauté the yellow and green onions and garlic until soft. Add to the potato-fish mixture with Tabasco, salt, pepper, parsley, and dill; mix well.

Heat some bacon drippings in a skillet and fry fish mixture until browned on the underside. Flip and brown second side, then serve immediately.

Eggs Edie

Serves 4

Two of the things I miss most in Baltimore are streetcars and the late Edie Massey. Edie is better known to some people as the Egg Lady in John Waters's film, Pink Flamingos. A beloved fixture on the Baltimore scene, Edie was really crazy about eggs. She came over one morning for breakfast and all I had in the fridge was a bunch of hard-cooked eggs. What I came up with was this dish, which Edie dearly loved. When friends come by early in the day, they always ask me if I'll fix those eggs Edie liked. And here they are . . . with love.

4 slices bacon
½ cup chopped fresh mushrooms
¼ cup chopped onions
2 tablespoons butter
2 tablespoons flour
2½ cups milk
1 tablespoon dry mustard

Juice of 1 lemon
1 whole clove
Salt and black pepper to taste
6 hard-cooked eggs, coarsely chopped
4 English muffins, split, toasted, and buttered

In a heavy-bottomed saucepan, cook the bacon. Remove the bacon with a slotted utensil and then chop in small pieces; reserve drippings in saucepan. Add the mushrooms and onion to the drippings and sauté until soft. Remove mushrooms and onion with a slotted spoon.

Add the butter to the same saucepan and heat until bubbly. Whisk in the flour and cook, stirring, 1 to 2 minutes. Off the heat gradually whisk in the milk; stir in mustard, lemon juice, clove, salt, and pepper. Return to the heat and bring to a boil, stirring constantly. Lower the heat and add the reserved bacon, mushrooms, and onion. Fold in the eggs. Serve on buttered muffin halves.

Steamed Shrimp with Tangy Cocktail Sauce

Serves a crowd

From the barrooms to the back-yards of Balamer, you'll find these spicy critters aplenty. Next to the blue crab there's not a seafood treat the locals prize more highly. Heavily spiced and served hot or cold, I suggest you eat them fast, for they have a tendency to disappear before your eyes. Rule of thumb for a shrimp feast: You snooze, you lose!

1 bottle (12 ounces) beer, allowed to go flat
1 cup white wine vinegar
1 onion, sliced
2 stalks celery, chopped
¼ cup Old Bay seasoning
4 teaspoons pickling spice
1 tablespoon black peppercorns
5 pounds medium to large raw shrimp in the shell
Lemon wedges and Tangy Cocktail Sauce (recipe follows), for accompaniment

In a large pot combine the beer, vinegar, onion, celery, Old Bay, pickling spice, and peppercorns. Bring to a boil, put in the shrimp, stir, and cover. Cook over a high heat, stirring occasionally, until the shrimp turn a bright pink, 5 to 7 minutes. Drain shrimp. Serve hot or cold with lemon wedges and plenty of cocktail sauce.

Tangy Cocktail Sauce

Makes about 2½ cups

2 cups ketchup
½ cup prepared horseradish
2 tablespoons Worcestershire sauce
1 teaspoon Tabasco sauce
Juice of 1 lemon

In a bowl combine all the ingredients and mix well.

Crabettes

Serves about 8

These little devils, whose name sounds suspiciously like a follies review over to the Steelworkers Hall, are actually the creation of a Johns Hopkins physics professor and myself. Rest assured they were perfected in his kitchen, not the lab. They look like miniature crab cakes, pack a zesty punch, and are perfect cocktail party pass-arounds. Serve with cocktail sauce (see recipe above) or a fresh salsa.

1 egg, beaten
3 tablespoons mayonnaise
1 teaspoon Tabasco sauce
½ teaspoon soy sauce
½ teaspoon Old Bay seasoning
½ teaspoon black pepper
1 teaspoon finely chopped fresh ginger
1 teaspoon chopped garlic
2 to 3 serrano or other hot chiles, finely chopped
2 tablespoons chopped fresh cilantro
1 pound claw crabmeat, picked over for shells
Dried bread crumbs, as needed
Vegetable oil, for deep-frying

Mix together all the ingredients except the crabmeat, bread crumbs, and oil. Whip by hand or in a blender until well mixed and frothy. Place the crabmeat in a bowl and pour egg mixture over it. Add the bread crumbs, a little at a time, tossing gently, until the mixture holds together and can be formed into patties. Mold into 1-ounce round patties.

In a deep skillet or fryer, heat oil for deep-frying to 375°F. Deep-fry patties, a few at a time, about 3 minutes, or until golden brown. Remove with a slotted utensil to paper towels to drain briefly, then serve.

Smoked Country Ham and Roquefort Pie

Makes one 9-inch pie, serves 6 to 8

A blend of hickory-cured ham and sharp Roquefort makes a delightful luncheon custard pie. The meal is perfectly balanced by a simple tossed salad.

Pastry Dough for single-crust 9-inch pie (recipe follows), partially baked
6 tablespoons butter
1 cup sliced leeks
6 ounces Roquefort cheese, softened
6 ounces cream cheese, softened
¼ cup heavy cream
3 eggs, lightly beaten
Salt and black pepper to taste
1¼ cups diced country ham

Prepare pastry dough and line a 9-inch pie pan; partially bake (see page 31). Set oven to 350°F.

Melt 3 tablespoons of the butter in a skillet. Add the leeks and cook over medium heat until soft.

While the leeks are cooking, cream the remaining 3 tablespoons butter, Roquefort, and cream cheese together. Beat in the cream and eggs and mix until smooth. Season to taste.

In the bottom of the pastry shell, arrange the ham and leeks. Pour in the cheese mixture and bake 35 to 40 minutes, or until nicely browned.

Pastry Dough

Double-Crust Pie

Makes pastry for one double-crust 9-inch pie

2¼ cups flour
1 teaspoon salt

¾ cup solid vegetable shortening
5 to 7 tablespoons cold water

Sift together the flour and salt into a mixing bowl. Work the shortening into the flour with fingertips or a pastry blender, until the mixture is the consistency of coarse meal.

Add the water, 1 tablespoon at a time, and mix with a fork after each addition. Dough should not be wet, but just moist enough to hold together. Form the dough into a ball. Wrap and refrigerate for at least 15 minutes before rolling.

Single-Crust Pie

Makes pastry for one single-crust 9-inch pie

1½ cups flour
¾ teaspoon salt

½ cup solid vegetable shortening
3 to 4 tablespoons cold water

Proceed with instructions for Double-Crust Pie recipe, above.

Partially Baked Shell

Prepare pastry dough (see recipes above). Line a 9-inch pie pan with rolled-out dough and form a fluted edge around the shell. Prick the bottom of the shell with a fork. Press aluminum foil into the bottom and sides of the shell, and cover foil with uncooked rice or dried beans to weight the pastry. This prevents the crust from swelling during baking.

Bake in a preheated 425°F oven for 8 minutes. Remove the foil and continue baking for another 5 minutes. Remove and allow to cool before filling.

Fully Baked Shell

Follow the preceding instructions for the Partially Baked Shell and, after removing the foil, continue baking 8 to 10 minutes, or until the crust is lightly browned. Cool before filling.

Shrimp in Sherry Sauce

Serves 6 to 8

El and Bern Farace get ready for friends and family with this crowd pleaser. El says that however many shrimp you think you'll need, you'll probably need more. She's worn the tread right off her tennis shoes running back and forth refilling the bowl. Supply plenty of toothpicks for your guests to spear their catch.

2 pounds shrimp
2 small onions, chopped
1½ cups olive oil
½ cup dry sherry
½ cup red wine vinegar
¼ cup fresh lemon juice

1 tablespoon Worcestershire sauce
1 teaspoon salt
½ teaspoon black pepper
2 tablespoons chopped fresh parsley
   or dill

Steam shrimp as directed in Steamed Shrimp with Tangy Cocktail Sauce (see page 29). Drain, peel, devein, and place in a bowl.

Mix together all the remaining ingredients. Pour the mixture over the shrimp, cover, and marinate 2 to 3 days in refrigerator.

Polish Marinated Herring

When Polish John's not operating his crane at the Dundalk Marine Terminal, you're likely to find him at his East Baltimore home eating or preparing this delicious snack from his homeland. Brine-cured herring have been preserved in salt and vinegar and can be purchased from most fish dealers. If pickled fillets are all that are available, John suggests soaking the fish in cold water several days longer. He also says, "If you like onions, use lots; if not, less." These Polish herring are great eaten as they are, or they make a great salad.

Brine-cured herring fillets
4 parts vegetable oil

1 part olive oil
Onions, thinly sliced

Remove the skin from the herring and soak fillets in cold water to cover overnight. The next day, discard the soaking water and rinse fillets in cold water. Cut in 2-inch pieces.

Combine oils. In a glass jar (1 quart, ½ gallon, or, for real herring lovers, 1 gallon), pour in a thin layer of the combined oils. Top with a layer of herring pieces and then a layer of onion slices. Add another layer of oil. Continue layering process until the jar is full or you've run out of herring. The top layer must be onions. Fill the jar with oil. Make sure the top layer of onions is completely immersed in oil. Cover jar tightly and refrigerate at least 7 days before serving.

Dandelion Soup

Serves 4

Weeds to some, but quite the summertime delicacy in Baltimore. Dandelion greens are versatile, used raw for a refreshing salad, or blanched, then lightly fried in olive oil and garlic for a vegetable dish.

This soup does wonders for the lower back, but only if you pick your own dandelions. While scouring the lawn or field, look for the small, tender leaves. The recipe is a variation on a theme from my friend Jo O'Dea.

1 pound tender dandelion greens, finely shredded
¼ cup (4 tablespoons) butter
1 small onion, chopped
3 cups Chicken Stock (recipe follows)

2 egg yolks
1 cup heavy cream
Salt and black pepper to taste
Dash Tabasco sauce

Soak the greens for 10 minutes in cold water to cover; drain. In a pot melt the butter and cook the onion a few minutes until soft. Add the greens and continue cooking until they are wilted. Add the stock and bring to a boil. Simmer 20 to 30 minutes.

In a small bowl, beat together the egg yolks and cream. Off the heat add to the soup, stirring rapidly with a wire whisk. Reheat the soup, but do not bring to a boil.

Add seasonings to taste. Serve hot or very cold.

Chicken Stock

Makes about 1 quart

2 to 2½ pounds chicken backs or necks
2 quarts water
2 onions, sliced
3 stalks celery, chopped

2 carrots, peeled and chopped
4 cloves garlic, unpeeled
2 bay leaves
2 teaspoons dried thyme
½ bunch fresh parsley

In a large pot combine all the ingredients and bring to a boil. Simmer slowly, uncovered, 4 to 5 hours, skimming off surface foam frequently. Strain through a fine sieve or cheesecloth. Chill and degrease.

NOTE: Stock freezes nicely, so it may be a good idea to make a double batch and freeze some.

Chesapeake Bay Bouillabaisse

Serves 8 to 10

Fresh seafood from the Bay makes a first-class fish soup on this side of the Atlantic. Mrs. Williams, from down on the Magothy River, gave me this recipe but did not include the rouille. *This sauce is a "fu-fu" touch from France, but one I feel adds nicely to the soup. The* rouille *is mayonnaiselike in texture, made from chiles, garlic, and olive oil. Pass plenty of hot crusty bread for dipping in the broth.*

¼ cup olive oil
1 large onion, diced
6 garlic cloves, unpeeled
2 leeks, halved and cut in pieces
⅓ cup chopped fennel bulb root, or 1 tablespoon fennel seed
5 pounds ripe tomatoes, chopped
2 small potatoes, peeled and diced
2 cups dry white wine
3 cups Fish Stock (see page 35)
1 teaspoon dried thyme
1 teaspoon dried oregano
1 bay leaf
Rind from 1 orange, grated

3 or 4 threads saffron
Salt and black pepper to taste
8 to 10 diagonally sliced pieces French bread
Melted butter and chopped garlic, for toast
2 pounds bass, cod, or other firm-fleshed fillets
1 pound backfin crabmeat, picked over for shells
1½ pounds clams in the shell, well scrubbed
Chopped fresh parsley
Hotsy-totsy Rouille (recipe follows)

In a heavy pot heat the oil and sauté the onion, garlic, leeks, and fennel until slightly softened. Add the tomatoes, potatoes, wine, stock, thyme, oregano, and bay leaf. Bring to a boil, reduce the heat, and simmer 30 minutes.

Purée the mixture in a blender or food processor. Pour through a fine sieve and return to the pot.

Add the orange rind, saffron, salt, and pepper. Continue cooking over medium-low heat, stirring frequently, until somewhat reduced, about 20 to 30 minutes.

Meanwhile, preheat the oven to 375°F. Brush bread slices with melted butter and top with garlic. Toast in oven until browned.

Cut the fish in chunks about 2-inch square. Add fish to the sauce and cook 8 to 10 minutes, or until the fish is almost done.

Add the crabmeat and clams. Stir, then cover. Cook a few minutes until clams have opened. Reserve 1 cup of the liquid for making *rouille*.

Prepare the *rouille*. Place 1 piece of garlic bread in each bowl, then spoon in the fish and broth. Arrange the clams on top. Garnish with parsley. Serve the *rouille* on the side.

Hotsy-totsy Rouille

Makes about 1½ cups

1 small potato, peeled
1 cup broth from recipe above

6 cloves garlic
4 fresh or dried red chiles

1 teaspoon Tabasco sauce   Salt to taste
½ cup olive oil

Quarter the potato and cook in the bouillabaisse broth. Drain, reserving liquid.

In a blender or a food processor, finely chop the garlic and peppers. Add the potato, Tabasco, and oil. Process until mixture forms a paste. Slowly add enough bouillabaisse liquid to give the mixture the consistency of heavy cream. Season with salt.

Cream of Crab Soup

Serves 4 or 5

There are as many versions of crab soup as there are homes on the Chesapeake. This Cream of Crab Soup is an elegant first course for that special dinner or luncheon.

¼ cup (4 tablespoons) butter
1 small onion, finely diced
¼ cup minced shallots
2 tablespoons flour
2 cups Fish Stock (recipe follows)
2 cups heavy cream
1 teaspoon Worcestershire sauce
1 teaspoon salt

⅛ teaspoon white pepper
1 bay leaf
Dash Tabasco sauce
1 pound backfin crabmeat, picked
    over for shells
¼ cup sherry
Lightly whipped cream and paprika,
    for garnish

In a pot melt the butter and sauté the onion and shallots until tender. Whisk in the flour and cook over medium heat, stirring constantly, about 2 minutes. Do not brown the flour.

Off the heat whisk in the stock and cream. Return to medium heat and stir frequently until the mixture thickens. Add the Worcestershire sauce, salt, pepper, bay leaf, Tabasco, crabmeat, and sherry; simmer about 20 to 25 minutes.

Ladle into soup bowls and garnish with whipped cream and paprika.

Fish Stock

Makes about 7 cups

3½ to 4 pounds fish heads, bones, or
    trimmings
2 quarts cold water
2 onions, sliced
3 stalks celery, chopped
2 carrots, peeled and chopped

4 cloves garlic, unpeeled
2 bay leaves
1 tablespoon black peppercorns
2 teaspoons dried thyme
½ bunch fresh parsley

In a large pot combine all the ingredients and bring to a boil. Simmer over medium heat for 30 minutes, skimming off surface foam frequently. Strain through a fine sieve or cheesecloth.

Crab Soup at Cross Street Market

Serves a crowd

A trip to the Cross Street Market carries the visitor back in time. Originally open air, the now-enclosed market houses century-old family-owned stalls displaying fish, meats, poultry, vegetables, and dairy products.

Jean Chagouris of Nick's Inner Harbor Seafood shared her locally famous recipe for crab soup. She said the recipe is not written in stone, so feel free to vary the amounts of crab or vegetables to your taste. Serve with plenty of Saltine crackers.

Tommy Chagouris and mother, Jean, at their Cross Street Market stall.

4 quarts water
5 cups peeled tomatoes or 2 cans (1 pound, 12 ounces) tomatoes
1 can (10 ounces) tomato sauce
2 bay leaves
½ cup pearl barley
½ cup chopped fresh parsley
1 tablespoon Old Bay seasoning
3 stalks celery, diced
1 large onion, chopped
2 ham shanks

1 beef bone
Salt and black pepper to taste
8 blue crabs, cleaned and quartered
½ head cabbage, chopped
2 medium potatoes, peeled and diced
4 cups fresh or frozen mixed vegetables (diced carrots, cut-up green beans, corn kernels, shelled peas, lima beans, in any combination)
2 pounds claw crabmeat, picked over for shells

In a large soup pot, combine the water, tomatoes, tomato sauce, bay leaves, barley, Old Bay, celery, onion, ham shanks, beef bone, salt, and pepper. Bring to a boil, reduce the heat, and simmer 1 hour.

Add the soup crabs and backs. Continue cooking another 30 minutes. Add the cabbage, potatoes, and mixed vegetables. When the vegetables are tender, add the claw meat and simmer a little longer. Discard the backs. Pick meat from the shanks and add to soup.

Crab Imperial, Baltimore Style

Serves 4

Here is the pièce de résistance of Chesapeake Bay blue crab dishes. It is reserved for the most special of family occasions, and is the showpiece selection at fine Chesapeake dinner houses. Restaurant reputations are often made—and unmade—on the basis of their success with this dish. "It'll make you or break you," says my imperial committee.

Basically, an imperial is a richly spiced crab casserole that is served in individual portions. It is said to be named after Queen Henrietta Marie. Want to start a fight? Ask two or more Marylanders how to make the best crab imperial and the situation becomes quite dangerous. The answer is a matter of fierce family pride and, in most cases, involves a recipe passed through seemingly countless generations.

After several scuffles, a few abrasions, and black-and-blue shins, I arrived at this delectable version of the fabled preparation.

¼ cup (4 tablespoons) butter
2 tablespoons diced green bell pepper
2 tablespoons diced red bell pepper or pimiento
½ cup chopped fresh mushrooms
¾ cup mayonnaise
1 tablespoon Dijon mustard
1 tablespoon Worcestershire sauce
1 teaspoon capers, drained and chopped
¼ teaspoon Tabasco sauce
½ teaspoon black pepper
1 teaspoon Old Bay seasoning
1 pound lump crabmeat, picked over for shells
Imperial Topping (recipe follows)

Preheat oven to 350°F.

In a small skillet melt the butter and sauté the bell peppers and mushrooms until soft. Put aside.

Combine all the remaining ingredients, except the crabmeat and topping, in a small bowl and mix well. Add the sautéed peppers and mushrooms to the mixture.

Place the crabmeat in a mixing bowl and pour the pepper mixture over it; toss gently. Spoon the mixture into 4 small individual casserole dishes or well-cleaned crab shells. Bake 20 to 25 minutes.

Meanwhile, prepare the topping. Remove casseroles from the oven. Preheat the broiler. Spoon the topping evenly over each casserole. Place under the broiler 1 to 2 minutes, or until nicely browned. (If a broiler is unavailable, brown the top in the oven. It will take a bit longer.) Serve immediately.

Imperial Topping

1 egg, beaten
¼ cup mayonnaise
Pinch paprika
1 tablespoon chopped fresh parsley

In a small bowl, combine all the ingredients and mix well.

Gertie's Crab Cakes

Serves 4

If you ask someone what comes to mind when they think of the Chesapeake, nine times out of ten it'll be "crabs." And when they think of crabs, the first thought is always crab cakes. These delicious broiled or fried mounds of precious spiced crab are found in nearly every eatery and kitchen along the Bay. As with many traditional Bay recipes, there are several variations on the crab cake theme. This was the recipe used by my grandmother Gertie, and to be sure I think it's the best by far. I've served this version at my restaurant on the West Coast, and now have countless crab cake devotees.

For the full experience, serve with Tartar Sauce (see page 15), Coleslaw (see page 54), and french fries. Locals require Saltine crackers to carry the crab cakes to their lips.

1 egg
2 tablespoons mayonnaise
1 teaspoon dry mustard
½ teaspoon black pepper
1 teaspoon Old Bay seasoning
2 teaspoons Worcestershire sauce
Dash Tabasco sauce
1 pound backfin crabmeat, picked over for shells
¼ cup cracker crumbs
Vegetable oil, for deep-frying

In a blender or mixing bowl, combine the egg, mayonnaise, mustard, pepper, Old Bay, Worcestershire, and Tabasco. Mix until frothy.

Place the crabmeat in a bowl and pour the mixture over the top. Sprinkle on cracker crumbs. Gently toss together, taking care not to break up the lumps of crabmeat.

Form the cakes by hand or with an ice-cream scoop into 3-inch wide, 1-inch thick rounded mounds. Do not pack the crab-cake batter together too firmly. Keep as loose as possible, yet still holding form.

Heat oil in a deep skillet or fryer to 375°F. Deep-fry crab cakes, a few at a time, until golden brown on all sides, about 3 minutes. Remove with a slotted utensil to paper towels to drain. (Alternatively, slip under a preheated broiler until nicely browned, turning to cook evenly.) Serve at once.

Crabmeat-Stuffed Sole Fillets with Saffron Cream Sauce

Serves 6

If you need to impress your boss or are having the future in-laws to dinner, this classy dish is sure to please. Country Asparagus (see page 228) and buttery rice are perfect accompaniments. For a dapper presentation, top each sauced fillet with a thin strip of sautéed red bell pepper.

4 tablespoons butter
¼ cup diced red bell pepper or pimiento
¼ cup diced green bell pepper
⅓ cup mayonnaise
½ teaspoon dry mustard
½ teaspoon salt, plus salt to taste
¼ teaspoon white pepper, plus white pepper to taste
2 lemons
2 tablespoons chopped fresh dill or parsley

1 pound backfin crabmeat, picked over for shells
6 sole fillets
1½ cups dry white wine, heated to boiling point
Saffron Cream Sauce (recipe follows; see Note)
Chopped fresh parsley or sautéed or roasted bell pepper strips, for garnish

Preheat oven to 375°F.

In a small skillet, melt 2 tablespoons of the butter. Sauté the bell peppers until soft. In a small bowl combine the mayonnaise, ½ teaspoon salt, ¼ teaspoon white pepper, juice of 1 lemon, and dill. Add the sautéed peppers and mix well.

Place the crabmeat in a bowl and pour the mixture over the top. Gently toss together.

Spread the fillets with the crabmeat mixture and roll up. Arrange, seam side down, in a glass baking dish. Melt the remaining butter and brush on tops of rolled fillets. Sprinkle lightly with salt and pepper. Top each fillet with a squeeze of juice from the remaining lemon. Pour the hot wine into the bottom of the baking dish. Cover dish with aluminum foil and bake 20 to 25 minutes. Remove the fillets with a slotted utensil to a heated platter; keep warm while making the sauce. Strain the cooking juices and use for making the sauce.

Ladle sauce over fillets and garnish with parsley.

Saffron Cream Sauce

Makes about 1 cup

2 tablespoons butter
2 to 3 threads saffron, soaked in a little warm water at least 30 minutes
1 teaspoon minced shallots
1½ tablespoons flour

Strained pan juices or ¼ cup Fish Stock (see page 35)
1 cup heavy cream
Salt and black pepper to taste
1 tablespoon fresh lemon juice

In a saucepan melt the butter and sauté the shallots for several minutes. Whisk in the flour. Cook, stirring, 1 to 2 minutes; do not brown the flour.

Off the heat stir in the pan juices, saffron, and cream. Return to heat and bring to a boil. Season with salt, pepper, and lemon juice. Simmer 1 to 2 minutes.

NOTE: If you would rather make the sauce while the fillets are baking and you have some fish stock on hand, simply use the stock in place of the pan juices.

Jumbo Shrimp with Seafood Stuffing

Serves 6

This delightful dish of shrimp with a seafood-infused stuffing will thrill even those guests who aren't usually disposed to seafood. Serve it with fluffy white rice.

1 cup (½ pound) butter
½ cup minced green bell pepper
½ cup minced red bell pepper
¼ cup minced onion
½ cup dry white wine, plus white wine for baking dish
¼ cup fresh lemon juice
1 tablespoon chopped garlic
1 pound backfin crabmeat, picked over for shells
¼ pound scallops, poached or sautéed and then finely diced

1 cup finely diced, peeled, steamed shrimp (see page 29)
1 tablespoon chopped fresh parsley
Salt and black pepper to taste
Dried bread crumbs, as needed
2 pounds jumbo shrimp, peeled, deveined, and butterflied
Melted butter, for drizzling on shrimp

Preheat oven to 375°F.

In a skillet melt the butter and sauté the bell peppers and onion briefly. Add the wine, lemon juice, and garlic. Bring to a boil and remove from the heat to cool.

In a mixing bowl combine the crabmeat, scallops, and diced shrimp. Pour the butter-vegetable mixture over the top. Add parsley, salt, and black pepper and mix well. Add enough bread crumbs as needed for the mixture to hold together.

Place jumbo shrimp, spread open, in a shallow casserole or baking dish and mound the stuffing on top. Drizzle a little melted butter over the top of each shrimp. Pour a little white wine in the bottom of the dish. Bake 18 to 20 minutes.

Baltimore Grilled Oysters with Lemon-Celery Cream Sauce

Serves 4

Inspired by a dish served at Baltimore's grand old Southern Hotel, this recipe calls for broiling the oysters rather than grilling them. The only thing you grill is the ham.

Lemon-Celery Cream Sauce
(recipe follows)
24 large oysters, shucked, drained,
    and liquor reserved
½ cup (¼ pound) butter, melted

Black pepper
Dried bread crumbs
4 slices country ham
4 slices bread, toasted and buttered
Lemon wedges for garnish

Preheat the broiler. Prepare the sauce, using the reserved oyster liquor; keep warm.

Dry the oysters on paper towels. Dip them in the melted butter, sprinkle with pepper, and roll in bread crumbs. Arrange on a broiler pan and broil until golden brown, turning once. It doesn't take long, so keep an eye out.

Grill or panfry the ham and place 1 slice on each slice of buttered toast. Arrange the oysters on top. Spoon the Lemon-Celery Cream around the edges of the toast. Garnish with lemon wedges.

Lemon-Celery Cream Sauce

Makes about 2¼ cups

6 tablespoons butter
⅓ cup finely chopped celery
2 tablespoons minced onion
3 tablespoons flour
2 cups half-and-half

Reserved oyster liquor
Salt and black pepper to taste
2 tablespoons fresh lemon juice
Few dashes Tabasco sauce

In a saucepan, melt the butter and sauté the celery and onion until tender. Whisk in the flour and cook 1 to 2 minutes. Do not brown.

Off the heat gradually whisk in the half-and-half and oyster liquor. Return to the heat and bring to a boil. Season with salt, pepper, lemon juice, and Tabasco.

Fried Perch with "Burn Yo Mouth Sauce" (or Perch Till It Hurts)

Serves 6 or 7

Tina Louise down to church gave me this recipe. She got it from her momma who said that if it was just hot enough, you'd feel like the Holy Ghost had got a-hold of you. Now that's a religious experience!

½ cup vegetable oil or butter, plus oil for panfrying
1 yellow onion, diced
1 bunch green onions, finely chopped
1 green bell pepper, diced
1 red bell pepper, diced
2 stalks celery, diced
2 tablespoons chopped garlic
3 to 6 fresh hot chiles, minced
4 large ripe tomatoes, chopped
½ cup tomato juice

½ cup white wine
Juice of 1 lemon
1 teaspoon Worcestershire sauce
1 bay leaf
Salt, black pepper, and Tabasco sauce to taste
2 pounds perch fillets
Flour seasoned with salt and black pepper
Milk, as needed
Yellow cornmeal, for coating

To make the sauce, heat the ½ cup oil in a pot. Cook the yellow and green onions, bell peppers, and celery 10 minutes. Add the garlic, chile peppers, tomatoes, tomato juice, wine, lemon juice, Worcestershire, and bay leaf. Bring to a boil. Season with salt, pepper, and Tabasco. Reduce the heat and simmer about 1 hour.

For the fish, pour oil into a large skillet to a depth of about ¼ inch. Dust the fillets with the seasoned flour. Dip fillets first in the milk and then the cornmeal. Shake off excess, then fry in the hot oil until golden brown and crisp. Transfer fillets to a heated platter and serve topped with the tomato sauce.

Shad Roe Sauté

Serves 4

Those shad are quick, so you better get 'em while you can! They only run in the Bay and its tributaries during the spring, primarily March, making them a short-lived delicacy. The season is heralded by the sign annually hung outside Danny's restaurant on Charles Street: The Run Is On! And run they do, to get as much shad and shad roe as possible during those precious few weeks.

The two most important things to remember when cooking shad roe are don't overcook and stand back so you don't get burned when the sacks of roe start to pop during sautéing.

4 pairs shad roe (see page 12)
Salt and black pepper
4 to 6 tablespoons butter
Juice of 1 lemon

Lemon wedges and hot melted or browned butter, for accompaniment

Season the shad roe with salt and pepper. Melt the butter in a skillet and cook the roe over medium-low heat. Turn roe several times to make sure it is cooked through. This takes about 15 minutes.

Remember, take care when cooking that you aren't burned by the popping roe. When finished, squeeze the lemon juice over the roe and remove from the skillet. Serve with lemon wedges and hot melted butter.

NOTE: Many locals top their sautéed roe with a strip of cooked bacon when serving.

Mrs. Tovey's Chicken and Waffles with Gravy

Serves 5 or 6

Perfect for a Sunday supper or for those times when the whole family's at home. Mary likes to simmer the chicken over a real low flame so that it takes longer to cook—because "it fills the whole kitchen with a wonderful perfume." A slice of jellied cranberry sauce goes very nicely with this rich concoction.

2 tablespoons butter
1 small onion, diced
4 stalks celery, diced
4 cups Chicken Stock (see page 33)
   or bouillon
1 bay leaf

4 boneless whole chicken breasts
Waffles (recipe follows)
4 tablespoons flour
Salt and black pepper to taste
Jellied cranberry sauce, for accompaniment

In a pot melt the butter and sauté the onion and celery until soft, about 10 minutes. Add the stock or bouillon and bay leaf. Bring to a boil. Add the chicken breasts, reduce the heat to low, and simmer 1½ hours.

Prepare the waffles and keep warm.

Remove the breasts from the pot and set aside. Pour the cooking liquid into a bowl and skim the fat from the surface; reserve 4 tablespoons of the fat.

In the same pot, heat the reserved fat, add the flour, and cook, stirring, several minutes. Gradually stir in the liquid, then bring to a boil. Season with salt and pepper.

Skin the breasts and slice the meat. Arrange the meat on the waffles. Cover with the gravy and serve with a slice of jellied cranberry sauce.

A NOTE ON PAN GRAVY: After roasting or braising meats, fowl, or poultry, drain off all liquids from the pan and skim fat off the top. Reserve liquid and fat separately. For one cup of gravy, put 2 tablespoons reserved fat back into the pan and heat on the top of the stove. Whisk in 2 tablespoons flour and cook for several minutes until slightly browned—this is a *roux*. Off the heat, whisk in one cup of the reserved cooking liquid (or stock or water if that's all you have). Bring to a boil, stirring constantly, reduce the heat and simmer for 5 minutes. Season according to taste with salt and pepper, herbs, or whatever you like.

Waffles

Makes 10 to 12 waffles

2 cups flour
1 tablespoon baking powder
½ teaspoon salt
1 tablespoon sugar

1¾ cups milk
3 eggs, separated
3 tablespoons butter, melted

Preheat the waffle iron. In a large bowl sift together flour, baking powder, salt, and sugar. In a second bowl, mix together the milk, egg yolks, and butter. Gradually add the wet ingredients to the dry. Beat the egg whites until stiff peaks form. Gently fold the beaten whites into the batter; do not overmix.

Cook in the waffle iron, according to manufacturer's directions, until golden brown.

Grandma Rita's Irish "Biled" Chicken

Serves 4

On the boat to America from County Wexford in Ireland, Brigid Stacia Reville told her sister she was changing her name to Rita. She was sick and tired of people at home calling her "Biddy." She may have left her name in the old country, but she brought this dish with her to the shores of the Chesapeake. An absolute delight, as is Grandma Rita. Make plenty of mashed or boiled potatoes to go along with the chicken.

1 chicken (3½ to 4 pounds), cut in serving pieces
3 tablespoons vegetable oil
2 or 3 large leeks, halved and cut in 1-inch pieces
2½ cups Chicken Stock (see page 33) or bouillon
¼ cup fresh lemon juice

½ teaspoon dried thyme
½ teaspoon salt
1 bay leaf
Freshly ground black pepper to taste
½ pound fresh mushrooms, quartered
2 tablespoons flour

Preheat oven to 375°F.

Dry chicken pieces with paper towels. In a heavy pot or dutch oven, heat the oil and sear the chicken on all sides. Remove from the pot. Add the leeks and cook until wilted. Pour in the stock and lemon juice. Add the thyme, salt, bay leaf, and pepper.

Return the chicken to the pot and bring to a boil. Cover tightly and place in the oven. Bake 20 minutes. Add the mushrooms and continue baking another 30 minutes.

With a slotted spoon remove the chicken, leeks, and mushrooms to a heated platter; set aside and keep warm.

For the gravy pour the cooking juices into a bowl and remove fat from surface; reserve 2 tablespoons of the fat. In the pot, heat the reserved fat, add the flour, and cook, stirring, several minutes. Gradually stir in the cooking juices, then bring to a boil. Adjust seasonings.

Spoon gravy over the chicken and vegetables. Serve remaining gravy in a bowl alongside.

Mom Mom's Braised Chicken and Drop Dumplings (Loves Perdue)

Serves 6

My mother is a woman of many names. "Mom Mom" came about with the arrival of her grandchildren.

Monday is roast chicken night at the homestead, and Mom Mom is quite agitated with me for calling her famous roast chicken dish "braised," but that's the truth of the matter. Call it what you will, just don't call me late for supper! It's one of my favorites. I know you'll like it, too. Fill the bird with your tastiest stuffing, if you like.

1 roasting chicken (5 to 6 pounds)
Salt and black pepper to taste
1 bay leaf
4 cups Chicken Stock (see page 33) or bouillon, heated
1 onion
2 cloves garlic
Drop Dumplings (recipe follows)

Preheat oven to 350°F.

Dry the chicken with paper towels. Place it in a deep roasting pan and bake, uncovered, 20 minutes.

Pour in the hot stock. Add the bay leaf, onion, and garlic. Cover, reduce the heat to 325°F, and continue cooking 1 hour.

Remove the chicken to a heated platter. Skim the fat from the pan juices. Prepare dumpling dough. Bring defatted juices to a simmer and cook dumplings in the roasting pan as directed. After all the dumplings have been cooked, strain the juices and then thicken for gravy. (See page 44 for gravy instructions.) Season to taste.

Drop Dumplings

2 cups flour, sifted
1 tablespoon baking powder
1 teaspoon salt
1 tablespoon butter
1 egg, beaten
¾ cup milk

In a large mixing bowl, sift together flour, baking powder, and salt. Work in the butter with fingertips.

In a separate bowl mix together the egg and milk. Gradually add wet ingredients to dry ingredients, mixing them to make a soft dough.

Drop dough by the tablespoonful into hot, simmering pan juices. Cook until firm, around 10 minutes.

Rabbit with Basil and Cream

Serves 3 or 4

I grew up on the border between an Irish and an Italian neighborhood. From early on, I leaned culinarily to the Italians. Many of the families raised rabbits and I feasted on dishes such as this.

1 rabbit (3 to 3½ pounds), cut in serving pieces
Flour seasoned with salt and black pepper
½ cup olive oil
1 onion, sliced
2 stalks celery, chopped
1 tablespoon chopped shallots
2 tablespoons chopped garlic

1 cup dry white wine
1 cup Chicken Stock (see page 33) or bouillon
1 bay leaf
6 to 8 fresh basil leaves, coarsely chopped
1½ cups heavy cream
Salt and black pepper to taste
Chopped basil, for garnish

Dry the rabbit pieces with paper towels. Dust pieces lightly with the seasoned flour. In a dutch oven or flameproof casserole, heat the oil. Brown the rabbit pieces well on all sides. Remove from the casserole.

Add the onion, celery, shallots, and garlic to the pot. Sauté 5 minutes. Add the rabbit and its juices. Pour in the wine and stock. Put in the bay leaf and basil. Bring to a boil. Cover, reduce heat, and simmer about 40 minutes, or until tender.

Remove the rabbit with a slotted utensil to a heated platter; keep warm. Strain the cooking juices through a fine sieve. Return the juices to the pot and add the cream. Turn up the heat and cook until reduced and slightly thickened. Season with salt and pepper.

Spoon sauce over the rabbit and garnish with basil.

Grandma Wissman's Sour Beef and Dumplings

Serves 8 to 10

Here is my great grandmother's recipe for this classic German pot roast. Friends and family from the old neighborhood where I grew up have fond memories of this dish. I never met my great grandmother. But from the severe Germanic portraits I've seen of her, I assumed a certain degree of the sourness of the beef came from her staring the meat down. After relatives sampled my attempt at her signature dish, however, I was assured it was every bit as pungent and tender as they remembered.

1 rump roast (5 to 6 pounds), rolled
   and tied
2 cups red wine vinegar
1 cup dry red wine
1 cup water
1½ tablespoons salt
2 cloves garlic, peeled
2 medium onions, sliced
2 stalks celery, chopped
2 carrots, peeled and sliced

2 bay leaves
12 black peppercorns
3 whole cloves
3 whole allspice
¼ cup sugar
½ cup bacon drippings
Potato Dumplings (recipe follows)
3 tablespoons flour
1 cup gingersnaps, finely crushed
1 cup sour cream

Put roast in a deep glass or ceramic bowl. In a saucepan combine the vinegar, wine, water, salt, garlic, onions, celery, carrots, bay leaves, peppercorns, cloves, allspice, and sugar. Bring to a boil and pour over meat. Cover bowl and refrigerate in marinade 2 to 3 days, turning meat 2 or 3 times a day with wooden spoons.

Remove meat from marinade, reserving marinade. Wipe meat dry with paper towels. Dredge meat in flour. In a dutch oven or other heavy-bottomed pot, melt bacon drippings. Brown meat on all sides. Remove roast. Pour off fat from pot and reserve. Return meat to pot and pour reserved marinade over it. Bring to a boil. Cover, reduce heat to a simmer, and cook 3 hours.

Remove meat to a heated platter and keep hot. Strain cooking liquid and reserve. Cook dumplings and keep warm.

In the pot heat 3 tablespoons of the reserved fat. Stir in the flour and cook 1 to 2 minutes, stirring constantly. Add gingersnaps. Whisk in reserved liquid and heat, stirring, until sauce thickens. Reduce heat and stir in sour cream. Adjust seasonings. Serve gravy over the sliced meat and dumplings.

Potato Dumplings

2 pounds potatoes, peeled, boiled,
   and mashed
2 eggs, lightly beaten

½ to ¾ cup dried bread crumbs
Salt and black pepper to taste

Bring a deep pot filled with salted water to a boil. In a mixing bowl, combine all the ingredients, adding only enough bread crumbs so that mixture can be formed into balls. Using a tablespoon, form mixture into balls, dusting them with bread crumbs as you form them.

Gently drop dumplings into boiling water. Reduce heat and simmer 6 to 8 minutes. Remove with a slotted spoon.

Christmas Day Roast "Beast" with Yorkshire Pudding

Serves 10 or more (up to 16)

"Hey hon, where's the salt?" During the testing for this book, I approached the beasty roast beef with kosher salt in hand, only to have Bernie—the beast master of Rogers Forge—wrestle me to the kitchen floor. Sprawled out on a bed of salt, I was culinarily dressed down by the beastmaster. "Are you outta your mind? Don't ever put salt on a beautiful specimen of meat like that! Salt will suck the juices right out of it! Might as well eat fast-food hamburger."

Needless to say we roasted the meat salt-free, and my host knew his stuff. Never have I tasted such a juicy and tender slice of beef.

1 rib roast (16 pounds or 6 to 8 ribs—a real beast)

Yorkshire Pudding (recipe follows)

Preheat oven to 325°F.

Put meat in a shallow roasting pan. Roast uncovered 12 to 15 minutes per pound for medium-rare. (To better insure desired degree of doneness, use a meat thermometer.)

When the meat is done, remove it from the pan and let stand at least 20 minutes before carving.

While the beast is at rest you can prepare the Yorkshire Pudding.

Yorkshire Pudding

Serves 10 or more

4 eggs
2 cups milk
2 cups flour

½ teaspoon salt
Beef drippings

Preheat oven to 500°F. In a large mixing bowl, beat the eggs until frothy, then mix in milk. Beat in flour and salt until a smooth batter forms. Do not overbeat. Cover the bottom of a shallow pan or muffin-tin wells with beef drippings to a depth of ½ to ¾ inch. Put pan or muffin tins in oven for several minutes to get very hot.

Remove pan(s) and pour in batter. Return to oven for 10 minutes. Reduce heat to 400°F and cook 15 to 20 minutes more, or until browned.

Italian Sausage Braised with Peppers and Onions

Serves 4 or 5

Mrs. D'Lucca used to make this dish every Saturday night for her husband Tony. She told me, "Every week I'd get the sausages out and start cutting up the peppers. Next thing I knew, Tony'd slip his arm around my waist and whisper, 'You gonna make me my favorite?' I'd give him the elbow and tell him he better go to confession. He'd run up to church and I'd fix him the sausages . . . he always knew I would."

Serve the sausages with buttered fettuccine and a garden salad.

¾ cup olive oil
8 to 10 sweet or hot Italian sausages
2 red bell peppers, cut in strips
2 green bell peppers, cut in strips
2 small onions, sliced
6 cloves garlic, finely chopped
1 tablespoon red wine vinegar
2½ cups canned tomato sauce or Mealy's "Gravy" (see page 73)
Salt and black pepper to taste
Chopped fresh parsley

In a frying pan, heat ¼ cup of the olive oil. Brown sausages well on all sides and remove.

Add the remaining ½ cup olive oil to pan and sauté peppers, onions, and garlic until peppers are barely cooked. Add vinegar and tomato sauce. Return sausages to pan. Simmer, covered, about 30 minutes, or until sausages are cooked through.

Season with salt and pepper. Garnish with parsley.

Pork Chops with Apples and Maryland Rye Whiskey

Serves 6

This traditional Maryland recipe is just the thing for a crisp fall night. It goes well with pan gravy (see page 44), mashed potatoes, and sauerkraut with apples (see page 55).

¼ cup vegetable oil
6 thick loin pork chops
Flour seasoned with salt and black pepper
4 tablespoons butter
4 tart apples, peeled and sliced
¼ cup sugar
2 tablespoons fresh lemon juice
Freshly grated nutmeg to taste
¼ cup Maryland rye whiskey
Salt and black pepper to taste

Heat oil in a heavy skillet. Lightly dust pork chops with the seasoned flour. Brown on both sides, turning now and then for even cooking. They take about 20 to 25 minutes to brown properly.

Remove chops from skillet and pour off most of fat. Put butter in skillet and melt. Add apples and sauté briefly. Sprinkle apples with sugar, lemon juice, and a touch of nutmeg. When apples are just about tender, increase heat and pour in whiskey. Cook 1 to 2 minutes.

Serve chops on a heated platter, topped with apples.

Packets of Veal Stuffed with Crabmeat and Mozzarella

Serves 6

These mouth-watering bundles of crabmeat and melted cheese enclosed by tender veal take some time to prepare, but are more than worth the effort. When fresh basil is available, I like to substitute a few chopped leaves in place of the thyme. This dish is good with pasta tossed with olive oil and garlic. For a vegetable I suggest Fried Broccoli with Hot Peppers (see page 74) or Fried Watercress (see page 55).

1 tablespoon butter
1 tablespoon olive oil, plus oil for browning
½ cup tomato sauce or Mealy's "Gravy" (see page 73)
1 pound backfin crabmeat, picked over for shells
½ pound mozzarella cheese, coarsely shredded
Salt and black pepper to taste

2 pounds veal scallopinis, sliced ¼ inch thick and pounded thin
Flour seasoned with salt and black pepper
½ pound mushrooms, cut in quarters or sixths
2 tomatoes, chopped
1 tablespoon chopped garlic
1¼ cups dry Marsala
Pinch dried thyme

In a small pan heat butter and 1 tablespoon olive oil. Stir in tomato sauce and cook 1 to 2 minutes; remove from heat. In a bowl gently mix crabmeat and cheese. Pour sauce over and toss to mix. Season with salt and pepper.

Spread each scallopini with some of the crab mixture, leaving a bit of room at the edges. Roll up and tie with kitchen string.

Heat a few tablespoons of olive oil in a skillet. Lightly roll packets in the seasoned flour. Brown rolls on all sides; remove from pan. Adding more olive oil to pan as needed, sauté mushrooms briefly. Add tomatoes, garlic, Marsala, and thyme. Bring to a boil and return veal rolls to pan. Continue cooking 5 minutes, turning the packets occasionally.

With a slotted utensil remove veal packets to platter. Increase the heat and reduce juices until a slightly creamy sauce forms. Adjust seasonings and serve over veal.

Treasie's Crabmeat and Smithfield Ham Potato Salad

Serves 8 to 10

Here is Aunt "Treasie Utz-Utz's" now famous (up and down East Baltimore) summertime dish. She only prepares this treat on the Fourth of July, " 'cause it's too expensive to make all the time. Plus, the crabs is running big and heavy by the Fourth." Treasie keeps a watchful eye out for Uncle Elmer, who is disposed to picking the lumps of crabmeat out of the salad when he thinks no one is looking.

6 to 8 medium potatoes
Salted water to cover
4 stalks celery, diced
1 small yellow onion, finely chopped
5 green onions, minced
½ cup green bell pepper, diced
3 tablespoons dry mustard
½ teaspoon Tabasco sauce

1 cup mayonnaise
⅓ pound Smithfield ham, diced
1 pound backfin crabmeat, picked over for shells
Salt and black pepper to taste (Be careful! Smithfield ham is very salty.)

Put potatoes in a large pot, add salted water to cover, and bring to a boil. Cook until just tender. Test with a fork. Drain.

Peel off skins while potatoes are still somewhat hot. Cut into desired-sized pieces for salad and let cool.

In a small bowl combine yellow and green onions, bell pepper, mustard, Tabasco, and mayonnaise. Mix well.

In a separate large bowl, combine potatoes, crabmeat, and ham. Add mayonnaise mixture and toss very gently so as not to break up crabmeat.

Caesar Salad

Makes 3 cups dressing, serves a crowd

Now I don't expect you to believe Caesar was from Baltimore. But I also don't expect you to believe he invented this salad. All I can tell you for sure is that the salad is highly prized in this city. It's an-

2 eggs
¼ cup cloves garlic
6 ounces anchovy fillets
½ cup grated Parmesan cheese
⅓ cup sherry wine vinegar
2 teaspoons dry mustard
2 tablespoons fresh lemon juice

2 teaspoons Worcestershire sauce
2½ cups olive oil
Romaine lettuce, torn in pieces
Grated Parmesan cheese to taste
Garlic croutons
Freshly ground black pepper to taste

Bring a small saucepan of water to a boil. Slip eggs into it and imme-

other of those recipes that every-body feels they make best. This rendering of the classic Caesar was perfected by John Kelly, formerly maître d' of the Brass Elephant, one of Charles Street's finer dining establishments.

This recipe makes a lot of dressing. You can store any extra in the refrigerator for about a week.

diately remove the pan from the heat. Let stand 1 minute. Remove eggs and immerse them in cold water.

In a food processor or blender, process garlic. When finely chopped, add anchovies and process to form a smooth paste.

Add cheese, vinegar, mustard, lemon juice, and Worcestershire sauce. Break in eggs and blend very well.

With motor running, slowly pour in olive oil in a fine, steady stream.

In a large salad bowl toss romaine lettuce with a sprinkle of Parmesan cheese, some garlic croutons, and just enough dressing to coat. Serve with pepper.

NOTE: One head romaine lettuce is enough to serve 2 to 3 people.

Shrimp Salad

Serves 6 to 8

There are almost as many different shrimp salads floating around this city as there are crab cakes. Every bar, restaurant, tavern, and deli claims the prize for the best.

First it was judged by size of shrimp pieces. Or was it size of celery dice? No, no, I think it was the ratio of mayonnaise to lemon juice. Well, forget it. Now it's the type of chutney used or ripeness of the melons folded in at the end. Give me a break, Lorraine! The old-timers and I clamor for old-fashioned, unadulterated shrimp salad.

Try this one out. You just might throw your chutney in the trash can.

2 pounds shrimp
½ to ¾ cup mayonnaise
1 teaspoon Old Bay seasoning

1 cup chopped celery
2 tablespoons chopped fresh parsley
1 tablespoon fresh lemon juice

Steam shrimp as directed in Steamed Shrimp with Tangy Cocktail Sauce (see page 29). Drain, peel, devein, and cut in pieces. Place in a salad bowl.

In a small bowl combine mayonnaise, Old Bay, celery, parsley, and lemon juice; mix well. Pour over shrimp and toss.

Coleslaw

Serves 4

Coleslaw goes hand in hand with crab cakes, fried oysters, and any form of fried fish. Don't even try to host a cookout, picnic, or Sunday afternoon buffet without a large bowl of this slaw. To do so could mean social ruin.

1 cup mayonnaise
1 tablespoon red wine vinegar
1 teaspoon sugar
1 teaspoon Worcestershire sauce
1 tablespoon horseradish
1 teaspoon Dijon mustard
Few dashes Tabasco sauce
Salt and black pepper to taste
1 small head cabbage, thinly sliced
3 carrots, peeled and coarsely grated

To make the dressing, combine all the ingredients except cabbage and carrots in a small bowl. Mix well.

In a large bowl, toss together cabbage and carrots. Add dressing and mix thoroughly.

Sister Marlo's Potato Pancakes

Serves 8 to 10

Sis makes potato pancakes that won't quit—and I can't quit either when I'm eating them.

6 potatoes, peeled and grated
1 onion, grated
Juice of 1 lemon
3 eggs, beaten
1 teaspoon baking powder
3 tablespoons heavy cream
2 tablespoons flour
2 tablespoons dried bread crumbs
Vegetable oil, for frying
Sour cream and applesauce, for accompaniment

Place grated potatoes and onion in a tea towel and wring well to remove excess moisture. Transfer to a bowl and sprinkle with lemon juice to prevent discoloration.

Mix in eggs, baking powder, cream. Mix flour and bread crumbs together, add to mixture and mix well. Form into patties.

Heat oil in skillet and fry patties on both sides until golden brown. Remove to paper towels to drain.

Serve hot with sour cream and applesauce.

Sauerkraut and Apples

Serves 8

Baltimore is one of the sauerkraut capitals of the world. In fact, one mayor issued a decree that anyone caught eating turkey without sauerkraut inside the city limits would be shot. Anytime of the day or night, there are pots simmering with this zesty cabbage.

Try this recipe for a nice change from plain boiled kraut. I can't resist this with roast pork.

6 tablespoons butter
4 slices bacon, cut in ½-inch pieces
1 small onion, thinly sliced
3 tart apples, peeled, cored, and thinly sliced
2 jars (2 pounds each) sauerkraut, drained

1 bottle (12 ounces) beer, allowed to go flat
Salt and black pepper to taste
½ teaspoon caraway seed

In a heavy pot, melt the butter and render bacon a few minutes. Add onion and apples. Sauté 3 to 4 minutes.

Place sauerkraut in pot. Pour in beer and add salt, pepper, and caraway. Toss together, then bring to a boil. Cover tightly, reduce the heat, and simmer 45 minutes. Alternatively, bake in an oven preheated to 350°F 1 hour.

Fried Watercress

Serves 6

All along the streams and tributaries of the Chesapeake, watercress grows wild. Serve this garlicky treat with veal dishes or Panfried Pepper Steak with Mustard Butter (see page 199).

4 bunches watercress, large stems removed
6 tablespoons olive oil
1 teaspoon chopped garlic

Juice of 1 lemon
Salt and freshly ground black pepper to taste

Bring a pot of water to a boil. Blanch watercress 1 minute. Drain, rinse with cold water, and drain again.

In a skillet heat the olive oil. Add watercress and garlic. Cook briefly over high heat. Season with lemon juice, salt, and pepper.

• *Baltimore Breads* •

Two O'Clock Club Corn Bread

Makes one 8-inch-square loaf

*Years ago Trixie Shine was determined to head for New York to become a Broadway dancer. She had gotten a taste of the spotlight during a high-school production of **South Pacific**. Trixie found New York "too highfalutin" and returned to the Baltimore stage, making the rounds of Baltimore Street's more prestigious dance clubs. She also got a taste for corn bread from her grandmother, who had come up from the Deep South before World War II. This is Trixie's rendition of Grandma Shine's recipe. It's the melt-in-your-mouth kind.*

1 cup yellow cornmeal
1 cup flour
¼ cup sugar
5 teaspoons baking powder
½ teaspoon salt

2 eggs, lightly beaten
1¼ cups milk
2 tablespoons butter, melted and cooled

Preheat oven to 425°F.

In a bowl mix together cornmeal, flour, sugar, baking powder, and salt.

In another bowl combine eggs, milk, and butter. Add to dry ingredients and mix thoroughly without overbeating. Pour into a greased and floured, shallow 8-inch-square pan.

Bake 30 minutes, or until toothpick inserted in center comes out clean.

South Baltimore Ice Box Rolls

Makes about 4 dozen rolls

These light rolls are perfect for the host or hostess on the go. You can make the dough several days ahead and have it ready to bake before your meal.

1 package active dry yeast
¼ cup lukewarm (105°F to 115°F) water
1 cup warm mashed potatoes
½ cup potato water (reserved from cooking potatoes)
1 cup milk

½ cup (¼ pound) butter, melted
½ cup sugar
2 eggs, beaten
1½ teaspoons salt
4 to 5 cups flour

Dissolve yeast in lukewarm water; let stand until foamy, about 10 minutes. In a bowl, mix together warm potatoes, potato water, milk, butter, sugar, eggs, salt, and yeast mixture. Mix well. Beat in flour, 1 cup at a time, until a stiff dough is formed.

Turn dough out onto floured board and knead 8 to 10 minutes until smooth, adding flour as necessary to eliminate stickiness.

Place in an oiled bowl, cover with a towel, and let rise in a warm place until doubled in bulk, about 1 hour.

Punch down the dough, put in a bowl, and cover tightly. Refrigerate until ready to use, which can be up to several days. Check now and then to make sure dough isn't rising. If it is, punch it back down.

When ready to use, preheat oven to 375°F. Take out as much dough as needed and form into desired shape. Arrange rolls on a baking sheet and brush with melted butter. Let rise 30 minutes. Bake about 15 minutes or until golden brown.

Hot Cross Buns

Makes about 2 dozen buns

When I was a youngster these traditional treats brightened up for me what was otherwise a dismal time of the year. Beginning on Ash Wednesday, the austerity hit with purple-draped church statues, fasting, pennance, and giving up television, candy, cussing, and hitting your brothers and sisters. What a life! Just the same, I couldn't wait for Lent. I spent the month before counting down the days until our local bakeries started making my dreamt-about hot cross buns. After school I would buy a bag of the buns, go home, and settle down for a happy afternoon of eating. I still look forward to Lent for these hot cross buns!

1 cup milk
½ cup sugar
6 tablespoons butter
1 package active dry yeast
¼ cup lukewarm (105°F to 115°F) water
2 eggs, beaten
1 teaspoon ground cinnamon
½ teaspoon ground allspice
¼ teaspoon ground nutmeg
1 teaspoon salt
5 cups flour
1 cup raisins or dried currants
Grated rind of ½ lemon
1 egg yolk
1 teaspoon water
Cross Icing (recipe follows)

Scald milk and add sugar and butter. Heat until butter is melted and transfer to a large bowl. Dissolve yeast in water and let stand until foamy, about 10 minutes. Add to milk. Beat in the eggs.

Sift together spices, salt, and flour. Beat into liquid ingredients, 1 cup at a time, until a soft dough is formed. While beating sprinkle in raisins and lemon rind.

Turn out onto floured board and knead briefly 1 to 2 minutes. Place in an oiled bowl, cover with a towel, and let rise in warm place until doubled in bulk, 1½ to 2 hours.

Turn out onto floured board and knead briefly, 1 to 2 minutes. Return to oiled bowl, cover, and let rise again until doubled in bulk, about 1 hour.

Preheat oven to 350°F. Shape dough into biscuits and arrange on buttered baking sheet 1 inch apart. Cover and let rise 30 minutes. Mix together egg yolk and water and brush on buns.

Bake 25 to 30 minutes, or until golden brown. Prepare icing while buns are baking.

Remove buns from oven and brush a little icing on them while they are still hot. When buns are cool, use remaining icing to form crosses on tops of buns.

Cross Icing

1½ cups sifted confectioners' sugar
2 egg whites

1 tablespoon fresh lemon juice
Grated rind of ½ lemon

In a bowl beat sugar into egg whites, a little at a time. When mixed well, beat in lemon juice and rind. If too thick, use a little water or more lemon juice to make a thin glaze.

Lady Baltimore Cake

Makes one 9-inch cake, serves 8

A legendary dessert, famous throughout the South. This cake is said to have originated with the first Lord Baltimore's wife, for serving at afternoon teas.

The ladies I've spoken to don't hold many teas these days, but swear by this cake for first communions, bridal showers, and your more "upper-crust" Tupperware parties.

Trudy Paskowski, the undisputed Lady Baltimore of the Tupperware circuit, suggests doubling the Cognac in the filling and throwing a "touch" of it into the icing to increase sales.

1 cup (½ pound) butter, softened
2 cups sugar
3½ cups flour
1 tablespoon baking powder
¼ teaspoon salt

1 teaspoon almond or vanilla extract
1¼ cups milk
6 egg whites
Lady Baltimore Filling and Frosting
  (recipe follows)

Preheat oven to 350°F.

In a mixing bowl beat together the butter and sugar until pale and creamy.

In another bowl sift together the flour, baking powder, and salt. Add extract to milk.

Add a little of the dry ingredients to the butter-sugar mixture and mix in. Then stir in a little of the milk. Alternately add the remaining dry and wet ingredients in small amounts until both are completely incorporated. Beat until a smooth batter is formed.

Beat egg whites until stiff but not dry. Fold whites into the batter, one third at a time.

Pour into 2 greased and floured, 9-inch round cake pans. Bake 20 to 25 minutes, or until a toothpick inserted in middle of cake comes out clean. Let cool 5 minutes in pans, then turn out onto rack and cool completely.

Prepare frosting and filling while cake layers are cooling, then fill and frost.

Lady Baltimore Filling and Frosting

4 egg whites
1½ cups sugar
¼ teaspoon salt
1 teaspoon cream of tartar
⅔ cup water

2 teaspoons vanilla extract
½ cup chopped raisins
¾ cup chopped walnuts or pecans
8 figs, finely chopped
2 tablespoons Cognac

In the top pan of a double boiler, combine egg whites, sugar, salt, cream of tartar, and water. Beat with electric beater over simmering water until soft peaks form. This takes 5 to 8 minutes. Remove from water and beat in vanilla. Continue beating until the frosting is stiff. Put aside half of the frosting.

Beat into the remaining half of the frosting the raisins, nuts, figs, and Cognac. Use this mixture as a filling between the 2 layers of the cake. Ice the entire cake with the reserved frosting.

Alberta's Cheesecake

Makes one 8-inch pie, serves 8

Kids running under foot. Cats darting between her ankles. Nothing seems to bother Alberta as she whips up what many claim is the best cheesecake in town. I heartily agree, and I asked her what I should say about her cheesecake. Alberta responded with, "I don't care what you tell 'em, just don't tell 'em I beat my kids." So I won't and she don't. But do try this cheesecake. It's a little bit of heaven right here on earth!

Graham Cracker Crust (recipe follows)
3 packages (8 ounces each) cream cheese, softened
2 cups sugar

4 eggs
1 tablespoon vanilla extract
2 cups sour cream
Sweetened strawberries, blueberries, or other berries (optional)

Prepare pie crust and chill. Preheat oven to 350°F.

In a mixing bowl cream together the cream cheese and 1½ cups of the sugar until fluffy. Add the eggs, one at a time, mixing well. Add 1 teaspoon of the vanilla and mix well. Pour into the chilled crust and bake 50 minutes, or until firm in the center. When done, remove and let stand for 15 minutes out of the oven. Increase oven temperature to 450°F.

For the topping, mix together the sour cream, the remaining ½ cup sugar, and the remaining 2 teaspoons vanilla. Spoon over the cake and return to the oven 10 minutes.

Cool 24 hours or, at the very least, overnight, before serving. If desired, top with sweetened berries.

Graham Cracker Crust

Makes one 8-inch crust

1½ cups graham cracker crumbs
¼ cup sugar

½ cup butter, melted

Mix graham crackers and sugar together. Stir in the butter and mix thoroughly. Line the bottom of an 8-inch springform pan with mixture by pressing it firmly into place. Chill.

Jana Ringdinger's Rice Pudding

Serves 6 to 8

Jana and her best girlfriend Rosie worked over at the Domino sugar factory for years. Rice pudding is a must on every tavern menu in town, and the girls spent many long hours trying out different versions. They put on a few pounds along the way, but said it was worth it because Jana came up with the perfect recipe. She says using Domino sugar isn't absolutely necessary, but finds it makes a richer pudding. And I guess she should know.

4 cups half-and-half
4 cups milk
⅔ cup rice (long-grain white rice)
½ teaspoon salt
1 cup raisins
½ cup sugar

3 eggs
2 teaspoons vanilla extract
Ground cinnamon, for topping
Half-and-half or whipping cream, for accompaniment

In a saucepan, bring the half-and-half, milk, rice, and salt to a boil. Reduce the heat and simmer 30 minutes, stirring frequently. Add the raisins and continue cooking 15 minutes.

In a small bowl beat together the sugar, eggs, and vanilla. Add to the rice mixture. Bring to a boil and cook 1 minute, stirring constantly. Pour into a buttered, 3-quart casserole and sprinkle with cinnamon on top.

Cool to room temperature. Pudding will thicken as it cools. Serve with half-and-half or cream.

Apple and Walnut Pudding

Serves 6

While Bernie Curtis is wrestling with his Christmas Day Roast "Beast" (see page 49), his wife Judy is whipping up this luscious way to complete the holiday meal.

¼ cup (4 tablespoons) butter, softened
1 cup sugar
1 egg, beaten
4 tart apples, peeled, cored, and coarsely chopped
½ cup walnut pieces

1 teaspoon vanilla extract
1 cup flour
1 teaspoon baking soda
1 teaspoon ground cinnamon
Heavy cream, for accompaniment

Preheat oven to 350°F.

In a large bowl cream together butter and sugar. Add the egg and mix. Stir in the apples, walnuts, and vanilla.

Sift together the flour, baking soda, and cinnamon. Add to the apple mixture and stir to combine. Pour into a buttered 8- by 8- by 2-inch baking dish.

Bake 35 minutes, or until set. Serve warm with a little cream.

Mrs. Morrison's Mace Cake

Serves 6 to 8

When first I sampled this cake, I was unsure as to the classification of mace. Spice or chemical? After my initial ten pieces, I was sure. It's a drug. I simply could not stop until that rather large cake was gone!

I was given this recipe by Catherine LeVeque, who wrote down for posterity Mrs. Morrison's oral instructions. Mrs. Morrison was the housekeeper at St. Luke's Episcopal Church for at least two to three generations, and this cake was revered by each succeeding congregation.

Catherine, who is the wife of an Episcopal priest, says she loves this cake because not only is it a delightfully unusual dessert, but it's also great for funerals. Sometimes you need something for a large number of people quickly—and this cake surely fits the bill.

This cake needs no frosting, but for important occasions I have served mine topped with sliced strawberries and a dollop of sweetened whipped cream.

1 cup milk
½ cup (¼ pound) butter, softened
4 eggs, beaten
2½ cups sugar
2 cups flour

2 teaspoons baking powder
½ teaspoon salt
1 tablespoon plus ½ teaspoon ground mace

Preheat oven to 350°F.

In a saucepan combine milk and butter. Bring to a boil and remove from the heat.

Cream together the eggs and 2 cups sugar in a mixing bowl. Sift together the flour, baking powder, salt, and 1 tablespoon mace.

Mix the dry ingredients into the creamed mixture. Add the milk and butter while still hot and mix well. Mrs. Morrison always insisted on 300 strokes to blend the mixture well. Pour into a greased and floured 9-by-13-inch pan. For the topping, mix the remaining ½ cup sugar and ½ teaspoon mace together and then sprinkle the mixture overtop the batter. Bake 25 to 35 minutes. (Alternatively, bake the cake in a 10-inch tube pan at 325°F 1 hour.)

Vanilla-Butternut Pound Cake

Serves 10 to 12

El Farace says the secret to this incredible pound cake is how you treat the eggs. "You gotta leave the eggs out overnight or you might as well go up to the bakery, pick up a store-bought one, and forget the whole thing."
So, girls and boys, put a string around your finger and get those eggs out the night before!

½ cup vegetable oil
1 cup (½ pound) butter, softened
3 cups sugar
¼ teaspoon salt
6 eggs, at room temperature

3 cups flour, sifted
1 cup milk
1 tablespoon vanilla-butternut extract

Preheat oven to 325°F.

In a mixing bowl cream together the oil, butter, sugar, and salt. Beat in the eggs, one at a time. Alternately mix in the flour and milk in small amounts, ending with flour. Fold in the extract. Pour the batter into a buttered and floured 10-inch tube pan or two small loaf pans.

Bake for 1½ hours or until a toothpick inserted in the center comes out clean. Cool in the pan for 20 minutes, then turn out onto a wire rack and cool completely.

The LeVeque Man-Trap Cake

Makes one 9-inch cake, serves 8

This fairly historical cake has kept the girls in the LeVeque family up to their necks in men for generations. Legend has it that there was only one spinster aunt in the clan's entire history and that she thought cake or baked food of any kind unladylike. This was attributed to the fact that baking required one to bend over to put the product into the oven. She felt this was morally offensive.

I'm told this recipe is "surefire." So girls, get one of these in the oven 'cause time's a-wasting!

¼ cup (4 tablespoons) butter, softened
2 cups sugar
2 egg yolks
1½ cups milk
2 cups flour, sifted
2 teaspoons baking powder

2 teaspoons salt
2 egg whites
2 teaspoons vanilla extract
4 ounces unsweetened chocolate, melted and cooled
Fudge Topping (recipe follows)

Preheat oven to 350°F.

In a large mixing bowl cream together the butter and sugar. In a small bowl, beat the egg yolks and milk. Sift together the flour, baking powder, and salt.

Alternately mix dry and wet ingredients into the creamed mixture in small amounts; mix until a smooth batter is formed. Do not overbeat.

Beat the egg whites until stiff but not dry and add to batter with the vanilla and melted chocolate. Mix well. Pour into a greased and floured 9-inch-square cake pan. Bake 30 minutes. Turn out onto a rack to cool.

Ice with your favorite frosting, or, for the best results, prepare the Fudge Topping. For a good picnic cake, leave in the pan and ice only the top.

Fudge Topping

Makes 2 cups

2 ounces unsweetened chocolate
2 cups sugar
¾ cup milk

2 tablespoons light corn syrup
¼ cup (4 tablespoons) butter
1 teaspoon vanilla extract

Cut the chocolate into small pieces and place in a saucepan. Add the sugar, milk, corn syrup, and butter. Bring to a boil, stirring constantly. Continue cooking and stirring 1 minute more. Remove from the heat and stir in the vanilla. Cool slightly and beat until thick.

Laurie Torte

Makes one 10-inch torte,
serves 8 to 10

Laurie Plant, a one-time student of the Maryland Institute of Art and later a pastry chef, created this exquisite dessert. It highlights her artistic talents as well as her culinary expertise.

6 tablespoons butter, melted
¾ of an 8½ ounce box of chocolate
   wafers (Nabisco Famous Wafers)
2 oranges
1⅔ cups sugar
½ cup (¼ pound) butter, softened
5 eggs

2½ tablespoons flour
1 tablespoon yellow cornmeal
½ cup orange juice
¼ teaspoon vanilla extract
4 ounces semisweet chocolate
Sweetened lightly whipped cream, for
   accompaniment

Line the bottom of a 10-inch springform pan with waxed paper. In a food processor or blender, grind wafers until fine. In a bowl, mix wafers and the 6 tablespoons melted butter. Press mixture firmly onto bottom of pan. Cover and put in freezer.

Preheat oven to 350°F. Peel the zest from the oranges and grind zest in processor or blender. In a mixing bowl cream together the ½ cup butter, sugar, and ground zest. When very light in color, add eggs, one at a time. Add flour and cornmeal and mix well. Add orange juice and vanilla. Mix well.

Pour butter mixture into a heavy, nonaluminum pan. Cook over medium heat, stirring constantly with a wooden spoon, until mixture begins to thicken.

This is a good time for prayer and meditation since this step takes 8 to 12 minutes. When it begins to thicken you may want to use, alternately, a whisk and a spoon. *Do not boil!*

Pour into frozen crust and bake 30 to 35 minutes or until lightly browned.

While torte is baking cut chocolate in pieces and grind in processor. Remove torte from oven and sprinkle chocolate on evenly. Wait 1 minute, then smooth out softened chocolate with a small metal spatula.

Cover and refrigerate several hours or overnight before serving. Serve with whipped cream.

Strawberry Shortcake

Makes one 9-inch cake, serves 8

It's sure not summertime without strawberry shortcake! Just the ticket for recalling fond memories or creating new ones.

At least 2 pints ripe strawberries, hulled
Granulated sugar, for dusting strawberries, plus 2 tablespoons
2 cups flour
1 tablespoon baking powder
½ teaspoon salt
⅛ teaspoon ground mace

6 tablespoons butter, cut in pieces
¾ cup milk
Softened butter, for spreading on shortcake
Confectioners' sugar, for topping
Sweetened lightly whipped cream, for accompaniment

Preheat oven to 400°F.

Slice the strawberries in half (leave some whole for top) into a bowl and sprinkle lightly with granulated sugar. Let them sit while making the shortcake.

In a mixing bowl sift together the flour, baking powder, salt, 2 tablespoons granulated sugar, and mace. Work butter in with fingertips until mixture is the consistency of coarse meal. Stir in the milk to form a smooth dough that pulls away from the sides of bowl.

On a floured board roll out dough in a round to fit a greased and floured, 9-inch cake pan. Transfer dough round to pan. Bake 12 to 15 minutes.

Remove from oven and cool on wire rack. Turn cake out of pan and cut in 2 layers and butter. Arrange sweetened strawberries between layers and on top. Sprinkle top with confectioners' sugar and serve with whipped cream.

Frances's Sugar Cookies

Makes 10 dozen cookies

These cookies are favorites of the staff at Maryland Senator Barbara Mikulski's Inner Harbor office. Buttery rich and lightly scented with nutmeg, these treats are a welcome addition to any holiday baker's Christmas-cookie tins.

1½ pounds confectioners' sugar (about 5⅔ cups)
1½ cups (¾ pound) butter, softened
5 eggs, beaten
1 teaspoon baking powder
½ teaspoon salt
1 teaspoon ground nutmeg
1¼ cups milk
2 pounds flour (about 7½ cups)
Equal amounts flour and confectioners' sugar, for dusting

Preheat oven to 375°F.

In a mixing bowl, cream together the sugar and butter until fluffy. Mix in the eggs. Stir in baking powder, salt, nutmeg, and milk. Work in the flour slowly, making a dough stiff enough to roll out. Cover and refrigerate 5 to 6 hours before rolling out the dough.

Dust a board with flour-sugar mixture to prevent sticking. Roll out the chilled dough to ¼ inch thick and cut in desired shapes. Place on lightly greased baking sheets and bake 5 to 8 minutes, or until delicately browned. Cool on rack and serve.

Apple Marmalade

Makes 8 half-pints

The tart stewed apples produce a tangy, slightly sweetened, thick preserve perfect for the breakfast table.

1½ cups water
5 cups sugar
2 tablespoons fresh lemon juice

8 cups tart apples, peeled, cored and
  thinly sliced
1 orange, thinly sliced

In a large, heavy pot, bring water and sugar to a boil, stirring until sugar dissolves. Add lemon juice, apples, and orange. Boil rapidly until the mixture forms a thick syrup, about 30 to 60 minutes.

Remove from the heat; skin off the foam. Ladle into hot, sterilized jars, seal, and process in water bath according to standard canning procedures.

A NOTE ON CANNING: There are various methods employed in the canning of preserves, jellies, relishes, and the like. When referring to "standard canning procedures," I suggest using a reference cookbook such as *The Joy of Cooking* or *The Fannie Farmer Cookbook* for clear, detailed, and safe instructions.

Sister Judy's Hot Pepper Jelly

Makes 8 half-pints

Sister Judy grows her own peppers for this spicy jelly, which she makes at the Carmelite Monastery in Towson, Maryland. If you're too busy to make your own, but are in the area, stop by the monastery and stock up on Sister Judy's delicacy. The jelly is

1¾ cups distilled white vinegar
1 bell pepper, chopped
½ cup chopped fresh jalapeño chiles,
  plus additional chopped jalapeños
  as needed

6½ cups sugar
1¼ cups white vinegar
6 ounces liquid fruit pectin

In a blender, mix ½ cup of the vinegar, bell pepper and ½ cup jalapeños thoroughly. Whirl in additional jalapeños to bring volume to 1½ cups.

Combine sugar with 1 cup of the vinegar in a heavy pot. Bring to a slow boil, stirring to dissolve sugar. Add pepper mixture. Rinse blender with the remaining ¼ cup vinegar and pour into pot. Cook 15 to 20 minutes.

wonderful with cream cheese on crackers or can be used for basting meats or poultry

Stir in pectin. Pour into hot, sterilized jars and seal according to standard canning procedures.

NOTE: If doubling or tripling this recipe, divide mixture into halves or thirds before adding appropriate amount of pectin. Otherwise it will thicken too quickly.

Pickled Green Tomatoes

Makes 3 quarts

Green tomatoes are used widely in the Chesapeake area as a relish, in mock mincemeat, and fried.

3½ cups distilled white vinegar
3½ cups water
¼ cup kosher salt
72 firm medium-sized green tomatoes, cored and quartered
1 large green bell pepper, cut in ½-inch strips
1 red bell pepper, cut in ½-inch strips

4 whole dried hot peppers
6 cloves garlic
4 onions, coarsely chopped
3 stalks celery, cut in 2-inch pieces
¾ cup dill seed
4 tablespoons pickling spice

In a large pot combine vinegar, water, and salt and bring to a boil. Scald 3 quart jars. Pack tomatoes into each hot jar, evenly distributing peppers, garlic, onions, celery, dill seed, and pickling spice among jars. Pour boiling liquid into jars, leaving ½-inch headspace. Seal and process in water bath according to standard canning procedures. Store in a cool, dark place 4 to 6 weeks before eating.

El's Tomato Ketchup

Makes about 3 quarts

A welcome change from everyday ketchup. This zesty version is full of fresh tomato flavor. It's so good, you'll want to eat it right out of the jar.

4 quarts ripe tomatoes (about 24 large tomatoes), peeled, cored, and chopped
1 cup chopped onions
½ cup chopped sweet red peppers
½ tablespoon celery seed
1 teaspoon dry mustard
1 teaspoon ground allspice
1 stick cinnamon
1 cup sugar
1½ cups white vinegar
1 tablespoon paprika

Combine tomatoes, onions, peppers, and seasonings in a heavy-bottom pot and cook over medium heat until soft. Press through a food mill or sieve.

Return sieved mixture to pot. Cook rapidly until thick and reduced in volume. Ladle into hot, sterilized jars, seal, and process in water bath according to standard canning procedures.

Dirty Gertie

This nasty-sounding drink will "put hair on your chest," which was my Uncle Rob's selling point when persuading someone to try something of which they would otherwise be leery. It is actually a Baltimore "seafoodish" version of a Bloody Mary. For the ultimate in drink garnish, hang a peeled, deveined, and steamed jumbo shrimp on the glass.

1½ ounces vodka
1 tablespoon lemon juice
1 tablespoon Worcestershire sauce
¼ teaspoon Old Bay seasoning
Dash freshly ground black pepper
½ teaspoon prepared horseradish
3 dashes Tabasco sauce
2 parts tomato juice
1 part clam juice, fresh or bottled
Celery stick for garnish

Fill a tall glass with ice. Pour in the vodka, lemon juice, Worcestershire, Old Bay, black pepper, horseradish, and Tabasco. Stir. Fill the glass with a mixture of tomato and clam juice. Stir well. Garnish with the celery stick.

NOTE: To regulate chest hair growth, increase or decrease the amounts of horseradish and Tabasco accordingly.

Mealy Sartori and her granddaughter Sara Mae enjoy an intimate moment.

Mealy is sitting in her kitchen, in the home that she and her late husband Pete built by hand some forty years ago. She reminisces: "I grew up living right next to the harbor in Little Italy, in the early 1900s. There were ships from everywhere, loading and unloading stuff. The smells! Oh hell, there were banana boats from South America, boats of vegetables and fruits from the Eastern Shore, and watermelons. They were floating everywhere! As kids we loved to sit on the docks and watch them bobbing up and down in the water. The boys would try to spear them."

Her mother, who immigrated to Baltimore from Italy, was a great cook and Mealy says she learned the tricks of the trade from her. "We never wasted nothing. Hell, you couldn't afford to! By the time I was married and had the kids I was making my own breads, goat cheeses, ricotta, and pasta. I kept goats, chickens, ducks, and rabbits. Yea, right here in the backyard. I had a garden bigger than this one. It had everything! Fed us during the summer and gave us enough to put up for the winter. I love to cook! You know, you gotta love it. Nobody wants to bother with it no more. I don't know what the hell's wrong with them. They don't want to take the time to make something good, or take the time to sit with the family and eat. How you gonna get to know each other? I think they're all going crazy."

I asked Mealy what she would cook for a special occasion and this is her menu. The wonderful curly endive soup is a traditional Italian recipe, often made for weddings. For the rockfish with blue crab she calls the tomato sauce that is her classic braising medium "Gravy." It's the marvelous base for her pastas, lasagna, and raviolis. She ends this sumptuous meal with a light zabaglione sauce and stewed figs that have been picked from her backyard tree.

After watching Mealy enthusiastically prepare her food and then tasting the results, I know she loves to cook . . . and, yea, you gotta love it!

Curly Endive Soup
with Prosciutto and Parmesan

Salad of Mixed Field Greens
Tossed with Italian Dressing

Rockfish Braised in "Gravy"
with Blue Crab Clusters

Fried Broccoli with Hot Peppers

Stewed Fresh Figs
in a Warm Marsala Zabaglione

Curly Endive Soup with Prosciutto and Parmesan

Serves 6 to 8

4 quarts water
½ prosciutto bone, cut in several pieces
1 large onion, finely chopped
3 heads escarole lettuce, cored and washed

3 eggs, lightly beaten
4 ounces grated Parmesan cheese (about 1 cup)
Freshly ground black pepper

In a soup pot bring water and prosciutto bone to a boil. Reduce the heat and simmer, uncovered, 2½ to 3 hours. Remove bone and pick off any pieces of meat; add meat to pot. Return liquid to a boil and add onion and escarole. Lower heat and simmer 15 minutes.

In a bowl, mix together eggs and Parmesan. While soup is simmering, pour egg mixture into the pot in a slow stream, stirring constantly.

Remove from the heat and ladle into soup bowls. Top with freshly ground pepper.

Salad of Mixed Field Greens Tossed with Italian Dressing

Serves 8

Combination of greens for 8 servings: escarole, red lettuce, romaine, butter lettuce, and dandelion greens
1 large red onion, thinly sliced
10 radishes, thinly sliced
1 green bell pepper, thinly sliced
2 cucumbers, thinly sliced

2 ripe tomatoes, each cut in 8 wedges
Italian Dressing (recipe follows)
2 tablespoons chopped fresh or dried oregano
Freshly ground black pepper

Tear greens and place in a large bowl. Add onion, radishes, bell pepper, cucumbers, and tomatoes.

Toss salad with just enough dressing to coat lettuces. Sprinkle with oregano and freshly ground pepper.

Italian Dressing

Makes about 1¼ cups

¼ cup red wine vinegar
1 cup olive oil

1 clove garlic, pressed or minced
½ teaspoon salt

In a small bowl combine all the ingredients. Whisk well.

Rockfish Braised in "Gravy" with Blue Crab Clusters

Serves 6 to 8

"Gravy" (recipe follows)
2 rockfish or bass (3 to 4 pounds each), cleaned
16 alive and kicking blue crabs

Salt
Freshly ground black pepper
1 bay leaf

Prepare the "Gravy."

Cut off the head and tail of each fish. In a large flameproof casserole place fish side by side. Cover them two thirds of the way up with "Gravy." Bring to a boil. Cover, reduce the heat, and simmer 30 minutes.

While the fish is cooking, clean the crabs. Handle the crabs carefully because they'd love to bite you. Pick them up from behind. Remove bibs and top shell. Cut out gills and "devil" (see illustrations on page 7). Quarter crabs and put aside.

After fish has cooked for 30 minutes, add crab clusters to casserole and cover them with the remaining hot "Gravy." Cover and continue to simmer 20 minutes.

Place fish on a large serving platter and surround with crab clusters. Pout hot "Gravy" over fish and serve at once.

"Gravy"

Makes about 8 cups

¼ cup olive oil
2 cloves garlic, minced
½ large onion, finely chopped
¼ teaspoon hot-pepper flakes
1 can (12 ounces) tomato paste
3 cups water

1 can (14½ ounces) Italian plum tomatoes
1 teaspoon dried oregano
1 teaspoon dried basil
1 teaspoon salt, or to taste
1 tablespoon sugar

In a pot heat oil and sauté garlic, onions, and hot-pepper flakes until golden.

Stir in tomato paste. Rinse can with the water and add to the pot. Simmer 30 minutes.

Add all the remaining ingredients. Simmer at least 1½ to 2 hours. If you have more time, let it simmer even a little longer.

Fried Broccoli with Hot Peppers

Serves 6 to 8

2 pounds broccoli
Salted water
⅓ cup olive oil
2 cloves garlic, minced

¼ teaspoon hot-pepper flakes
Salt and freshly ground black pepper
to taste

Trim off tough bottom stems and outer leaves of broccoli. Bring a saucepan filled with salted water to a boil. Add broccoli and parboil 8 minutes. Remove broccoli with a slotted utensil and save water; set broccoli aside.

In a skillet heat olive oil. Sauté garlic and hot pepper. Add broccoli and cook 3 minutes.

Pour in 1 cup of the reserved water and simmer until broccoli is tender. Season with salt and pepper.

Stewed Fresh Figs in a Warm Marsala Zabaglione

Serves 8

½ cup sugar
½ cup water

2 pints ripe figs, stemmed
Zabaglione (recipe follows)

In a heavy-bottomed pot, bring sugar and water to a boil, stirring to dissolve sugar. Add the figs, cover, reduce the heat, and simmer slowly until tender, 15 to 20 minutes. Cool.

Prepare Zabaglione.

Spoon a little of the sauce into 8 wineglasses. Divide the figs among the glasses and top with the remaining sauce.

Zabaglione

8 egg yolks (save an eggshell half for
  measuring)

½ cup sugar
8 eggshell halves dry Marsala

Select a pot large enough to accommodate a mixing bowl resting in the top. Fill with water and bring to a boil.

In a stainless-steel mixing bowl, cream together egg yolks and sugar with a wire whisk until pale and creamy. Whisk in Marsala.

Rest bowl on top of pot above simmering water. Whisk mixture constantly until it becomes frothy and thickened. This generally takes several minutes. Do not overcook or sauce will scramble.

· Annapolis ·

Juxtaposed with the elegance of Annapolis' colonial surroundings is Chick and Ruth's Deli. Here, proprietor Charles "Chick" Levitt displays one of their famous over-stuffed sandwiches. Chick's son, Ted, provides the laughs with the deli's own joke book.

Whom entering the old town of Annapolis, one is immediately struck by the enormous sense of history. Situated on the Chesapeake, at the mouth of the Severn River, the town of Annapolis is full of streets lined with grand old homes dating back to the days before the American Revolution. When they speak of "the war" here, that is the one they mean.

Today the capital of Maryland, Annapolis served briefly as the capital of the United States, prior to the state giving up the land that became the District of Columbia. The presence of the United States Naval Academy, which was founded to "create a select group of gentleman and scholar officers," adds to the sense of tradition and chivalry that has always been a strong element of the city's culture.

Instead of tearing down and burying the past as so many other cities have done, Annapolis residents are devoted to the preservation and restoration of their city's proud history. Annapolis cooking reflects this heritage with an air of elegance and refinement. In the eighteenth century this colonial town was quite the cosmopolitan hot spot along the Chesapeake. Britain's influence undoubtedly shaped the styles of society and cuisine, but the fashions and flavors of France made their way into the manors and dining halls of Annapolis's most prominent families. Dishes such as Crabmeat and Shrimp Mousse, a Statehouse Seafood Ragout, and Sweetbreads of Veal with Backfin Crabmeat are testaments to the French influence on the capital city's kitchens. The historic dishes presented in Marjorie Steen's menu at the end of this section are fine representations of the mingling of the English and French cultures in colonial Annapolis cookery.

Annapolis is not totally absorbed in history, however. Do not forget the boats, for Annapolis is the most boat-oriented town on the East Coast. The locals are a sophisticated, pleasure-seeking lot whose leisure time is tied to the water. There are "weekend cap'ns" aplenty on the waters surrounding Annapolis, sharpening their boating skills at the helm as well as reaping the catches of the Chesapeake Bay.

Plantation Eggs

Serves 4

A lovely dish with which to start the day. As you bite into the smoky ham and creamy biscuits, visions of gentler times come to mind. A good cup of strong tea goes well with this substantial breakfast. If you don't have a biscuit cutter large enough to accommodate the eggs, I find the rim of a water glass does nicely for cutting a slightly larger round.

Cheese Sauce (recipe follows)
4 large Buttermilk Biscuits (see page 99), warm
Butter, for biscuits

8 thin slices Smithfield ham, grilled
8 eggs, poached

Prepare the sauce. Split the warm biscuits and spread with butter. Place a slice of grilled ham on each biscuit half. Place a poached egg on top of ham and cover with the hot sauce.

Cheese Sauce

Makes about 2 cups

¼ cup (4 tablespoons) butter
¼ cup flour
½ cup Chicken Stock (see page 33) or bouillon
1½ cups half-and-half

1 cup grated sharp Cheddar cheese
½ cup finely diced red bell pepper, sautéed in butter
Salt and white pepper to taste
Dash Tabasco sauce

In a saucepan melt the butter and stir in flour. Cook 2 to 3 minutes, stirring constantly.

Off the heat whisk in the stock and half-and-half.

Return to heat and bring to a boil. Cook 1 to 2 minutes. Stir in the cheese and bell pepper. Season with salt, pepper, and Tabasco.

Creamed Chipped Beef

Serves 4

A long-standing favorite on the Annapolis breakfast scene, chipped beef is actually dried beef that is sliced very thin. It is found at markets in packages and is sometimes quite salty, in which case it must be soaked briefly in hot water.

You will find vats of this creamy concoction percolating for the cadets at the United States Naval Academy, where it has a less-appetizing code name. Something to do with a shingle I think. Current Maryland Governor Schaefer has earned some fame for his early morning statehouse chipped beef breakfasts, to which he invites members of the legislature.

6 ounces chipped beef, cut in strips
1 cup sliced fresh mushrooms
12 tablespoons butter
6 tablespoons flour
5 cups milk
2 teaspoons Worcestershire sauce
Salt and black pepper to taste
1/8 teaspoon Tabasco sauce
8 slices white bread, toasted
Chopped fresh parsley or watercress, for garnish

Soak beef in hot water to cover to remove some of the saltiness. In a small skillet sauté the mushrooms in 4 tablespoons of the butter until soft; set mushrooms aside with their cooking juices.

In a saucepan, melt the remaining butter and stir in flour. Cook for 2 to 3 minutes, stirring constantly. Gradually whisk in the milk, and then the Worcestershire. Bring to a boil and add reserved mushrooms. Cook 3 to 5 minutes.

Drain the beef and add to pan with sauce. Simmer several minutes. Season with salt, pepper, and Tabasco.

Serve over toast and garnish with parsley.

Flannel Cakes

Makes about 2 dozen
3-inch pancakes

I am told these colonial-style yeast pancakes received their name from flannel cloths, or towels, placed over the bowl at night while the dough was rising. A scrumptious griddlecake that is more than worth the little extra bother of starting the dough the night before.

4 cups flour
1 teaspoon salt
1 package active dry yeast
¼ cup lukewarm (105°F to 115°F) water
3½ cups milk

3 tablespoons sugar
3 eggs, beaten
2 tablespoons butter, melted
Melted butter and maple syrup, for accompaniment

Before bed sift together the flour and salt into a bowl. Dissolve the yeast in lukewarm water and let stand until foamy, about 10 minutes. Combine the milk and sugar in a saucepan and scald, stirring to dissolve sugar. Remove from heat, pour into a large mixing bowl, and stir until lukewarm. Add the yeast mixture. Beat in the sifted ingredients to form a dough. Cover with a towel and let rise overnight in a warm place.

In the morning beat together the eggs and butter. Beat mixture into the dough.

Cook the cakes on a hot griddle as you would regular pancakes. Serve with melted butter and maple syrup.

Chicken Liver and Pecan Pâté

Makes one 3-pound pâté (6 cups)

Pâté has been on the Annapolis entertaining scene since colonial times. The original pâtés were whole pieces of boiled meats baked in a heavy pastry. They were cut in thin slices to be enjoyed by party goers.

Serve this luxuriously rich pâté with crackers or crusty French bread for spreading.

2½ cups (1¼ pounds) unsalted butter
1 small onion, chopped
2 tablespoons chopped shallots
1 pound chicken livers
½ cup dry Marsala wine
1 tablespoon dried thyme
Salt and black pepper to taste
¾ cup heavy cream
1 cup finely chopped pecans

In a skillet melt 1 cup of the butter and sauté the onion and shallots until soft. Add the chicken livers and cook 3 minutes. Then add the Marsala, thyme, salt, and pepper. Continue to cook until the livers are brown but still barely pink inside and the alcohol has cooked off.

With a slotted spoon transfer the liver mixture to a blender or food processor. Mix until very smooth.

Cut the remaining 1½ cups butter in small pieces and add to the mixture slowly. When the butter is incorporated, add the cream and fold in the pecans. The mixture will seem quite liquid.

Pour the mixture into a pâté mold or a 9- by 5- by 3-inch loaf pan. Cover and chill 24 hours. To unmold, set the pan in a larger pan of hot water, run a knife around edge of the pâté, and turn out onto a plate.

Crabmeat and Shrimp Mousse

Serves 6

A memorable first course suitable for a statehouse dinner, this mousse pairs shellfish and fin fish in a custard so light it practically floats off the plate.

¾ pound sole or flounder fillets
¼ pound shrimp, peeled and deveined
1 tablespoon fresh lemon juice
½ teaspoon salt
¼ teaspoon white pepper
4 egg whites
2 cups heavy cream
1 cup backfin crabmeat, picked over for shells
Boiling water
Dill-Shallot Butter Sauce (recipe follows)

In a food processor, combine the fillets, shrimp, and lemon juice. Process until very smooth. Season with salt and pepper. Add the egg whites and blend well. Then, with the motor running, slowly pour in the cream. As soon as all the cream is incorporated, turn off the processor.

Fold in the crabmeat. Spoon the mixture into six individual buttered 6-ounce custard cups. Place in a baking pan and pour boiling water in the pan to come halfway up the sides of the cups. Bake 25 to 30 minutes, or until a knife inserted in the center comes out clean.

While mousses are baking, prepare sauce. Gently turn mousses out onto plates and top with the Dill-Shallot Butter Sauce.

Dill-Shallot Butter Sauce

Makes about 1½ cups

2 cups dry vermouth
2 teaspoons minced shallots
¼ cup fresh lemon juice

1 cup (½ pound) unsalted butter, cut in small pieces
1 teaspoon chopped fresh dill
Dash salt

In a heavy-bottomed saucepan, combine the vermouth, shallots, and lemon juice and cook over high heat to reduce to about ¼ cup.

Over low heat whisk in the butter, piece by piece, until it is all used up. Remove from the heat and stir in the dill. Season with a touch of salt. Keep the sauce warm until serving time.

Stuffed Mushroom Caps

Serves 4 or 5 as a first course

These sherried mushroom caps, stuffed with a filling voluptuously endowed with crabmeat, can't be topped for a first course or for warm pass-arounds at formal cocktail parties.

Annapolis hostess Mrs. Louise Wright enjoys watching the expressions of utter delight on the faces of her guests when they first bite into one of these delectable morsels.

6 tablespoons butter
16 to 20 medium-sized mushrooms, stemmed
¼ cup dry sherry
Salt and black pepper to taste
¼ cup minced onion
¼ cup chopped fresh chives

2 tablespoons chopped fresh parsley
2 tablespoons chopped fresh dill or basil
¼ cup (4 tablespoons) butter, melted
½ cup sour cream
1 pound special or backfin crabmeat, picked over for shells

Preheat oven to 350°F.

In a skillet melt the 6 tablespoons butter and sauté the caps for 5 minutes, or until they are barely tender.

Pour in sherry, turn up the heat, and reduce liquid by half. Season with salt and pepper. Remove from the heat and cool.

To prepare the stuffing mixture, mix the onion, chives, parsley, dill, melted butter, and sour cream in a bowl. Season with salt and pepper. Gently fold in the crabmeat. Stuff the caps with mixture and arrange in a bakers dish.

Cover with waxed paper and bake 20 to 25 minutes. Serve hot or warm.

Crab Bisque

Serves 6 to 8

Originally the term bisque *referred to a method of preparing soup by thickening it with rice. Over the years it has become synonymous with a type of creamy soup made with shellfish.*

This bisque is a truly elegant, rich soup, sweetened with the flavors of sherry and Chesapeake blue crab.

6 tablespoons butter
1 cup finely diced onion
½ cup finely diced celery
½ cup minced leek
¼ cup flour
1 cup Fish Stock (see page 35)
4 cups half-and-half
¼ cup dry sherry, plus dry sherry to pass at table

½ teaspoon salt
¼ teaspoon white pepper
¼ teaspoon ground mace
Dash Tabasco sauce
1 pound backfin crabmeat, picked over for shells
Lightly whipped cream and paprika, for garnish

Melt the butter in a soup pot, then sauté the onion, celery, and leek until tender. Whisk in the flour and cook, stirring, several minutes; do not brown.

Off the heat whisk in the stock, half-and-half, sherry, salt, pepper, mace, and Tabasco. Return to the heat and bring to a boil, stirring often. Simmer 15 minutes. Stir in the crabmeat and continue to simmer another 5 minutes. Ladle into soup bowls.

Garnish each serving with a dollop of whipped cream and a dash of paprika. Pass dry sherry at the table and add to taste—a Chesapeake tradition.

Cream of Asparagus Soup

Serves 6 to 8

A beautiful puréed potage, with the blanched asparagus tips floating in the finished soup.

When you're putting on the ritz, garnish your soup with an asparagus tip nestled in a small spoonful of lightly whipped cream.

2 pounds asparagus
5 tablespoons butter
1 small onion, sliced
2 tablespoons chopped shallots
1 tablespoon chopped garlic
¼ cup flour

4 cups Chicken Stock (see page 33)
½ teaspoon dried thyme
1 cup heavy cream
2 tablespoons fresh lemon juice
Salt and black pepper to taste
Lightly whipped cream, for garnish

Cut the tips off the asparagus. Bring a saucepan of water to a boil and blanch asparagus tips 8 to 10 minutes. Drain and cool in ice water. Drain and reserve.

Cut off and discard the tough bottoms of the asparagus. Chop the remaining portions in pieces.

In a soup pot melt the butter and sauté the onion, shallots, and garlic 5 minutes. Whisk in the flour and cook, stirring, 2 to 3 minutes. Gradually whisk in the stock and then add the thyme. Add the asparagus pieces (not tips) and bring to a boil, stirring often.

Simmer 20 to 30 minutes, or until the asparagus pieces are tender. Remove from heat and purée the mixture in a blender or food processor. Pass through a sieve and return to the pot. Add the cream and heat almost to the boiling point. Now add the asparagus tips, reserving 6 to 8 for garnish. Season with lemon juice, salt, and pepper.

Ladle into bowls and garnish with whipped cream and reserved tips.

Maryland Diamondback Terrapin Soup

Serves 6 to 8

The diamondback terrapin, a water turtle, is one of the great stars of Chesapeake Bay cuisine. Recipes for the turtle are found in cookbooks from around the world. This local recipe is from Mrs. J. Millard Tawes, a former first lady of Maryland; she served the soup at formal dinners at the executive mansion.

The coveted terrapin, once the toast of presidents, governors, and the crowned heads of Europe, is no longer abundant. In fact, the supply has dramatically diminished; now only the older generations can recall the days when this delicacy was regularly pulled from the Bay waters. Since the turtle is scarce, I have included the recipe primarily for its historical importance.

Mrs. Tawes recommends serving the soup with Maryland Beaten Biscuits (see page 137) or Saltine crackers.

The former First Lady of Maryland, Avalynne Tawes, passed away in 1989 at the venerable age of ninety. Story has it that during her husband Millard Tawes' administration, she would send rations of her famous Terrapin Soup to Sir Winston Churchill.

3 live diamondback terrapins, 5 to 7 inches across
Boiling water
½ cup (¼ pound) butter
2 tablespoons flour
4 cups milk
6 hard-cooked eggs
1 cup heavy cram
½ cup dry sherry
Salt and black pepper to taste

To prepare the terrapins place them in a large pot filled with enough boiling water to cover the turtles completely. Cover and cook until tender, about 1 hour. To test, stick a fork into the sides. It will pierce the skin easily when the turtles are done. Remove them from the water and allow to cool enough to handle. Remove the top and bottom shells, scraping them for any adhering meat. Pull off the legs and remove meat from the top of the leg. Remove the liver, taking care not to break the bile pocket. Cut out and discard the bile pocket. Chop the liver and add to picked meat. Skin the legs and cut off the nails. If the meat is still somewhat tough, cook it in a little water.

In a saucepan melt the butter and whisk in the flour. Cook several minutes, stirring constantly; do not brown the flour. Gradually stir in the milk. Chop the egg whites and add to the saucepan. Mash the egg yolks and add them with the terrapin meat. Simmer, stirring all the while, until thickened. Add cream, sherry, salt, and pepper.

Heat through and ladle into soup bowls.

Oyster Pudding

Serves 4

This light and creamy pudding is a delectable way to serve plump oysters fresh from the Bay. The hint of cheese gives the dish a pleasant lift. The pudding, accompanied by a simple tossed salad, makes for an enjoyable meal.

6 slices bread, buttered and cubed
4 ounces sharp Cheddar cheese, shredded
1 pint shucked oysters, drained (reserve liquor for another use)
2 eggs
2 tablespoons grated yellow onion
¼ cup finely chopped green onions
1 teaspoon salt
¼ teaspoon black pepper
3 cups milk
⅛ teaspoon Tabasco sauce
3 tablespoons butter, for topping

Preheat oven to 325°F.

Butter a 2-quart casserole dish. Place half of the bread cubes in the bottom of the dish. Add the grated cheese on top. Distribute the oysters in casserole and top with the remaining bread cubes.

In a bowl beat together the eggs, yellow and green onions, salt, pepper, milk, and Tabasco. Pour over casserole. Dot the top of the casserole with butter and bake 1¼ hours.

Trout Stuffed with Spinach, Mushrooms, and Bacon

Serves 4

This wonderful spinach stuffing not only makes for a savory dish, but also helps to keep the flesh of the trout moist. If a sauce is desired, try Dill-Shallot Butter Sauce (see page 82) or Old Bay Hollandaise Sauce (see page 26).

3 slices bacon
2 tablespoons butter
¼ cup finely diced onion
1 tablespoon chopped shallots
1 cup coarsely chopped mushrooms
8 cups spinach leaves, stemmed (about 1 pound)
Salt, black pepper, and ground nutmeg to taste
Juice of 1 lemon
4 small trout (8 ounces each), boned
1 cup dry white wine or Fish Stock (see page 35)
Lemon wedges, for accompaniment

Preheat oven to 350°F.

In a large skillet fry the bacon until cooked but not crisp. Remove with slotted utensil and chop; set aside. Add the butter to the bacon drippings in the skillet and sauté the onion and shallots 2 to 3 minutes.

Add the mushrooms and cook 5 minutes. Stir in the spinach and cook until wilted. Add the reserved bacon and season with salt, pepper, nutmeg, and lemon juice.

Stuff the trout with spinach mixture and secure cavities closed. Pour wine in bottom of a glass baking dish. Place the fish side by side in dish and season with salt and pepper. Cover with well-buttered waxed paper.

Bake 25 to 30 minutes. Serve with lemon wedges.

Shad Roe Croquettes

Makes 18 to 20 croquettes

Early Annapolis residents adapted a French preparation to serve one of their most highly prized aquatic resources, shad roe.

A flavorful dish, it serves those well who like the taste of shad roe but are skittish about the texture.

For an alternative topping, try Lemon-Celery Cream Sauce (see page 41) or Old Bay Hollandaise Sauce (see page 26).

2 pairs shad roe (see page 12)
Salted water
5 tablespoons butter
5 tablespoons flour
2 cups heavy cream
2 tablespoons grated onion
¼ teaspoon Tabasco sauce
2 teaspoons fresh lemon juice
Salt and black pepper to taste

2 tablespoons chopped fresh parsley
  or chives
Dried bread crumbs, for dredging
2 eggs, beaten
Vegetable oil, for deep-frying
Lemon wedges and Tartar Sauce (see
  page 15) lightened with a little
  whipped cream, for accompaniment

Bring a saucepan filled with salted water to a gentle boil. Add shad roe and poach 10 minutes. Drain roe and cool.

In a saucepan melt the butter and whisk in the flour. Cook, stirring, 2 to 3 minutes. Gradually whisk in the cream, then add the onion, Tabasco, and lemon juice. Bring to a boil and cook, stirring, until thickened. Season with salt and pepper. Stir in the parsley.

Cut the shad roe into small pieces and fold into the sauce. Chill well. Form into 2½-inch-tall cone shapes.

Dip the cones into the bread crumbs, then the eggs and, once again, the bread crumbs.

Heat oil for deep-frying to 375°F. Fry cones, a few at a time, until golden brown, about 5 minutes. Remove with a slotted utensil to paper towels to drain.

Serve with lemon wedges and tartar sauce.

Statehouse Seafood Ragout

Serves 6

This fragrant seafood stew is served over rice, and is delicious accompanied with Two O'Clock Corn Bread (see page 56) or hot rolls. My Aunt Doris, a longtime Annapolis resident, gave me the recipe, which she says comes from a former chef who catered many statehouse receptions. Doris claims responsibility for the addition of the grated orange rind to the sauce, which she feels gives this dish panache. And she's right!

½ cup (¼ pound) butter or vegetable oil
½ cup flour
2 cups diced yellow onion
½ cup green onions
½ cup chopped celery
2 teaspoons chopped garlic
3 cups chopped ripe tomatoes
2½ cups Fish Stock (see page 35)
Grated rind and juice from 1 orange
1½ teaspoons salt
½ teaspoon black pepper
¼ teaspoon cayenne pepper
1 teaspoon dried thyme
1 bay leaf
½ pound backfin crabmeat, picked over for shells
½ pound shrimp, peeled and deveined
1 pound clams in the shell, well scrubbed
Fresh lemon juice to taste
Freshly cooked white rice, for accompaniment

In a heavy-bottomed pot, heat the butter. Whisk in the flour and cook over high heat, stirring constantly, 3 to 5 minutes or until the flour is lightly browned.

Lower heat and stir in the yellow and green onions, celery, and garlic. Cook, stirring frequently, 15 minutes. Add the tomatoes, stock, and orange rind and juice. Whisk well. Add the salt, peppers, thyme, and bay leaf. Bring to a boil and simmer 1 hour.

Add the crabmeat, shrimp, and clams. Cover and continue cooking until clams open. Add lemon juice.

Serve in bowls over rice.

Curried Crabmeat

Serves 4

Former slaves transported from the Caribbean brought with them the flavors and spices of the tropics. The meat of the Chesapeake Bay blue crab is a natural for this zesty ragout.

6 tablespoons butter
1 small onion, diced
1 teaspoon chopped garlic
1 pound backfin crabmeat, picked over for shells
1 medium hot green chile, chopped
½ teaspoon ground ginger
½ teaspoon ground turmeric
Pinch ground cinnamon
Pinch ground cloves
½ cup heavy cream
Salt and black pepper to taste
2 tablespoons fresh lemon juice
2 tablespoons chopped fresh parsley
Cooked white rice, for accompaniment

In a saucepan melt the butter. Sauté the onion and garlic until tender. Stir in crabmeat and toss with butter. Add all the remaining ingredients and simmer 5 minutes.

Serve over rice.

Smoked Chicken Pot Pie with Yam Pastry

Serves 6 to 8

Smoked chicken is now available in many specialty food stores and poultry shops. The hint of smokiness that comes through in the pot pie is delightful.

Salted water
1 large chicken (4 to 4½ pounds)
1 large onion, sliced
2 whole cloves
Yam Pastry (recipe follows)
15 pearl onions
1 cup medium diced carrots
1 cup medium diced celery

1 cup corn kernels
1 cup fresh peas
1 cup coarsely cut smoked chicken meat
½ cup (¼ pound) butter
½ cup flour
1 cup heavy cream
Salt, black pepper, and ground nutmeg to taste

Bring a large pot filled with salted water to a boil. Add chicken, sliced onion, and cloves; reduce the heat and simmer until chicken is tender, 1 to 1½ hours. While chicken is cooking, cook and chill the yams for the pastry. Remove the chicken from the pot and pick off the meat; set aside. Strain and reserve the liquid from the cooking pot. Skim off the fat.

In a saucepan combine pearl onions, carrots, celery, corn, and peas. Pour in the strained cooking liquid to cover and simmer until tender.

Preheat oven to 350°F. In a 4-quart baking dish, arrange the reserved chicken meat, smoked chicken, and vegetables.

To make the sauce melt the butter in a saucepan and whisk in the flour. Cook, stirring 2 to 3 minutes. Gradually whisk in 3 cups of the strained cooking liquid and the cream. Bring to a boil and cook until thickened. Season well with salt, pepper, and nutmeg. Pour over the chicken and vegetables. Finish making the pastry and fit it on the top of the baking dish.

Bake pie about 45 minutes, or until top is nicely browned and filling is piping hot.

Yam Pastry

Makes one 12-inch top crust

1 or 2 yams (enough to yield 1½ cups mashed)
1½ cups flour
1 teaspoon salt

2 teaspoons baking powder
½ cup solid vegetable shortening
2 eggs, beaten

Preheat oven to 400°F. Bake the yams until soft, about 40 to 60 minutes, depending upon size. (Prick with fork tines when half-cooked to prevent them from bursting.) When cool enough to handle, scoop out the flesh and mash. Chill.

In a bowl, sift together the flour, salt, and baking powder. Add the chilled yams and shortening. Work into the flour with the eggs.

Turn the dough out onto a lightly floured board and roll it to a size that will cover the baking dish.

Miss Lorraine's BBQ Chicken

Serves 5 or 6

Miss Lorraine is notorious for her Magothy River cookouts. She loves getting her grill hot and loading it up with chicken while sipping beer.

Once, though, she thinks maybe because of too much chicken on the grill at one time, the flames shot up and her wig caught fire. She says it was quite the sight. Due to jangled nerves she's adapted her recipe for the oven.

For you outdoor barbecuers, don't pile too much chicken on at one time. And baste the chicken with the sauce for only the last ten to fifteen minutes. Once you start basting, keep the chicken moving or it tends to burn. Make up a batch of Miss Silvia's Potato Salad (see page 16) to go along with the birds.

Oh yeah, I forgot, Lorraine's boyfriend Teddy describes the BBQ sauce as "kick ass" (if you'll pardon the expression).

½ cup ketchup
¼ cup apple cider vinegar
1 tablespoon brown sugar
¼ cup water
1 tablespoon Worcestershire sauce
2 tablespoons fresh lemon juice
2 tablespoons grated onion

1 teaspoon chopped garlic
2 teaspoons dry mustard
¼ teaspoon cayenne pepper
Tabasco sauce to taste
2 frying chickens, cut into quarters
Vegetable oil or melted butter

To make the barbecue sauce, combine all the ingredients, except the chicken and oil, in a pot. Simmer 15 minutes. Remove from the heat and let stand at least 1 hour before using. Meanwhile, preheat oven to 400°F.

Put the chicken in a roasting pan and brush the skin with oil. Place in the oven and roast about 1 hour. Baste the chicken occasionally with the pan juices the first 40 minutes. Baste it with the barbecue sauce the last 20 minutes.

Serve with plenty of napkins for sticky fingers.

Stewed Pheasant with Sour Cream and Walnuts

Serves 4

Miss Alma's brother Lou, of South River, was an avid hunter. Each season she would make this succulent stew from one of his bagged birds. The rich dark meat of the pheasant, together with the hearty red wine, makes for a dining experience that will excite both olfactory and taste receptors. Potato Dumplings (see page 48) are a good accompaniment.

¼ cup (4 tablespoons) butter
2 large onions, sliced ¼ inch thick
3 carrots, peeled and sliced ¼ inch thick
3 stalks celery, diced
2 pheasants (about 2½ pounds each), cut in serving pieces
2 cups dry red wine
1 teaspoon rubbed sage
½ teaspoon dried marjoram
¼ teaspoon ground mace
2 teaspoons salt
½ teaspoon black pepper
Flour mixed with water, for thickening
1 cup walnut pieces
1 cup sour cream

In a flameproof casserole or dutch oven, melt the butter and sauté the onions for several minutes. Add the carrots, celery, and pheasant pieces. Pour in the wine and then add enough water to cover birds. Add the sage, marjoram, mace, salt, and pepper and bring to a boil. Cover and simmer about 1½ hours, or until pheasant pieces are tender. Remove the pheasant pieces to a platter and keep warm. Over medium heat thicken the pan juices with flour-water mixture. Add the walnuts. Adjust seasonings. Off the heat whisk in the sour cream.

Serve the pheasant pieces on a platter with the sauce spooned over them.

Veal Sweetbreads and Crabmeat

Serves 4

The pairing of delicate sweet-breads and backfin crabmeat may sound a bit odd, but I assure you this match makes for first-class dining. For a tasty variation top each piece of toast with a thin slice of grilled Smithfield ham.

2 pairs veal sweetbreads
Salted water
Juice of 1 lemon
Ice water
6 tablespoons butter
1 cup coarsely chopped mushrooms
2 tablespoons flour
1 cup veal or Chicken Stock (see page 33)
1 cup heavy cream

½ teaspoon salt
¼ teaspoon white pepper
¼ teaspoon ground mace
½ pound backfin crabmeat, picked over for shells
¼ cup dry sherry
4 slices white bread, toasted

Soak the sweetbreads in cold water to cover 1 hour; drain. Bring a saucepan filled with salted water to a boil. Add sweetbreads and lemon juice and simmer 20 minutes. Drain and cool in ice water. Remove all membranes, tubes, and strings from the sweetbreads. Cut in small dice.

In a saucepan melt 3 tablespoons of the butter. Sauté the sweetbreads and mushrooms 5 minutes. Remove with a slotted spoon and set aside.

Melt the remaining 3 tablespoons butter in the pan and whisk in the flour. Cook, stirring, 2 to 3 minutes. Gradually stir in the stock and cream. Add the salt, pepper, and mace. Heat until thickened, stirring frequently.

Stir in the reserved sweetbreads and mushrooms, crabmeat, and sherry. Simmer 10 minutes. Serve on toast.

Spring Lamb Chops with Mint

Serves 4

These lamb chops are braised in a mint-scented broth that is flavored by the rendered lamb fat. The chops go well with whipped garlic potatoes and steamed baby carrots.

8 thick lamb chops
Olive oil, for marinating
2 tablespoons chopped garlic
Salt and black pepper to taste
3 tablespoons butter
3 tablespoons vegetable oil

1 large onion, thinly sliced
¾ cup white wine
¾ cup water
2 tablespoons chopped fresh mint
1 bay leaf
Ms. Jamie's Apple Chutney (see page 106)

Marinate the lamb chops for several hours in a little olive oil and 1 tablespoon of the garlic.

In a skillet, heat the butter and vegetable oil. Salt and pepper the chops, add them to the skillet, and brown well on both sides. Remove from the pan and set aside.

In the same pan cook the onion and garlic until limp and starting to color, 3 to 5 minutes. Return the chops to the skillet and add the wine, water, mint, and bay leaf. Cover and simmer 30 to 40 minutes, or until done.

Remove the chops from the pan. Increase the heat and slightly reduce the juices. Adjust seasoning. Serve the chops with the hot pan juices and apple chutney on the side.

Roast Fresh Ham with Fried Apples

Serves 12

One is hard-pressed to find a more typical Bay country pork dish than this one. A fresh ham is sheer gastronomic bliss. It is actually a leg of pork, but it's been "fresh ham" to us Bay folks for generations. Serve it with Fried Apples, mashed potatoes, and, don't forget the Sauerkraut and Apples (see page 55)!

1 large (8 to 10 pounds) fresh ham
3 cloves garlic, cut in slivers
1 tablespoon rubbed dried sage

Salt and pepper to taste
Fried Apples (recipe follows)

Preheat oven to 350°F.

Score the skin of the ham with a sharp knife. Push slivers of garlic under the skin, then rub skin with sage, salt, and pepper.

Place the ham on a rack in a shallow baking pan. Reduce the heat to 325°F and bake 20 minutes per pound.

Remove ham to a platter and keep warm. Make a gravy from pan juices (see page 44) and cook the Fried Apples. Carve ham and serve with gravy and apples on the side.

Fried Apples

6 large apples, peeled and cored
8 to 12 tablespoons butter

1 teaspoon sugar
A few drops fresh lemon juice

Slice the apples into rounds about ½ inch thick. In a skillet melt the butter. Add the apple slices and sauté with a sprinkling of sugar and lemon juice until tender and lightly browned.

Succotash

Serves 4

This vegetable dish is as southern as corn bread. But you don't find it around too much these days. It's one of my favorites, and I think an effort should be made to save our succotash heritage. I'm printing bumper stickers as we speak!

1 cup shelled young lima beans
Salt
1 cup corn kernels

3 tablespoons butter
Black pepper to taste

In a saucepan place the limas and add water just to cover. Lightly salt the water. Bring to a boil and simmer until the beans are barely tender.

Add the corn and simmer 10 minutes. Drain off the water and season with butter, salt, and pepper.

Asparagus Soufflé

Serves 4

A grand treatment for this summer treasure. This recipe can be served as an appetizer, an elegant vegetable course, or a wonderful luncheon entrée.

Salted water
1 cup asparagus tips
Ice water
2½ tablespoons butter
1 tablespoon chopped shallots
3 tablespoons flour
1 cup milk

4 egg yolks
Salt, as needed
Black pepper and freshly grated nutmeg to taste
½ cup grated Swiss cheese
6 egg whites

Preheat oven to 375°F.

Bring a saucepan filled with lightly salted water to a boil. Add the asparagus tips and parboil 8 to 10 minutes. Drain, cool in ice water, then drain again and set aside.

In an enamel saucepan, melt the butter and sauté the shallots 1 to 2 minutes. Whisk in the flour and cook several minutes, stirring constantly.

Off the heat whisk in the milk. Return to the stove and bring the mixture almost to the boiling point, stirring all the while. Remove from heat and beat in the egg yolks, one at a time, until a smooth mixture is formed. Season with salt, pepper, and nutmeg. Stir in all but 2 tablespoons of the cheese. Mix in the asparagus tips.

Beat egg whites with a pinch of salt until stiff but not dry. Gently fold whites into the asparagus mixture.

Butter a 6-cup soufflé mold. Sprinkle the bottom with the reserved cheese. Pour in the soufflé mixture.

Bake about 30 minutes, or until nicely brown and firm. Serve at once.

Stuffed Tomatoes

Serves 4

When your summer tomato vines are producing more than you can slice or put up, try this recipe. These stuffed treats go well with Panfried Pepper Steak with Mustard Butter (see page 199) or Miss Sara's Ham Loaf (see page 197).

4 large firm, ripe tomatoes
2 tablespoons finely chopped onion
2 stalks celery, finely chopped
1½ cups corn kernels

½ cup (¼ pound) butter
Salt and black pepper
Dried bread crumbs
Chopped fresh parsley

Preheat oven to 375°F.

Cut about ½ inch off tops of the tomatoes. Scoop out the seeds and pulp and reserve. Turn the tomatoes upside down on a rack to drain while making the stuffing.

Drain off the liquid from the tomato pulp. In a mixing bowl, combine the pulp, onion, celery, and corn. Melt ¼ cup of the butter. Add to bowl with pulp and season with salt and pepper. Mix well.

Stuff the tomatoes with pulp mixture. Top each tomato with a sprinkling of bread crumbs and parsley. Cut the remaining ¼ cup butter into 4 equal pats and place a pat on each tomato. Generously butter a baking dish in which tomatoes will fit snugly. Arrange tomatoes in dish and bake about 20 minutes, or until heated through.

Colonial Gingerbread

Makes one 8-inch-square loaf, serves 8

Chesapeake gingerbread recipes date back to the early colonial days. Most of the baking done in the 1700s did not use white sugar, since it was not a readily available commodity. Instead molasses was used as a sweetener. You will find many traditional recipes for pies, cakes, and confections that call for molasses. Generally, precious refined sugar was used only for dusting on the dessert after baking or cooking.

Since the beautiful Domino sugar factory is right up the Bay from Annapolis, this recipe has been updated to include a touch of the once-scarce sweetener.

½ cup (¼ pound) butter
½ cup sugar
2 eggs
1 cup dark molasses
1 cup boiling water
2½ cups flour

1½ teaspoons baking soda
½ teaspoon salt
½ tablespoon ground ginger
1 teaspoon ground cinnamon
¼ teaspoon ground cloves
Whipped cream, for topping

Preheat oven to 350°F.

In a mixing bowl, cream together the butter and sugar until light. Add the eggs and beat until fluffy. Mix together the molasses and water. Stir into the creamed mixture.

Sift together the flour, baking soda, salt, ginger, cinnamon, and cloves. Add to the batter and beat until smooth. Pour batter into a prepared 8-inch-square baking pan.

Bake 40 to 45 minutes. Serve warm or at room temperature with whipped cream.

Sweet Potato Rolls

Makes about 3 dozen rolls

What a treat it is to be offered a basket of these hearty, richly flavored yeast rolls. Serve them hot from the oven and have plenty of butter on the table.

6 tablespoons lard or solid vegetable shortening
1 cup mashed, cooked sweet potatoes or yams
1 package active dry yeast
1¼ cups lukewarm (105° to 115°F) water

2 tablespoons sugar
1 tablespoon salt
1 egg, beaten
⅛ teaspoon ground allspice
⅛ teaspoon ground nutmeg
4 to 4½ cups flour

In a mixing bowl work the lard into the sweet potatoes.

In a large bowl dissolve the yeast in the warm water and let stand until foamy, about 10 minutes. Stir in the sugar and salt. Beat in the egg. Mix in the sweet potato mixture, allspice, and nutmeg. Beat in the flour, one cup at a time; add flour just until the dough pulls away from the sides of bowl.

Turn out onto a lightly floured board and knead for about 10 minutes. Form into a ball and put in a well-oiled bowl, turning to coat all sides of ball. Cover bowl with a tea towel and let rise in a warm place until doubled in bulk, about 1 hour.

Preheat the oven to 400°F. Divide the dough into thirds and cut each portion in 12 pieces. Roll each piece into a ball with the palms of your hands and set out on flat surface. Cover with a towel and let rise 30 minutes.

Arrange balls on a greased baking sheet. Bake 15 to 20 minutes, or until nicely browned.

Buttermilk Biscuits

Makes 12 to 14 biscuits

The Troutmans, longtime residents of Annapolis and dear friends of my grandmother Gertie, gave her this splendid recipe for some of the most tender, light biscuits imaginable.

A sound biscuit recipe is a must for every self-respecting Bay household. It is the cornerstone of many local meals and an invaluable tool for dipping into gravy!

2 cups flour
1¼ teaspoons baking powder
½ teaspoon baking soda
1 teaspoon salt

10 tablespoons lard or solid vegetable
  shortening
¾ to 1 cup buttermilk

Preheat oven to 450°F.

Sift together the flour, baking powder, soda, and salt into a large bowl. Work in the lard with fingertips or a pastry blender until mixture is the consistency of coarse meal. Beat in the buttermilk until a stiff (not wet) dough is formed. Knead dough in bowl lightly for 1 minute.

Roll the dough out on a lightly floured board about ½ inch thick and cut out 12 to 14 rounds. Place biscuits on a baking sheet.

Bake 12 minutes, or until nicely browned. Serve hot.

Chocolate-Bourbon Pecan Pie

Makes one 9-inch pie,
serves 6 to 8

Accenting this rich pecan pie with chocolate gives a new twist to a southern classic.

Pastry Dough for single-crust 9-inch pie (see page 31)
3 eggs, beaten
1 cup sugar
1 cup dark corn syrup
6 tablespoons butter, melted and cooled
1 tablespoon flour

1 teaspoon vanilla extract
3 ounces unsweetened chocolate, melted and cooled
¼ cup bourbon whiskey
1½ cups pecan halves or pieces, lightly toasted
Sweetened whipped cream, for accompaniment

Prepare pastry dough and line a 9-inch pie pan.

Preheat oven to 400°F.

In a large bowl, beat together the eggs and sugar. Mix in the corn syrup, butter, flour, vanilla, chocolate, and bourbon. Pour into the pie crust and arrange the pecans on top.

Bake 20 minutes, then reduce heat to 325°F and continue baking 30 minutes, or until set and a knife inserted in center comes out clean. Serve warm with sweetened whipped cream.

Maryland Black Walnut Cake

Makes one 10-inch cake, serves 8

Another traditional recipe from the Old Line State, this delicate cake is permeated with the fragrance of black walnuts. These nuts, which grow in abundance around the Bay, have a strong, distinctive flavor.

2 cups flour
1 tablespoon baking powder
¼ teaspoon salt
1 cup (½ pound) butter
1½ cups granulated sugar
1 teaspoon vanilla extract
3 eggs, separated

¾ cup milk
1½ cups ground black walnuts
Confectioners' sugar, for topping
Vanilla ice cream and/or fresh strawberry sauce, for accompaniment (optional)

Preheat oven to 350°F.

Sift together the flour, baking powder, and salt. In a large bowl, cream together the butter and sugar until light and fluffy. Add the vanilla and egg yolks. Beat the mixture well.

Alternately add the dry ingredients and the milk in small portions to the batter. Mix well. Beat the egg whites until stiff but not dry and gently fold them and the walnuts into the batter. Pour the mixture into a greased and floured tube pan and bake 30 minutes. Cool on a wire rack.

Dust with confectioners' sugar and serve with vanilla ice cream or surround with a fresh strawberry sauce. Or if you feel like pulling out all the stops, try all three.

Apple Cake

Makes one 10-inch cake,
serves 8 to 10

This pleasing cake is not exactly from Annapolis, but it is eaten in Annapolis at the Maryland Department of Agriculture. You see, Mrs. Jordan of Carroll County is famous for this recipe and makes it for her son Glenn, who works for the department. Since Glenn was always bringing the cake to work, it caught on like wildfire. Thus, Annapolis and the folk at the Department of Agriculture have claimed it as their own. The cake is so moist that it is quite delicious plain, without any frosting.

1 cup vegetable oil
2 cups sugar
3 eggs, beaten
1 teaspoon vanilla extract
2½ cups flour
2 teaspoons baking soda
1 teaspoon salt
1 teaspoon ground cinnamon
1 cup chopped black walnuts
1 cup raisins
3 cups diced apples

Preheat oven to 375°F.

In a large bowl cream together the oil and sugar until light and fluffy. Add the eggs and vanilla. Mix well.

Sift together the flour, baking soda, salt, and cinnamon into a bowl. Beat flour mixture into the batter. Mix in the walnuts, raisins, and apples. Pour the batter into a greased and floured 10-inch tube pan.

Bake 1 hour. Cool on a rack.

Lord Baltimore Cake

Makes one 9-inch cake, serves 8

After sampling his wife's egg white–laden cake (Lady Baltimore Cake, see page 59), Maryland's first governor, Lord Baltimore, noticed the large amount of egg yolks her ladyship was letting go to waste. After giving her a sound tongue-lashing, the governor snatched the yolks from his wife and dashed off to the kitchen looking for the manor's head cook, Miss Florine.

Putting their heads together, Lord Baltimore and Florine worked into the wee hours of the morning sipping sherry and perfecting a yolk-rich cake. As the sun was rising, and with the sherry nearly gone, Lord Baltimore and Miss Florine, in a fit of culinary ecstasy, threw everything but the kitchen sink (lucky for us they didn't have sinks back then) into the mixing bowl to provide a filling for their masterpiece. The result was a richly textured cake and one of the most festive fillings since the Queen of Sheba's birthday cake in 900 B.C.

During my research I was unable to confirm the complete accuracy of the details of this historic occasion. Since my grandfather recounted this tale at every Fourth of July cookout, however, I am sure it is very close to what actually happened.

2¼ cups flour, sifted
½ teaspoon salt
1 tablespoon baking powder
1 cup (½ pound) butter, softened
1½ cups sugar
8 egg yolks

¾ cup milk
1 teaspoon lemon or vanilla extract
Lord Baltimore Filling and Frosting (recipe follows)
Candied cherry halves, for garnish

Preheat oven to 375°F.

Sift together the flour, salt, and baking powder. In a large bowl cream together the butter and sugar until light in color and creamy. Beat in the egg yolks, one at a time, and mix well. Alternately, add the dry ingredients and the milk in small portions to the batter. Mix well. Add the extract and mix well.

Pour the batter into 3 greased and floured 9-inch cake pans. Bake 20 minutes, or until a toothpick inserted in the center comes out clean. Let cool 5 minutes in pans, then turn out onto rack and cool completely.

Prepare frosting and filling while cake is cooling, then fill and frost. Garnish with cherry halves.

Lord Baltimore Filling and Frosting

1½ cups sugar
½ cup water
2 egg whites
Pinch salt
½ teaspoon vanilla extract
½ cup macaroon crumbs

½ cup chopped black walnuts
¼ cup chopped almonds
½ cup chopped candied cherries
2 teaspoons fresh lemon juice
1 tablespoon sweet sherry

Combine the sugar and water in a saucepan and bring to a boil, stirring to dissolve sugar. Boil until a syrup forms, about 10 minutes. In a bowl beat the egg whites and salt until stiff peaks form. Pour a little of the boiling syrup into the egg whites and beat well. Continue cooking the syrup until thin threads form from the tip of a spoon that is dipped in and then pulled out of the syrup (about 230°F on a candy thermometer).

Beat the syrup into the egg-white mixture. Add the vanilla. Continue beating until the frosting is stiff and forms tall peaks. Transfer two thirds of the frosting to another bowl and put aside.

Beat the macaroon crumbs, walnuts, almonds, cherries, lemon juice, and sherry into the remaining one third of the frosting.

Use this nut mixture as a filling between the layers of the cake. Ice the entire cake with the reserved frosting.

Mudd Cake

Makes one 9-inch cake, serves 8

Miss Ferguson of Severna Park, on the Magothy River, has had this dense-chocolate-cake recipe in her family for years. Any similarity to mud is strictly coincidental. I enjoy mine topped with a bit of lightly whipped cream or sitting on a bed of Sweet Cream (see page 105).

1¾ cups brewed coffee
¼ cup bourbon whiskey
5 ounces unsweetened chocolate
1 cup (½ pound) butter, cut in pieces
2 cups sugar

2 cups flour
1½ teaspoons baking soda
⅛ teaspoon salt
2 eggs, lightly beaten
1 teaspoon vanilla extract

Preheat oven to 275°F.

In the top of a double boiler placed over simmering water, heat the coffee, bourbon, and chocolate. Stir until the chocolate melts. Whisk in the butter, a little at a time, until all of it is melted. Remove from the heat and beat in the sugar.

Sift together the flour, soda and salt into a bowl. Put the coffee mixture in a large bowl and add the sifted ingredients. Beat well for about 1 minute. Add the eggs and vanilla and beat until the batter is smooth.

Pour the batter into a greased and floured cake pan 9 inches round and 2 inches deep. Bake 1½ hours, or until a toothpick inserted in the center comes out clean.

Paca House Snickerdoodles

Makes about 5 dozen cookies

After finishing my Christmastime tour of the historic William Paca House, I fell in love with these cookies offered in the restored colonial kitchen.

½ cup (¼ pound) margarine or butter, softened
½ cup solid vegetable shortening
1½ cups plus 2 tablespoons sugar
2 eggs

1 teaspoon vanilla extract
2⅔ cups sifted flour
2 teaspoons cream of tartar
1 teaspoon baking soda
1 teaspoon ground cinnamon

Preheat oven to 400°F.

In a large bowl cream together the margarine and shortening until light. Add the 1½ cups sugar and beat until fluffy. Beat in the eggs and vanilla.

Sift together the flour, cream of tartar, and baking soda. Add to the margarine mixture. Mix well.

Combine the cinnamon and the 2 tablespoons sugar. With your palms, roll the dough into one-inch balls. Roll the balls in the cinnamon mixture and arrange two inches apart on an ungreased baking sheet.

Bake 8 to 10 minutes. Remove and cool on racks.

Poached Peaches on Sweet Cream

Serves 8

An exceptional dessert of gently poached peaches that have taken on the fragrance of mulled wine. Served on a bed of lightly thickened sweet cream, this is a luscious finale to any dinner.

4 cups dry white wine
1½ cups sugar
1 stick cinnamon
1 teaspoon ground cinnamon
2 teaspoons whole cloves
1 teaspoon vanilla extract

1 lemon, sliced
1 bay leaf
8 firm, ripe peaches
Sweet Cream (recipe follows)
Fresh berries or mint sprigs,
  for garnish

In a pot bring the wine, sugar, cinnamon stick and ground cinnamon, cloves, vanilla, lemon, and bay leaf to a boil. Boil about 3 minutes.

Add the peaches and cover the pot with a light towel or cloth. Reduce the heat and simmer until the peaches are tender, 15 to 20 minutes.

Remove the peaches from the liquid with a slotted utensil and set aside in a bowl. Chill the poaching liquid. When it is cold, pour it over the peaches. Cover the bowl holding the peaches with a towel and place in the refrigerator until well chilled.

Before serving prepare the Sweet Cream and cool. Pour a bed of the cream on a plate or large saucer. Remove the peaches from the liquid and slide off the skin.

Place a peach in the center of each plate. Garnish with berries. Serve with a knife, fork, and spoon.

Sweet Cream

Makes about 4 cups

6 egg yolks
1 cup sugar
3 cups half-and-half

½ split vanilla bean, or 1 teaspoon
  vanilla extract

In an enamel pot beat together the yolks and sugar until pale and ribbonlike. In a stainless-steel pot, combine the half-and-half and vanilla and bring almost to a boil. Whisk the hot milk into the yolk mixture. Cook over low heat, stirring constantly with a wooden spoon. Continue cooking until the mixture becomes heavy, creamlike, and thoroughly coats the back of the spoon. Remove from heat.

If a vanilla bean was used, remove it and scrape the seeds from the bean into the cream. Cool at room temperature, stirring occasionally. Refrigerate until ready to use.

Ms. Jamie's Apple Chutney

Makes about 6 pints

Unlike traditional chutney recipes, this version of the spicy apple condiment includes green tomatoes. These Chesapeake staples add a pleasant flavor and texture to the chutney. To make a delightfully unusual dipping sauce for crab cakes or grilled or fried fish, lighten the chutney with a bit of sour cream and chopped mint just before serving.

4 cups chopped green tomatoes
    (about 1 pound)
2 tablespoons plus 2 teaspoons salt
3 cups cider vinegar
1 cup fresh lemon juice
5 cups granulated sugar
5 cups firmly packed dark brown
    sugar
8 cups chopped tart apples (about 3
    pounds), peeled and cored

½ cup chopped fresh ginger or
    3 tablespoons ground ginger
1 pound raisins
2 teaspoons salt
1 teaspoon powdered cayenne pepper
2 onions, chopped
1 green bell pepper, chopped
1 red bell pepper, chopped

Place the tomatoes in a colander. Sprinkle with 2 tablespoons salt and leave overnight.

In a heavy pot combine the vinegar, lemon juice, and sugars and bring to a boil. Add the tomatoes and all the remaining ingredients. Bring back to a boil and simmer until thick.

Pack into hot, sterilized jars, seal, and process in a water bath according to standard canning procedures.

Horseradish, Bay Style

This prepared horseradish is widely used with seafood and beef.
Peel 1 or 2 pounds of horseradish root and cover with cold water. Squeeze a lemon into the water and let the horseradish soak about 30 minutes. This will keep it from turning brown.

Drain off the water and chop the horseradish very fine in a food processor. Spoon horseradish into half-pint glass jars and top each with 1 teaspoon salt. Pour distilled white vinegar, or half white and half cider vinegar, into the jars to cover horseradish completely. Screw on caps, let cool at room temperature, and refrigerate.

Paca House Christmas Punch

Serves a crowd

A warming and tangy punch for your holiday entertaining.

1 gallon cranberry juice
1 gallon apple juice
1 quart ginger ale

1 cup fresh lemon juice
1 cup Spiced Tea Concentrate (recipe follows)

Combine all ingredients in a large saucepan and heat. Serve warm.

Spiced Tea Concentrate

2½ cups boiling water
4 tea bags
4 whole cinnamon sticks

2 tablespoons whole allspice
2 tablespoons whole cloves

Combine all the ingredients in a saucepan and simmer 15 minutes; strain.

Marjorie Steen at Annapolis' William Paca House where she demonstrates colonial cooking.

Annapolis, Maryland, the onetime capital of the United States, is steeped in Early American history. It was, by the beginning of the eighteenth century, one of the larger cities in the New World and was deeply involved in colonial politics. Marjorie Steen has brought that history one step closer to us by introducing the foods and techniques of eighteenth-century Chesapeake cookery to present-day Annapolis.

Mrs. Steen, an Annapolis schoolteacher, first became interested in the historical cooking of the Chesapeake region through her husband. He had begun spending weekends with groups that organized authentic reenactments of colonial military battles; they included everything from the uniforms right down to the meals prepared in the army camps. It quickly became apparent to Mrs. Steen that if she didn't want to spend her weekends alone, she would have to roll up her sleeves and join the battle. And that she did, with the rest of the family soon to follow.

While simulating the foods and cooking methods on a battlefield, Marjorie became fascinated with Early American cookery. She has spent vast amounts of time researching and perfecting the colonial recipes of the Annapolis area.

Several times a year at the beautifully restored William Paca House in Annapolis, Marjorie demonstrates fireplace cooking and gives historical accounts of the cookery of the early Chesapeake Bay townspeople. She explains that in those days Annapolis was referred to as "the New World Paris."

The colonial menu presented here blends English and French influences. There are such Gallic-inspired recipes as Ham Pâté, Stewed Oysters, and fireplace-roasted Rock Cornish Game Hens with Bread Stuffing. The English tastes come through in Carrot Pudding, Poor Man's Pudding, and the molasses-rich Lemon Pot Pie.

As was the custom at Early American dinner tables, Marjorie offers a wide variety of items for the repast, rather than large quantities of just one or two dishes. This menu illustrates the foundations of present-day Chesapeake Bay cooking.

Stewed Oysters

Ham Pâté

Rock Cornish Game Hens with Bread Stuffing

Mrs. Steen's Fried Apples

Green Beans with Herbs

Pickled Peaches

Baked Pumpkin

Carrot Pudding

Poor Man's Pudding

Tidewater Delight

Vinegar Pie

Lemon Pot Pie

Stewed Oysters

Serves 4

Sixteenth-century writers speak of oyster dishes containing "one oyster sufficient to fill the dish; with two such oysters it is hearty to fill a man's stomach." This same account mentions that a single crab would serve four men and calls for lobsters one to six feet in length, although one to one and a half feet was desirable at the table. It seems that they knew how to raise shellfish in those days.

1 pint shucked oysters, drained and liquor reserved
½ cup dry white wine
½ cup water
⅛ teaspoon ground pepper

⅛ teaspoon ground mace
1 tablespoon flour
1 tablespoon butter, softened
Sippets (small pieces of bread) and lemon slices, for garnish

In a pot combine the oyster liquor, wine, water, pepper, and mace. Bring to a boil. Add the oysters and bring almost to a boil.

Mix the flour and softened butter together. Stir it into the stew, a little at a time, until thickened.

Serve with sippets floating in the stew. Garnish with lemon slices.

Ham Pâté

Serves a crowd

In colonial times the word pâté referred to foods enclosed in dough. Often this crust was hard enough to be a storage container for fruits and meats for months at a time. These crusts were either thrown away or used as plates and or serving dishes. Late eighteenth-century recipes describe "fine crusts" as "crispy and tender enough for eating."

A mustard cream sauce made with dry mustard or prepared Dijon goes well with the pâté.

Fine Crust Pastry (recipe follows)
2 pounds ground turkey
2 cups soft bread crumbs, soaked in half-and-half
3 egg whites
1 teaspoon salt, plus salt to taste
½ teaspoon black pepper, plus pepper to taste
Pinch ground nutmeg

1 medium ham (6 to 8 pounds), boned, topped with ground ginger and whole cloves, partially baked at 325°F for 2½ hours, and thinly sliced
Mixture of 1 part brandy to 4 parts dry white wine, as needed
1 egg, beaten

Prepare the pastry, wrap, and chill.

In a bowl mix together the turkey, soaked crumbs, egg whites, 1 teaspoon salt, ½ teaspoon pepper, and nutmeg.

Preheat oven to 350°F.

Divide the pastry into 2 balls, one slightly larger than the other. On a lightly floured board, roll out the smaller ball ½ inch thick and large enough to line the bottom of a small roasting pan. Line the pan as for a pie, covering the bottom and sides.

Place a 1- to 1½-inch-thick layer of the turkey mixture on the pastry. Top with a ¼- to ⅓-inch-thick layer of thin ham slices. Sprinkle with a small amount of salt and pepper.

Repeat layers of stuffing and ham slices until all is used, ending with a layer of stuffing and a generous amount of stuffing along the sides.

Roll out the remaining pastry ½ inch thick and cover pan with it. Crimp the edges, moistened with water, to ensure a good seal.

Reroll any pastry scraps, make small cutouts, and use to decorate top of pastry. Brush with beaten egg. Make a hole in the middle of the crown, or perhaps 2 or 3, if the dish is long and narrow. Bake 1 hour.

Remove from the oven and place a funnel in the pastry hole. Slowly pour in as much of the brandy-wine mixture as the dish will allow. Return to the oven 1 hour more.

Serve hot or chilled. Slice the pâté to reveal the ham layers.

Fine Crust Pastry

4 cups flour
1 teaspoon salt
1½ cups solid vegetable shortening

⅓ cup cold water
2 tablespoons distilled white vinegar

In a large bowl mix the flour and salt together. Cut in the shortening with fingertips or a pastry blender until mixture has the consistency of coarse meal. Mix together the water and vinegar and work it into flour mixture. Form into a ball, wrap, and chill at least 1 hour.

Rock Cornish Game Hens with Bread Stuffing

Serves 2

2 Rock Cornish game hens
Salt and black pepper to taste
3 cups dried or soft bread crumbs, soaked in brandy or milk
1 egg, beaten

1 teaspoon rubbed sage
½ teaspoon dried oregano
¼ teaspoon ground mace
¼ teaspoon ground nutmeg
2 tablespoons butter, softened

Preheat oven to 400°F.

To prepare the hens, wash out their cavities and then rub inside and out with a small amount of salt and pepper.

In a bowl combine the soaked bread crumbs and their soaking liquid with all the remaining ingredients except the butter. If the mixture is too wet, add more bread crumbs. Season with salt and pepper. This mixture should be sufficient to stuff 2 Cornish hens, plus, later, enough to be the foundation for Poor Man's Pudding (see page 114). Stuff both the forward and back openings of the hens and truss closed. Rub the outside of the hens with softened butter.

Bake until the hens are tender and browned, 40 to 45 minutes.

If a fireplace is available for cooking, wrap the hens with strong cord (grocers' twine) and suspend them 8 to 12 inches above the fire. Roast until no juices run when thigh is pierced with a fork. The heat of the fire will cause the birds to rotate on their cords. If they become dry before they are finished cooking, brush with more butter.

Mrs. Steen's Fried Apples

Serves 6

These apples can be used as a side dish with meats, poultry, and fowl.

6 tablespoons butter
1 teaspoon ground cinnamon
¼ teaspoon ground nutmeg
¼ teaspoon ground mace

⅛ teaspoon ground cloves
8 apples, peeled, cored, and sliced
Apple cider, as needed

In a deep skillet, melt the butter. Add the cinnamon, nutmeg, mace, and cloves; mix well. Add the apples and cook over medium heat, turning often, about 3 to 5 minutes. Cover the apples with cider and bring to a boil. Reduce the heat and simmer until the apples are tender, about 20 minutes.

Serve hot or cold.

Green Beans with Herbs

Serves 6

Salted water
2 pounds green beans, trimmed
2 teaspoons finely chopped burnet
(herb with cucumberlike taste)
1 tablespoon finely chopped chives
1 tablespoon finely chopped tarragon

2 tablespoons chopped fresh parsley
½ cup olive oil or vegetable oil
2 tablespoons red wine vinegar
¼ teaspoon salt
¼ teaspoon ground pepper

Bring a saucepan filled with salted water to a boil. Add beans and cook about 10 minutes, or until tender. Drain and place in a bowl.

In a small bowl mix together the burnet, chives, tarragon, and parsley. Toss with the beans.

Combine the remaining ingredients and stir well. Pour over the warm beans when ready to serve.

Pickled Peaches

Serves 4

These peaches keep well in the refrigerator. The syrup can be reused to pickle additional peach halves.

1 quart ripe peaches (about 2 pounds)
¾ cup firmly packed brown sugar
½ cup cider or distilled white vinegar

2 sticks cinnamon, broken in half
1 teaspoon whole cloves
1 teaspoon whole allspice

Bring a saucepan filled with water to a boil. Place the peaches in the pot a few minutes so that the skins can be easily removed; drain and reserve 2 cups of the blanching water. Remove the skins and halve and pit the peaches.

In a pot, mix the reserved water, brown sugar, vinegar, cinnamon, cloves, and allspice. Bring to a boil and continue boiling 8 minutes, or until the mixture begins to get syrupy. Add the peach halves and simmer 5 minutes. Remove from the heat and chill in syrup several hours before using.

Baked Pumpkin

Preheat oven to 350°F.

Cut a pumpkin into large bite-sized pieces. Remove all the seeds and strings, but leave the rind on.

Arrange pieces on a baking sheet. Brush with softened butter and sprinkle with salt. Cover and bake 30 to 45 minutes or until tender.

Pour melted butter to taste over the pumpkin and serve.

Carrot Pudding

Serves 5 to 6 as a side dish

1 onion, finely chopped
3 large carrots, peeled and shredded
1 cup water
⅛ teaspoon salt, plus salt to taste
1 egg, beaten

½ cup cracker crumbs
1 tablespoon butter, melted
½ cup milk
¼ teaspoon ground cinnamon
Black pepper to taste

Preheat oven to 350°F.

Combine the onion, carrots, water, and 1 teaspoon salt in a saucepan. Bring to a boil and cook 5 minutes. Drain.

Stir in the egg, cracker crumbs, butter, milk, cinnamon, and salt and pepper to taste. Turn the mixture into a buttered 4-cup casserole. Bake 20 to 30 minutes, or until pudding is set.

Poor Man's Pudding

Serves 4

This versatile pudding can be served as a sweetened dessert or mixed with leftover meats to make a hearty entrée.

About 2 cups leftover stuffing from Rock Cornish Game Hens with Bread Stuffing (see page 111)
1 egg, beaten
¼ cup sugar
1 teaspoon ground cinnamon, nutmeg, or mace (see Note)

1 apple, peeled, cored, and chopped
½ cup raisins
2 tablespoons vegetable oil
2 tablespoons butter

Preheat oven to 350°F.

In a bowl combine the stuffing, egg, sugar, cinnamon, apple, and raisins.

If baking in an oven: Pour the oil into a small iron skillet and place the skillet in the oven until it is very hot. Remove from the oven and pour in the pudding mixture. Smooth top so it is flat and dot with butter. Return to the oven and bake about 20 minutes, or until set.

If baking in a fireplace: Pour oil into a dutch oven with a lid and heat in the fireplace. Add the pudding, smooth the top, cover with the lid, and return to the fireplace. Heap coals on the lid, then remove from fire. Allow the pudding to cook at the edge of the fireplace, replacing coals on the lid if they stop glowing. Check pudding after about 20 minutes. If not yet set, repeat the process.

NOTE: If instead of a spice you add a "heavy" spice, such as thyme, sage, tarragon, or rosemary, add black pepper and chopped onion as well. Omit the sugar and serve this as a savory side dish. If bits of cooked meat, especially roast beef, are added with the onion and "heavy" spice, this pudding can be served as a main dish.

Tidewater Delight

Makes one 9-inch pie, serves 6 to 8

This pie recipe has been handed down through many generations. It is said to have originated on the Eastern Shore.

Wafer Crust (recipe follows)
1 tablespoon unflavored gelatin
¼ cup water
3 eggs, separated
½ cup sugar

¼ teaspoon salt
1 cup milk
1 teaspoon vanilla extract
½ teaspoon almond extract
1 cup heavy cream, lightly whipped

Prepare the crust, cover, and chill.

Sprinkle the gelatin over the water and let stand 10 minutes to soften. In a bowl, cream together the egg yolks, sugar, and salt until pale colored. Stir in the milk. Pour into the top pan of a double boiler placed over simmering water. Stir constantly with a wooden spoon until the mixture thickens and coats the back of the spoon. Stir in the softened gelatin, vanilla, and almond extracts. Remove from the heat.

Beat the egg whites until stiff peaks form. Gently fold beaten whites into yolk mixture.

Whip the cream until soft peaks form. Fold into the egg mixture, then pour into the chilled crust. Sprinkle the top with some of the leftover wafer crumbs and chill well.

Wafer Crust

Makes one 9-inch crust

1¼ cups vanilla or chocolate wafer crumbs

⅓ cup butter, melted

Combine the crumbs and melted butter and mix well. Press onto the bottom and sides of a 9-inch pie pan. Reserve any leftover crumb mixture for topping pie.

Cover and chill at least 1 hour before filling.

Vinegar Pie

Makes one 9-inch pie, serves 6

By the eighteenth century desserts had become part of every family's evening meal. When fresh fruit was not available, custards and dried fruit were the main ingredients. When all other ingredients were exhausted, this Vinegar Pie found its way to the table.

Vinegar Pastry Dough, prebaked (recipe follows)
1 cup sugar
2 eggs, beaten
2 tablespoons flour
1 cup water
2 tablespoons butter, melted
2 tablespoons cider vinegar

Cream together the sugar and eggs. Add the flour, water, butter, and vinegar. Mix well.

Cook the mixture in the top pan of a double boiler over simmering water, stirring often, until thickened. Pour into the prebaked pie shell (see page 31) and cool.

Serve with sweetened whipped cream.

Vinegar Pastry Dough

Makes pastry for one 9-inch pie

1½ cups flour
¾ teaspoon salt
½ cup solid vegetable shortening
2 tablespoons water
1 tablespoon distilled white vinegar

In a large bowl mix together the flour and salt. Cut in the shortening with fingertips or a pastry blender until mixture has the consistency of coarse meal.

Mix together the water and vinegar. Work it into the flour mixture. Form into a ball, wrap, and chill at least 1 hour before rolling out the dough.

Lemon Pot Pie

Makes one 10-inch pie

2 or 3 lemons, thinly sliced and
   seeded
½ cup sugar
1½ cup molasses
4 cups water
½ cup lard

2½ cups flour
1 teaspoon salt
3 to 4 tablespoons water
Flour, for dusting
Whipped cream or vanilla ice cream,
   for accompaniment

Preheat oven to 350°F.

In a 10-inch cast-iron skillet, combine the lemon slices, sugar, molasses, and water. Bring to a boil and cook about 20 minutes, or until the mixture becomes syrupy.

In a bowl mix together the flour and salt. Cut in the lard with fingertips or a pastry blender until mixture has the consistency of coarse meal. Work the water into the flour mixture to make a stiff dough.

Form the dough into a ball. On a lightly floured board roll it out ¼ inch thick. Cut it into diamond-shaped pieces, about 3 inches long by 3 inches wide.

Sprinkle a few dough pieces with flour and drop them into the syrup bubbling in the skillet. Continue in this manner until all the dough is in the skillet. Remove some syrup if it begins to overflow the skillet rim. Leave just enough syrup to cover the dough before the last pieces are added.

Transfer skillet to the oven and bake 30 minutes. Serve warm, sliced in wedges. Top with whipped cream or vanilla ice cream.

· St. Mary's County ·

*J. Edward Knott, born at Sotterley Plantation in St. Mary's County,
operates the plantation smokehouse as did his father before him.
Here, southern Maryland hams are flavored with the aromatic
smoke of hickory or apple wood and then hung to dry in paper
bags for about one year. Like the ham of Smithfield, Virginia,
Chesapeake ham is best served sliced paper thin.*

A drive through St. Mary's County brings to mind bygone days. One imagines families sitting on broad plantation porches in retreat from the summer sun, sipping iced tea and mint juleps, or of sultry July picnics beneath a sprawling shade tree with everyone eating fried chicken.

In 1634 two ships, the *Ark* and the *Dove,* arrived from England to the shores of what was to become the first settlement of the Maryland colony. St. Mary's City was originally a Catholic settlement, but the Protestants got wind of the crabs, oysters, and other delights being pulled from the Bay, and it wasn't long before the culinary gold rush was on. As more colonists arrived, and new and larger towns sprang up along the shore, St. Mary's City began losing its footing as the center of the colony. Today work has begun on excavating and restoring the site of the city.

Tobacco is king in St. Mary's County. It has been and still is one of the primary cash crops on the southern part of the Bay. The old tobacco plantations were also the source of smoked hams, sausages, and a rich bounty of fruits and vegetables.

Bordered by the Chesapeake Bay and the Patuxent and Potomac rivers, this area hosts numerous inlets and creeks along its shores. The locals fish, crab, and harvest the surrounding waters and fields, providing some of the finest seafood, ham, game, waterfowl, and agricultural products of the Bay region. These culinary resources work together to create a delightful gastronomic experience that is marked by the tastes and flavors of the Old South. Full-bodied country hams become the focal point of a St. Mary's breakfast that includes fried tomatoes and a cream gravy. A tangy Southern barbecue sauce atop briny Chesapeake oysters translates into the locally infamous Barbecued Oysters recipe. The many sauces and gravies of the St. Mary's recipes all beg for sopping up with the legendary Maryland Beaten Biscuits.

The smells, tastes, and graceful manner of living are alive and well on the shores of St. Mary's County.

Scrapple

You don't think I'd write a Chesapeake Bay cookbook and not include a scrapple recipe, do you? Of course not. And for those of you with bad nerves, I've used quite a tame one at that. Oh, do I have scrapple stories! Too bad this is a cookbook. Guess I'll save them for a scrapple novel.

Some of the best scrapple in the country is made around St. Mary's way. Try this scrapple with eggs, covered with maple syrup, or as a sandwich with scrambled eggs and ketchup on toast. Don't laugh at me until you've tried it. I love scrapple!

2 parts pork shoulder
2 parts pork liver
1 part pork scraps (feet, jowl, kidneys, or whatever)
Yellow cornmeal

Salt, black pepper, and dried sage to taste
Flour
Bacon drippings or butter

Cut the pork shoulder into chunks. Wash the shoulder, liver, and scraps with cold water. Put all the meats into a heavy pot and add just enough water to cover them. Cook until the meat is quite tender, about 2 to 3 hours. Remove the meats from the pot with a slotted utensil. Grind them in a meat grinder or a food processor.

Return the ground meat to the pot with the cooking juices and continue cooking. Add just enough cornmeal for the mixture to become mushlike. Season well with salt, pepper, and sage. Pour the mixture into loaf pans, cover, and chill.

To serve, cut scrapple in ¼- to ½-inch-thick slices, according to taste. Dust slices with flour and fry in bacon drippings for several minutes on each side, browning well.

NOTE: If all of this is too much for you to handle, there are many excellent brands of scrapple on the market.

Country Ham and Fried Tomatoes with Cream Gravy

Serves 4

This breakfast feast is simply some of the best eating country life has to offer. It's the kind of meal that can bring on tears of joy. After cooking the ham and tomatoes in the skillet, please do not clean the skillet out before making the gravy. The cooking residue gives the gravy such a flavor! Whip up a batch of hot Buttermilk Biscuits (see page 99).

4 to 6 tablespoons butter or oil, for frying
4 slices country ham, about ½ inch thick
2 to 3 green tomatoes, cored, sliced ½ inch thick, and soaked in milk
Flour seasoned with salt and black pepper
Pinch sugar
Cream Gravy (recipe follows)

In a heavy skillet, melt the butter and sauté the ham slices about 3 minutes on each side. Remove ham to heated platter and keep warm.

Drain the tomatoes and dust them with the seasoned flour. Add more butter to pan if necessary and fry the tomatoes several minutes on each side, sprinkling each side with a little sugar. Remove and drain on paper towels, then arrange on platter with ham.

While tomatoes are cooking make the gravy. Pour the gravy over the ham and tomatoes and serve immediately.

Cream Gravy

Makes about 1¾ cups

¼ cup (4 tablespoons) butter
¼ cup flour
2 cups milk or half-and-half
Salt and black pepper to taste

Melt the butter in the same skillet used for cooking the ham and tomatoes. Whisk in the flour. Cook, stirring, 2 to 3 minutes. Gradually stir in the milk. Bring to a boil and cook, stirring constantly, until thickened. Season with salt and pepper.

Barbecued Oysters

Serves 4 to 6

This is a great dish to design a party around. All you need is a bushel or two of oysters, plenty of cold beer, and some friends with good strong wrists for shucking.

24 oysters
1½ to 2 cups Jimmy's Barbecue
  Sauce (see page 134)

24 pieces bacon (2-inches square)
Rock salt

Preheat oven to 450°F.

Shuck the oysters, keeping the oyster meat in the deep part of the shell. On each oyster place about 1 tablespoon of the barbecue sauce. Top with a bacon piece.

On a heatproof tray, make a layer of rock salt and arrange the oysters on it. Bake 6 to 8 minutes, or until oysters begin to curl at edges and bacon begins to brown slightly.

Smoked Cod Hors d'Oeuvres

Makes about 50 canapés

Here's a lip-smacking buffet dish that will keep them coming back for more. This appetizer showcases the smoked hams and fish from the famous smokehouses of St. Mary's County.

6 tablespoons butter
3 tablespoons finely chopped onion
3 tablespoons finely chopped green
  bell pepper
¼ cup flour
1½ cups heavy cream
4 egg yolks

½ cup grated Swiss cheese
1½ cups chopped smoked cod
½ cup ground smoked ham
2 tablespoons chopped fresh dill
Salt and black pepper to taste
50 bread slices (approximately)
Buttered dried bread crumbs

Preheat oven to 375°F.

In a saucepan, melt the butter and sauté the onion and bell pepper until soft. Stir in the flour and cook, stirring, several minutes. Gradually stir in the cream and cook until thick.

Off the heat beat in the egg yolks, one at a time. Stir in the cheese. Mix in the cod, ham, and dill. Season with salt and pepper.

Cut out small 2-inch rounds of bread and toast them on one side. Arrange rounds, untoasted side up, on a baking sheet. Spoon mounds of the mixture on rounds. Top with bread crumbs and bake until browned. Serve at once.

Summer Tomatoes and Shrimp Aspic

Serves 4 as a first course or light entrée

A visually stunning first course or ladies' luncheon entrée that bursts with the sweet flavor of summer tomatoes.

1 envelope unflavored gelatin
¼ cup water
1½ cups strained fresh tomato juice
2 tablespoons red wine vinegar
2 tablespoons fresh lemon juice
½ teaspoon Old Bay seasoning
¼ teaspoon white pepper
1 tablespoon grated onion
¼ teaspoon Tabasco sauce
2 tablespoons chopped fresh dill

½ pound shrimp, steamed, peeled, and sliced in half lengthwise (about 1 cup)
½ cup peeled, seeded, halved cucumber slices
¼ cup finely diced celery
A few sprigs fresh dill
Dill Sauce (recipe follows)
Lettuce leaves, for garnish

Sprinkle gelatin over water in a small pan. Place over low heat and stir to dissolve. In a bowl mix the dissolved gelatin with tomato juice, vinegar, lemon juice, Old Bay, white pepper, onion, Tabasco, and chopped dill.

Cover and chill the mixture. When it begins to thicken, fold in the shrimp, cucumbers, celery, and dill sprigs. Pour the mixture into a well-oiled 2-cup ring mold.

Cover and chill until set. Prepare Dill Sauce. Dip base of mold in warm water, then invert on lettuce-lined platter. Serve napped with the Dill Sauce.

Dill Sauce

½ cup mayonnaise
¼ cup sour cream
2 teaspoons chopped fresh dill

1 teaspoon red wine vinegar
Salt and white pepper to taste

In a small bowl combine all the ingredients and mix well.

• St. Mary's Soups •

Summer Garden Soup

Serves 10 to 12

A gardener's harvest brought to- gether in a simple soup brimming with fresh, natural tastes. Take care when cooking the vegetables that you do not leave them on the heat too long. Each vegetable should hold its own—stand out as an individual—and at the same time make a contribution to the team effort.

6 tablespoons butter
2 small onions, chopped
2 leeks, halved and chopped
2 tablespoons chopped garlic
6 cups Chicken Stock (see page 33)
8 tomatoes, chopped
½ pound zucchini, cut in ¾-inch-thick slices

½ pound green beans, trimmed and cut in 2-inch-long pieces
1 cup corn kernels
1 cup cut-up okra
1 cup shelled peas
2 teaspoons salt
½ cup coarsely chopped fresh basil
Freshly ground black pepper

In a pot melt the butter and cook the onions, leeks, and garlic 5 minutes. Add the stock and tomatoes. Bring to a boil.

Reduce the heat and add the zucchini, green beans, corn, okra, peas, salt, and basil. Simmer 25 to 30 minutes, or until the vegetables are tender but not mushy. Adjust the seasonings and add black pepper to taste.

Oyster Bisque

Serves 10 to 12

A rich, lovely, creamy bisque that is delicately flavored with sautéed vegetables and the oyster's own liquor. Please notice that the bisque is briefly cooked at the end, to preserve the integrity of the oysters.

6 tablespoons butter
½ cup diced onion
¼ cup diced celery
¼ cup diced carrot
1 quart shucked oysters with liquor
4 cups Fish Stock (see page 35)
½ cup white rice

1 teaspoon salt, plus salt to taste
2 cups heavy cream
Black pepper to taste
Few dashes Tabasco sauce
Whipped cream and cayenne pepper, for garnish

In a skillet melt the butter and sauté the onion, celery, and carrot 5 to 10 minutes. Drain oysters, reserving liquor; chop 3 or 4 oysters and set the remaining oysters aside. Add the chopped oysters to the skillet and cook 3 to 4 minutes.

In a pot, bring the stock to a boil. Add the rice, 1 teaspoon salt, and the contents of the skillet. Reduce the heat and simmer 40 minutes.

Press the soup through a fine sieve. Return to the pot and place over the heat. Add the cream and reserved oyster liquor. Season with salt, pepper, and Tabasco. Add the reserved oysters and heat briefly until the edges of the oysters begin to curl.

Serve bisque in bowls. Garnish each serving with a dollop of whipped cream and a sprinkling of cayenne pepper.

Crab and Oyster Gumbo

Serves a crowd

When I mentioned to some of my culinarily correct food friends that I was researching a Chesapeake gumbo recipe, they were surprised. To them, gumbo only comes from Louisiana. Don't tell that to my girls in St. Mary's County. I did and they responded, "Honey, they ain't had gumbo till they had our gumbo!"

The Bay region is a natural for gumbo, to be sure. The seafood, smoked sausage, and the Sassafrass (gumbo filé is ground sassafrass leaf) River ain't known for bananas. The African word for okra is gombo, thus the name gumbo, and there's plenty of good-looking okra grown along the shores of the Bay.

What gives this gumbo its wonderfully distinctive taste is the use of veal knuckles as opposed to fish stock. The veal makes a flavorful broth that accents the seafood but does not overpower it.

1 cup vegetable oil
1 cup flour
2 cups chopped yellow onions
1 cup chopped green onions
1 cup chopped celery
1 cup chopped bell peppers
¼ cup chopped garlic
4 cups cut-up okra (about 1 pound)
1 pound country ham, diced
4 cups chopped tomatoes (about 2 pounds)
7 cups water
2 veal knuckles

2 teaspoons salt
1 teaspoon ground pepper
½ teaspoon cayenne pepper
1 teaspoon dried thyme
2 bay leaves
1 teaspoon Tabasco sauce
1½ cups corn kernels
1 pound claw crabmeat, picked over for shells
1 pint shucked oysters with liquor
Freshly cooked white rice
Filé powder (optional)

To make the roux heat the oil in a heavy-bottomed soup kettle until it is smoking hot. Whisk in the flour and stir constantly over a high heat until the mixture turns dark or reddish brown. Keep it moving or it will burn and stick to the bottom. Be careful not to splash it on your skin!

When the roux is browned, stir in the yellow and green onions, celery, bell peppers, and garlic. Cook over medium heat, stirring all the while, about 5 minutes.

Stir in the okra, ham, and tomatoes. Mix well, cover, and simmer 10 minutes, stirring now and then. Add the water, veal knuckles, salt, ground pepper, cayenne, thyme, bay leaves, and Tabasco. Bring to a boil and simmer 1 to 1½ hours.

Just before serving add the crabmeat and oysters with their liquor. Simmer until the oysters begin to curl at the edges, about 5 minutes.

Serve the gumbo in large bowls, spooned over the rice. Pass the filé.

· St. Mary's Seafoods ·

Fish Cakes

Serves 6 to 8

I've tried substituting part smoked cod in this old-fashioned recipe for Friday nights, and the result is delicious. If you do use smoked fish, go lightly on the salt when seasoning the mixture. A pot of baked beans traditionally accompanies these cakes.

2 cups cooked cod or other firm fish fillet
2 cups mashed, cooked potatoes
2 tablespoons bacon drippings
2 tablespoons butter
1 onion, finely minced
1 egg, beaten

½ teaspoon Worcestershire sauce
¼ teaspoon Tabasco sauce
Pinch ground nutmeg
Salt and black pepper to taste
3 tablespoons chopped fresh parsley
Butter or bacon drippings, for frying cakes

Mix together the cod and potatoes in a bowl.

In a skillet heat the bacon drippings and butter. Add the onions and sauté until soft; add to the cod mixture. Add egg, Worcestershire, Tabasco, nutmeg, salt, pepper, and parsley to bowl. Mix well.

Form mixture into 12 to 16 cakes, then brown on both sides in a skillet in a little butter. Drain on paper towels before serving.

Shad Roe with Bacon and Mushrooms

Serves 4

This is a very simple preparation of shad roe, and is precisely the idea to keep in mind when preparing the delicate roe. This dish goes nicely with buttered boiled potatoes and a fresh vegetable.

4 slices bacon
12 tablespoons butter
1½ cups thinly sliced mushrooms (about 6 ounces)

Salt and black pepper to taste
4 pairs shad roe (see page 12)
Juice of 1 lemon
1 tablespoon chopped fresh parsley

Fry the bacon in a skillet until fairly crisp. Remove bacon to paper towels to drain; reserve drippings in skillet.

Melt 3 tablespoons of the butter in the skillet with the drippings. Sauté the mushrooms 2 to 3 minutes, or until cooked. Season with salt and pepper. Remove from the skillet and keep warm.

Melt 6 tablespoons of the butter in the same skillet. Sprinkle the roe with salt and pepper. When the butter is hot, add the roe. Cook the roe pairs, covered, over medium-low heat, turning now and then. Be careful when handling the roe sacks, for they have a tendency to pop during cooking.

Total cooking time is about 12 minutes. Remove the roe from the skillet and place on a heated platter. Top with the mushrooms and bacon strips. Keep warm.

Place the remaining 3 tablespoons butter in pan over high heat. When melted and just beginning to brown, add lemon juice and parsley. Remove from the heat immediately and pour over the roe.

Ham and Oyster Pie

Serves 6

Here's a signature dish of Chesapeake regional cuisine: succulent, creamy oysters are steamed beneath a flaky pastry crust in an unsurpassed partnering of ham and bivalve.

Pastry Dough for double-crust 9-inch pie (see page 31), bottom shell partially baked
3 tablespoons butter
3 tablespoons flour
1 pint shucked oysters, drained and liquor reserved

Heavy cream, as needed
Salt and ground pepper to taste
Pinch ground mace
¾ cup grated Swiss cheese
1½ cups minced country ham
1 egg, beaten
1 tablespoon water

Prepare pastry dough. Line a 9-inch pie pan with half of the dough and partially bake crust.

Preheat oven to 375°F.

In an enamel or other heavy-bottomed pan, melt the butter. Whisk in the flour and cook, stirring, 2 to 3 minutes. Remove from the heat.

Measure oyster liquor and add cream to make 2¼ cups. Whisk cream mixture into the butter-flour mixture. Return pan to the heat and stir constantly until mixture comes to a boil. Season well with salt, pepper, and mace. Stir in cheese to melt.

Arrange the oysters and ham in partially baked crust. Pour in the cream sauce and gently blend with the oysters and ham.

Roll out the remaining pastry on a lightly floured board and fit it over the pie, crimping edges. Make 2 or 3 slits in the top crust for vents. Mix together the egg and water and brush on top of pie.

Bake about 45 minutes, or until golden brown.

Catfish and Waffles

Serves 4

The sweet-fleshed catfish is literally smothered in a flavorful sauce. The addition of crabmeat to the sauce at the end transports this meal from "down home" to "country elegance."

4 medium-sized catfish fillets
Milk, to cover
4 Waffles (see page 45)
3 tablespoons butter
3 tablespoons oil
Flour seasoned with salt and black pepper
1 cup chopped tomatoes

1 cup heavy cream
¼ cup minced green onions
Few drops Tabasco sauce
Juice of 1 lemon
¾ cup backfin or special crabmeat, picked over for shells
Salt and black pepper to taste

Place fish in a shallow dish and add milk to cover; let stand 1 hour. Prepare Waffles and keep warm.

In a skillet large enough to hold the fish fillets, heat butter and oil over medium heat. Pat the fillets dry and coat well with seasoned flour. Put into skillet and fry about 2 minutes on each side. Pour off excess oil.

Add the tomatoes, cream, green onions, Tabasco, and lemon juice. Bring almost to a boil. Gently stir in crabmeat and cover. Simmer gently for 10 minutes.

Arrange Waffles on a heated platter. Remove the fish and crab with a slotted utensil and arrange on top of the Waffles. Increase the heat and reduce the cooking juices slightly. Season with salt and pepper. Spoon the sauce over the fish and crab.

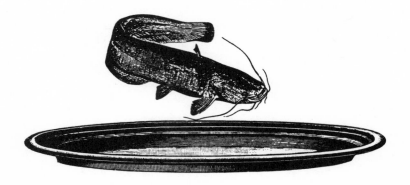

Roast Turkey with Oyster Dressing

Serves 10 to 12

The locals take great pride in this regional stuffing, and with good reason. The briny quality of the oysters gives a deliciously unusual tang to the dressing. A good deal of the credit for the wonderful flavor goes to the oyster liquor, which embodies the essence of the oyster.

Oyster Dressing (recipe follows)
1 turkey (10 to 12 pounds)

Salt and black pepper
2 tablespoons butter, softened

Preheat oven to 325°F. Prepare the Oyster Dressing.

Wash the cavity of the turkey with cold water and dry with paper towels. Sprinkle cavity with salt and pepper. Stuff cavity loosely with the dressing. (If there is any extra dressing, bake separately in a buttered pan during the last hour the turkey is roasting.)

Truss the turkey. Rub the skin with butter. Place turkey on a rack in a roasting pan. To prevent the turkey breast from drying out, roast breast side down the first 2 hours. Roast 25 minutes per pound.

Oyster Dressing

1 cup (½ pound) butter
1 cup chopped onion
1 cup chopped celery
7 cups day-old bread cubes
2½ teaspoons salt

½ teaspoon black pepper
¼ teaspoon ground mace
1 pint shucked oysters, drained, liquor reserved, and chopped
About 1 cup milk

Melt the butter in a skillet and sauté the onions and celery until soft.

In a bowl combine all the remaining ingredients except the milk and oyster liquor. Mix well. Pour in the oyster liquor, then slowly add enough milk to moisten stuffing. Do not make it too wet.

Smoked Chicken Croquettes

Serves 5 or 6

The smokiness of the chicken and the tiny flecks of crisp bacon give this old favorite a new attitude. I find that after preparing the croquette mixture, it is helpful to chill it thoroughly before forming it. Otherwise it gets stuck between your fingers and doesn't make for a pretty picture.

If desired, serve croquettes with a chicken gravy and cranberry sauce.

6 tablespoons butter
6 tablespoons flour
½ cup chicken stock or bouillon
1 cup heavy cream
Salt and black pepper to taste
Pinch cayenne pepper
Pinch ground nutmeg
1½ cups chopped, cooked chicken

1 cup chopped smoked chicken
2 tablespoons finely chopped cooked bacon
2 tablespoons chopped chives or parsley
3 eggs, beaten
Dried bread crumbs, for coating
Vegetable oil, for deep-frying

Melt the butter in a saucepan. Whisk in the flour and cook several minutes, stirring all the while.

Off the heat slowly whisk in the stock and cream. Return to the heat and whisk constantly until thick. Season with salt, peppers, and nutmeg. Cover and chill.

In a bowl combine the cooked chicken, smoked chicken, bacon, chives, and chilled sauce. Mix well, cover, and chill.

Form mixture into 2½-inch-tall cone-shaped croquettes. Dip into beaten egg, then roll in bread crumbs. In a deep pan, heat oil to about 365°F. Deep-fry the croquettes, a few at a time, until golden brown, 2 to 4 minutes. Remove with a slotted utensil to paper towels to drain. Serve hot.

Maryland Panfried Chicken with Cream Gravy

Serves 4

You'll have no trouble getting anybody to the table with this one! In fact, it'll take a lot of "shooing" to keep them out of the kitchen while you're frying. This world-famous dish puts the Colonel to shame.

When you put the chicken pieces in the bag, it's your basic "shake and bake" technique. But you don't bake, and the shaking has to come from the hips. I suggest putting some soul-vibrating music on the Victrola before beginning.

The differences between Maryland fried and southern fried are that, after browning in very hot oil, we cover the pan and reduce the heat to let the steam go all through the chicken. This keeps the meat remarkably moist while producing a crispy outside coating. I promise. The addition of cream gravy made from those delicious pan drippings is another big difference. I serve my Maryland fried chicken with buttery mashed potatoes and South of the Mason-Dixon Greens (see page 136).

1 frying chicken (3 to 4 pounds), cut in serving pieces
Buttermilk, as needed
Salt and black pepper
2 cups flour seasoned with 2 tablespoons salt
Lard or vegetable oil, for frying
¼ cup flour, for gravy
2 cups milk, for gravy

Place chicken pieces in a shallow dish and pour in buttermilk to cover. Cover dish and refrigerate overnight.

When ready to fry, remove the chicken from the buttermilk and wipe off the excess. Rub the chicken with salt and pepper. Put 2 cups flour and 2 tablespoons salt in a plastic or paper bag. Place the chicken in the bag and shake to coat well.

In a cast-iron skillet, melt lard to a depth of about 1¼ inches. Heat until very hot but not smoking. Brown the chicken on both sides, turning frequently. Reduce heat to medium and cover skillet. Cook chicken, turning occasionally. Total cooking time should be about 25 to 30 minutes. Remove the chicken with a slotted utensil to paper towels to drain.

Pour off all but 3 tablespoons of the cooking fat. Stir in ¼ cup flour and cook, stirring, 1 to 2 minutes. Slowly whisk in the milk; stir constantly until thickened. Season with salt and pepper. Serve over the chicken or on the side.

Country Fried Rabbit

Serves 2 or 3

A true country dish, the rabbit picks up a distinctive flavor from the use of salt pork in the frying process. The mustard in the gravy provides a nice bite. Have plenty of hot biscuits on hand for dipping. Mighty fine eating!

1 rabbit, cut in serving pieces
Salted water
Milk
Flour seasoned with salt and black
    pepper
¼ pound salt pork, cut in pieces
2 tablespoons flour

1 tablespoon Dijon mustard
½ cup chicken stock (or bouillon)
1½ cups heavy cream
¼ teaspoon dried thyme
Salt and black pepper to taste

In a bowl cover the rabbit pieces with salted water. Let stand 2 to 3 hours. Drain rabbit, dip in milk, and then roll in the seasoned flour.

In a large skillet render the salt pork. Brown the rabbit slowly on all sides in the hot fat. Remove rabbit.

Pour off all but 3 tablespoons of fat. Whisk in the flour and mustard and cook, stirring, several minutes. Slowly whisk in the stock and cream. Add thyme, salt, and pepper.

Return the rabbit pieces to the skillet and bring to a boil. Reduce the heat and simmer, covered, 1½ hours, or until tender.

• St. Mary's Meats •

Baked Maryland Ham

How long to presoak a ham depends largely on its age. Most aged hams are about two to three years old and require twenty-four hours of soaking. If a ham is older, it is a good idea to soak it for two days.

1 aged country ham
Water
1 part cider vinegar

4 parts brown sugar
Dry mustard to taste
Whole cloves

Scrub the ham well with a stiff-bristled brush. Place in a large vessel and add water to cover. Soak 24 to 48 hours.

Throw out the soaking water, place ham in a large pot, and re-cover with fresh water. Bring to a boil, then simmer for 2 to 2½ hours, or until bone becomes loose. Let the ham cool in the cooking liquid.

Preheat oven to 350°F. Make a paste of the cider vinegar, brown sugar, and mustard. Carefully remove the skin from the ham while still warm; do not remove the fat. Cover ham with the paste. Stick whole cloves into the fat.

Bake, basting often, 20 to 30 minutes, or until glaze has browned.

Let ham sit for at least 30 minutes before slicing. Cut in thin slices and serve warm or cold.

Pork Chops with Corn Bread and Pear Stuffing

Serves 4

A marvelous dressing up for big, fat, juicy chops. The combination of pears and corn bread goes together like bread and butter. Should your pears not be quite ripe enough to be soft, sauté them in a little butter until tender. Serve with mounds of mashed potatoes and Sauerkraut and Apples (see page 55).

¼ cup (4 tablespoons) butter
½ cup finely chopped onion
¼ cup finely chopped celery
1 cup dried corn bread crumbs or pieces
1 cup diced ripe pears
½ teaspoon dried sage

¼ teaspoon ground nutmeg
Milk, as needed
Salt and black pepper to taste
4 pork chops, about 1 inch thick
6 tablespoons vegetable oil or rendered pork fat, for frying
Stock or bouillon, if needed

To prepare the stuffing melt the butter in a skillet. Add the onion and celery and sauté until soft. Mix the crumbs and pears together in a bowl and add the sautéed onion and celery. Add the sage and nutmeg. Sprinkle with a little milk to moisten. Season with salt and pepper.

Preheat oven to 350°F. Have your butcher cut pockets in the pork chops. Fill the pockets with stuffing and secure closed with toothpicks.

In a flameproof casserole heat the oil. Salt and pepper the chops and brown well on both sides. Pour in just enough water to cover the bottom of the casserole. Cover tightly and bake 45 minutes.

Remove the chops and make a pan gravy from the juices (see gravy Note, page 44). If there is not enough liquid, add a little stock or bouillon to the casserole and thicken.

Jimmy Le Blue's Barbecued Ribs

Serves 5 to 6

Jimmy and his brother Leroy have had a feud going for a number of years about how to fix the finest spareribs. Leroy likes to throw them right on the grill. Jimmy twists his face up when he hears that, saying you get a tough, fatty rib that will, "if you ain't careful, fly back and hit you square in the face."

Not wanting facial lacerations, I took Jimmy's side. Here is Jimmy's recipe. The ribs turn out as tender as butter and very moist. Sorry, Leroy!

Jimmy's Barbecue Sauce (recipe
  follows)
Salted water
5 to 6 pounds pork spareribs
2 onions, sliced

Bay leaf
Vegetable oil, for marinating
1 tablespoon chopped garlic

Prepare barbecue sauce and set aside to blend flavors.

Bring a large pot filled with salted water to a boil. Add the ribs, onions, and bay leaf. Cover, reduce the heat, and simmer 45 minutes. Drain.

Pour a little oil and the chopped garlic into a shallow dish. Add the ribs and marinate until ready to grill, at least 1 hour.

Grill over hot coals 15 to 20 minutes, turning often. Baste with the barbecue sauce after each turn. Serve with extra sauce on the side.

Jimmy's Barbecue Sauce

Makes about 2½ cups

1½ cups ketchup
½ cup cider vinegar
2 tablespoons brown sugar
2 tablespoons dry mustard
2 tablespoons grated onion
1 tablespoon minced garlic

1 tablespoon Worcestershire sauce
2 tablespoons prepared horseradish
2 tablespoons fresh lemon juice
1 teaspoon salt
3 tablespoons butter

Mix all the ingredients together in a saucepan and bring to a boil. Simmer 15 minutes. Let stand for at least 1 hour to let the flavors mingle.

Spinach Timbales

Serves 4

Individual spinach custards can make any luncheon or dinner a special occasion. I cook the spinach in a few tablespoons of butter with half an onion, finely minced. Serve the timbales plain or topped with Old Bay Hollandaise Sauce (see page 26).

2 cups well drained, finely chopped, cooked spinach (about 1½ pounds)
3 tablespoons butter, melted
2 eggs, beaten
1 cup half-and-half

Salt and black pepper to taste
Pinch ground nutmeg
Juice of 1 lemon
Hot water

Preheat oven to 300°F.

Prepare the spinach and let cool.

In a mixing bowl combine all the ingredients except the spinach and hot water. Stir in the spinach and mix well. Pour into 4 buttered individual 6 ounce custard cups or individual timbale molds.

Place in a baking dish and add hot water to reach two thirds up the sides of the mold. Bake about 40 minutes, or until the custard is set.

Remove from the oven and let the timbales rest in water about 10 minutes before serving. To unmold, loosen edges of custards with a knife and invert on individual plates.

Candied Yams

Serves 5 or 6

Yams play a major role in the kitchens of the Bay. This candied version is positively addictive. Be careful when the yams are served piping hot, because they tend to stick to the lips.

6 yams or sweet potatoes
Salted water
¾ cup firmly packed brown sugar
½ cup water

¼ cup (4 tablespoons) butter
¼ cup maple syrup
½ cup chopped black walnuts

Preheat oven to 375°F.

Bring a large pot of salted water to a boil. Add the yams and boil until just tender, about 40 minutes. Drain and peel yams. Cut them in quarters and place in a well-buttered baking dish.

Meanwhile, in a heavy-bottomed pan, combine the brown sugar, water, butter, and maple syrup. Bring to a boil, stirring to dissolve sugar, and cook until mixture forms a syrup, about 10 minutes.

Sprinkle the yams with chopped nuts and pour the syrup over all. Bake until browned and well glazed.

South of the Mason-Dixon Greens

Serves 6

The Chesapeake ain't exactly in Dixie, but it is, to be sure, on the south side of the Mason-Dixon Line. These ham-flavored greens slide down easy and can pack a wallop, depending on the wrist action when adding the black pepper and hot-pepper flakes. Don't give me any stuff about over-cooked greens! Loosen up a bit and try them the good old-fashioned country way. They're great with Maryland Panfried Chicken with Cream Gravy (see page 131), Jimmy Le Blue's Barbecued Ribs (see page 134), or just about any ham dish to your liking.

4 cups water
1 to 1½ pounds smoked ham hocks
2 pounds collard or mustard greens

Salt, black pepper, hot-pepper flakes and cider vinegar to taste

In a pot bring the water and ham hocks to a boil. Cook over medium heat about 1 hour. Remove and discard the large stems from the greens and add the greens to the pot. Simmer a long time, at least 2 hours.

Strain off most of the liquid, leaving a little to keep the greens moist. Take out the ham hocks and pick off the meat. Season greens with salt, pepper, hot-pepper flakes, and vinegar. Add the ham pieces back to the greens and stir well.

Maryland Beaten Biscuits

Makes about 3 dozen biscuits

The oldest and most famous biscuit recipe of the Chesapeake Bay region originated on the plantations of southern Maryland. The traditional preparation can be termed, at the very least, a culinary-cardiovascular-aerobic exercise.

Its execution is best described by Joanne Pritchett, who's great-great grandmother was a cook on a St. Mary's plantation: "Honey, every time I know I'm gonna make these here biscuits, I get myself good and mad. Normally I think about my sister-in-law, Darlene, who ran off with my husband, right after Granny Pritchett's funeral. That was years ago, but it still galls me into making some of the tenderist biscuits around."

4 cups flour
1 teaspoon salt
1½ teaspoons lard or solid vegetable
   shortening

1¾ to 2 cups water

"It's very simple. I just sift the flour and salt together in a bowl. Some people, nowadays, like to use Crisco or something like that. But I believe in lard. It gives it that certain taste.

"So then, I cuts the lard into the flour with the tips of my fingers, working it real quick. During this step I make believe I'm putting out Darlene's eyes.

"Then, little by little, I pour in the cold water, until I get a good stiff dough. Put it on a real solid table with flour. Now if your table is weak, honey, the legs'll fall right off. I've seen it happen!

"Depending on my mood, I use an ax or big ole mallet. I make a ball out of the dough to look like Darlene's head and, baby, I let her have it. Use the flat side of the ax or mallet, and beat the hell out of the dough till it blisters good. Takes about half an hour, but honey, it makes 'em tender as butter.

"Form the dough into balls, the size of little eggs, and flatten 'em a bit on the board. Put a few pokes in the center with a fork, then bake in a hot 425°F oven for about 20 to 25 minutes. Serve hot and put some liniment on your arm, or it'll be acting up the next day."

Black Walnut Cake Doughnuts

Makes about 3 dozen doughnuts

Mrs. Delores Clinton of St. Mary's has spent many hours making doughnuts for her twelve grandchildren. She says that she has used this basic recipe since she was a little girl, but started adding black walnuts about fifteen years ago, to "jazz 'em up."

3⅔ cups flour
4 teaspoons baking powder
½ teaspoon salt
1 cup sugar, plus sugar for sprinkling
3 eggs

1 cup milk
3 tablespoons butter, melted
1 teaspoon ground cinnamon
1 teaspoon walnut extract
⅔ cup finely chopped black walnuts
Vegetable oil, for deep-frying

Sift together the flour, baking powder, and salt into a bowl.

In a large bowl cream together the 1 cup sugar and eggs until fluffy. Mix in the milk and butter. Beat in the sifted ingredients and cinnamon. Add the walnut extract and walnuts. Mix well.

Turn out onto a floured board and roll out ½ inch thick. Cut out doughnuts with a doughnut cutter. Heat oil to 375°F and deep-fry doughnuts, a few at a time, until golden brown, about 3 minutes per side (depending on size). Drain well on paper towels and sprinkle with sugar.

Johnny Cake

Makes one 8-inch cake, serves 6 to 8

This is an Early American recipe that I don't see made often these days. For years my grandmother had me believing that she baked up these cakes for me and that's how they got their name. What a world! If you can't believe your own sainted grandmother, who can you believe? The secret to getting this cake to cook up nice is the "hot as the dickens" skillet. Works every time. Serve the cake with sweet butter.

1 egg
1 tablespoon sugar
1½ cups milk
½ teaspoon salt
¾ cup yellow cornmeal

¼ cup flour
2 tablespoons butter, melted
2 tablespoons bacon drippings, melted

Preheat oven to 400°F.

In a bowl beat the egg and sugar together. Stir in the milk and salt. Beat in the cornmeal and flour. Mix in the butter and bacon drippings.

Generously grease an 8-inch cast-iron skillet with bacon drippings. Put in the hot oven about 5 minutes. Remove from the oven (with mitts) and pour in the batter.

Bake 30 to 40 minutes, or until well browned.

Indian Pudding

Serves 8 to 10

The creation of this pudding is attributed to some of the Bay's earliest inhabitants. The cornmeal and molasses make for a flavorful combination.

5 cups milk
¼ cup yellow cornmeal
½ cup molasses
¼ teaspoon salt
¼ cup butter, softened

1 teaspoon ground cinnamon
½ teaspoon ground ginger
¼ teaspoon ground nutmeg
3 eggs, beaten

Preheat oven to 300°F.

In the top pan of a double boiler over simmering water, combine the milk, cornmeal, and molasses. Heat, stirring frequently, until the mixture is smooth and just beginning to thicken. Cover and reduce heat.

Cook about 30 minutes, stirring occasionally. Off the heat beat in the butter, cinnamon, ginger, nutmeg, and eggs. Pour into a buttered 2-quart baking dish.

Bake 1 hour and 15 minutes, or until a knife inserted in the center comes out clean.

Apple Dumplings

Serves 6

Not only an endearment, but a loving act of baking. Few other desserts connote to me the care and feeling that goes into the preparation of this time-honored apple pastry.

You see, kids do remember.

1 cup firmly packed brown sugar
1 cup plus 6 teaspoons granulated sugar
2 cups water
½ teaspoon ground cinnamon, plus cinnamon to taste
¼ teaspoon ground nutmeg, plus nutmeg to taste
12 tablespoons butter

3 cups flour
1 teaspoon salt
1 tablespoon baking powder
1 cup solid vegetable shortening
¾ cup milk
6 apples, peeled and cored
Vanilla ice cream or sweetened whipped cream, for serving (optional)

To make the glaze, bring brown sugar, 1 cup granulated sugar, water, ½ teaspoon cinnamon, ¼ teaspoon nutmeg, and 6 tablespoons of the butter to a boil, stirring to dissolve sugar. Cook until mixture becomes a light syrup, about 10 minutes. Remove from the heat and set aside.

In a bowl sift together the flour, salt, and baking powder. Work in shortening with fingertips or a pastry blender until mixture is the consistency of coarse meal. Stir in milk and beat until a fairly stiff dough forms.

Preheat oven to 375°F.

To assemble the dumplings, roll out the dough about ¼-inch thick on a lightly floured board. Cut dough into six 5-inch squares. Place an apple on each square. Sprinkle each apple with 1 teaspoon granulated sugar and cinnamon and nutmeg to taste. Dot each apple with 1 tablespoon butter. Bring the dough together at the top of the apple and twist to seal.

Put dumplings in a buttered baking dish 1 inch apart. Pour the reserved syrup over the dumplings. Bake 35 to 45 minutes, basting them with the syrup as they are baking. I like mine served with vanilla ice cream or a bit of whipped cream.

Molasses Cake

Makes one 10-inch cake, serves 8 to 10

This rich, moist cake is another fine example of the Early American use of molasses and brown sugar as a primary sweetener in desserts.

½ cup (¼ pound) butter, softened
1 cup firmly packed brown sugar
2 eggs
1 cup milk
3 cups flour
½ teaspoon salt
2 teaspoons baking soda

¼ cup hot water
1 cup molasses
1 teaspoon ground cinnamon
½ teaspoon ground ginger
½ teaspoon ground nutmeg
Rind and juice of 1 orange
Confectioners' sugar

Preheat oven to 325°F.

In a large bowl cream together the butter and brown sugar until smooth. Add the eggs and beat until fluffy. Add the milk and mix well. Beat in the flour and salt. Dissolve the baking soda in hot water and add to the batter. Mix in the molasses, cinnamon, ginger, nutmeg, and orange rind and juice. Mix well, but do not overbeat.

Pour into a buttered and floured tube pan. Bake 45 to 50 minutes, or until a toothpick inserted in the center of the cake comes out clean.

Dust with confectioners' sugar.

Apple Butter

Makes about 5 pints

This smooth, spicy bread is a perfect partner for breakfast rolls or buttered warm toast. A great way to start the day with a steaming cup of tea or coffee.

5 pounds tart apples
2 cups apple cider
Water
2 cups sugar

2 teaspoons ground cinnamon
1 teaspoon ground cloves
1 teaspoon ground allspice
¼ cup apple cider vinegar

Cut the apples into quarters. It is not necessary to peel or core them.

Place the apples in a heavy-bottomed pot. Pour in the apple cider and enough water to come about halfway up the depth of the apples. Cook until apples are very soft. Press the mixture through a sieve and return to the pot.

Add the sugar, cinnamon, cloves, allspice, and vinegar. Cook over medium heat, stirring frequently, until thick and smooth.

Pour into hot, sterilized jars and seal according to standard canning procedures. Cool and refrigerate what will be eaten soon. Freeze the remainder.

Corn and Pepper Relish

Makes 6 to 8 pints

A delicious, simple-to-prepare relish you'll want to have on hand the whole year.

12 ears corn
6 red bell peppers
6 green bell peppers
1 bunch celery
4 onions
1 medium head cabbage

1 quart cider vinegar
3 cups sugar
2 tablespoons salt
2 teaspoons mustard seed
2 teaspoons celery seed

Cut the kernels from the corn cobs. Chop the peppers, celery, onions, and cabbage in ⅛-inch pieces. Place all the vegetables in a pot, cover with water, and bring to a boil. Drain and return vegetables to the pot. Add all the remaining ingredients and simmer 30 to 40 minutes, stirring occasionally. Remove from the heat and cool.

Pour into hot, sterilized jars, seal, and process in a water bath according to standard canning procedures.

Mint Julep

Serves 1

A classic mint julep is the drink of true southern gentlemen. The principal variation from state to state is the type of liquor used. In Kentucky the rule is bourbon whiskey. In Georgia, better pour peach brandy. And here on the Bay, the order of the day is rye whiskey.

Into a tall frosted glass, dissolve 1 teaspoon sugar in ¼ cup spring water. Pick a few fresh mint leaves, give them a slight twist, and then drop them into the bottom of the glass (the "twist" releases the scent and flavor of the mint).

Pour the glass one quarter full with Maryland rye whiskey. Fill with finely cracked ice. Garnish with a mint sprig.

• A Country Buffet with William Taylor •

William Taylor of St. Mary's County enjoys a mint julep in a plantation field of springtime flowers.

William Taylor resides in St. Mary's County at Klahanie, his beautiful cottage home in a grove of trees on the edge of Nat Creek. Mr. Taylor is the full-time goodwill ambassador of charming St. Mary's County. His gracious manner, quick wit, and winning smile are the epitome of southern hospitality.

And Mr. Taylor has the hospitality market covered. He is a much-sought-after Chesapeake food designer, cooking instructor, and foremost expert on both the old and new cooking styles and recipes of St. Mary's.

At Sotterly, the oldest working plantation on the Chesapeake and a place where southern Maryland country hams are still smoked in the traditional manner, one could easily imagine Mr. Taylor as the master of the plantation in a bygone era. Here he can be found hosting clients, students, and visiting dignitaries to eighteenth-century candlelight dinners, afternoon teas, and the Grand Oyster Gala Dinner, the annual feast for the National Oyster Festival.

St. Mary's County Stuffed Ham is legendary in the

Old South and serves as the focal point in Mr. Taylor's country buffet menu. He offers remarkably detailed, yet manageable instructions on the preparation and cooking of the ham. Perhaps due to today's heightened pace of life, such culinary treasures are becoming harder to find.

The accompanying recipes are some of the signature dishes of southern Maryland: Oyster Fritters, Corn Pudding, and Green Beans with Country Ham and Sautéed Peanuts. There is also a recipe for a delicious treat of Mr. Taylor's creation, the Crabbit, which incorporates crabmeat in a Welsh Rabbit Sauce on a toasted crumpet. Warm Bourbon-Apple Crisp with Vanilla Ice Cream is the perfect close to a culinary visit to this southern county on the Bay.

Chesapeake Oyster Stew

St. Mary's County Stuffed Ham

Oyster Fritters

Corn Pudding

Green Beans with Country Ham and Sautéed Peanuts

Crabbit

Bourbon-Apple Crisp with Vanilla Ice Cream

Chesapeake Oyster Stew

Serves 8 to 12

1 pound slab bacon, chilled
1 cup finely minced onions
1 cup finely minced celery
2 quarts half-and-half
3 tablespoons flour
Butter, as needed

1 quart shucked oysters with liquor
Salt and white pepper to taste
Cayenne pepper to taste
1 teaspoon Old Bay seasoning
2 tablespoons Worcestershire sauce

Place bacon in freezer 20 minutes, then slice in thin strips. In a heavy-bottomed pan, fry bacon until crisp. Remove bacon with a slotted utensil to paper towels to drain. Reserve the bacon drippings in the pot.

Add the onion and celery to the pot and cook in the bacon fat, stirring now and then, until their shapes almost disappear.

In a separate pan heat the half-and-half, stirring, until quite hot.

Blend the flour into the vegetables and cook, stirring, over low heat a few minutes. Add some butter if there is not enough bacon fat.

Heat the oysters with liquor in a separate pan, just until the edges begin to curl. Immediately drain the liquor into the hot milk. Cover oysters and set aside.

Stir the hot milk into the vegetable-flour mixture. Cook over medium heat, stirring constantly, until slightly thickened.

Season lightly with salt, white pepper, cayenne, Old Bay, and Worcestershire. (You want the stew to be very savory, but not salty.)

To serve, pour the stew into a soup tureen, add the oysters, and stir. Drop a chunk of butter into the center and sprinkle with cayenne. Put a small piece of butter into each wide soup bowl and ladle in stew. Crumble the reserved bacon and sprinkle over the top.

NOTE: Never serve this dish with oyster crackers. In the old days crackers were passed so that they could be crumbled into the hot milk to thicken it.

St. Mary's County Stuffed Ham

Serves a crowd with plenty left for
the week

½ bushel kale (about 8 pounds),
thick stems removed

2 medium cabbages, cored and cut in
wedges

12 bunches wild field cress (if possible) or watercress, tough stems removed

12 bunches green onions

1 bunch celery

½ cup salt

2 tins (1¼ ounces each) mustard
seed

¼ cup hot-pepper flakes

1 corned ham (20 pounds), fat removed, boned, and tied

1 new, extra-large white cotton
T-shirt

Watercress bunches and ripe tomatoes, for garnish

Coarsely grind or chop all the vegetables. Put them in a large deep tub
and work in the salt, mustard seed, and pepper flakes with your hands.

Place the ham on a large baking sheet or tray with an edge. With a
boning knife, cut deep half-moon slits in the ham, checkerboard fashion, 3
slits, then 4, 3, then 4, from one end to the other.

With your fingers, poke some of the vegetables into the holes, filling
them. Turn the ham over and repeat the process of cutting the slits and
filling them.

On a clean tray, spread out the T-shirt. With scissors cut it up the front
and lay it open.

Spread half of the remaining vegetables on the T-shirt and place the
stuffed ham on the vegetables. Pack the rest of the vegetables over the top
of the ham.

Bring up the T-shirt over the ham, stretching it. Tie the ham round
and round with strong twine (fishing line is also good), adding a stout loop
for lifting.

Put a small rack in the bottom of a deep canning kettle and half fill
the kettle with cold water. Put in the ham and add additional water to cover.

Put a lid on the kettle and bring to a boil. Lower heat and boil slowly
4 hours. After 4 hours, remove from the heat and take the lid off the kettle.
Leave the ham in the pot liquor overnight.

In the morning drain well, put the ham in a plastic bag, and refrigerate
for 1 day. To serve, cut away the T-shirt and lift the ham onto a large platter.
Scoop up any vegetables remaining on the shirt and pat them all over the
top of the ham and around the edges. Decorate the platter with watercress
and sliced red-ripe field tomatoes.

Carve the ham in thin slices, exposing the green veining. Serve extra
greens and always serve cold.

NOTE: When corned ham is unavailable, substitute a fresh ham. In either case, the ham is delicious with drinks. Place the thin slices of cold ham on cocktail biscuits with a little mayonnaise, then cover and heat biscuits very slightly in the oven.

Oyster Fritters

Serves 12 to 16

Vegetable oil, for deep-frying
2 cups flour
1 teaspoon baking powder
1 teaspoon salt
2 eggs
¾ cup milk

2 quarts shucked oysters with liquor, drained and liquor reserved
2 tablespoons vegetable oil
Tartar Sauce (optional, see page 15) and lemon wedges, for accompaniment

Heat oil to 375°F (an electric wok will keep constant heat).

In a large bowl mix together flour, baking powder, and salt.

In a small bowl beat the eggs lightly with the milk, ¾ cup of the reserved oyster liquor, and vegetable oil. Stir into the dry ingredients.

Gently stir the drained oysters into the batter. Using 2 spoons, drop oysters, one at a time, into the hot oil. (You can cook 12 to 15 oysters in the wok at one time.)

When the fritters are just golden and not yet brown, remove with a slotted spoon and drain on paper towels in a metal pan. Keep warm in a very slow oven.

Serve warm with Tartar Sauce, if desired, and lemon wedges.

Corn Pudding

Serves about 12

2 cans (15 or 16 ounces) cream-style corn, or 4 cups corn kernels
2 cups milk

6 eggs, separated
2 tablespoons butter
2 tablespoons sugar

Preheat oven to 350°F.

In a saucepan heat the corn and milk together about 5 minutes, stirring constantly. Off heat, beat the egg yolks and add to corn-milk mixture with the butter and sugar.

In a bowl beat the egg whites until soft peaks form. Fold the whites into the corn mixture.

Pour into a buttered 2-quart casserole. Bake 30 to 35 minutes. Do not peek while baking. Serve warm.

Green Beans with Country Ham and Sautéed Peanuts

Serves 10 to 12

Virginia hogs are peanut-fed, hence the sautéed peanuts are a tribute to those delicious porkers.

2 pounds green beans
Salted water
½ cup (¼ pound) plus 6 tablespoons butter
Juice of 2 lemons
2 tablespoons Dijon mustard
Salt
Freshly ground black pepper
2 cups julienned Smithfield ham
1½ cups peanuts, coarsely chopped

Using scissors snip off the ends of the beans on the diagonal; leave the beans whole. Bring a saucepan filled with salted water to a boil. Add beans and cook, checking constantly, until done but still crisp. Drain immediately and place in a large deep bowl.

Cut the ½ cup butter in chunks over the beans. Add the lemon juice and mustard. Season with salt and pepper. Add the ham and stir gently to mix all ingredients.

Sauté the peanuts in the remaining 6 tablespoons butter for just a few minutes, stirring constantly; drain off any excess butter.

Arrange the beans on an oval platter and spoon a long line of sautéed peanuts down the center.

Crabbit

Serves 6

6 authentic English crumpets or English muffins
Butter for crumpets, plus 1 tablespoon
1 pound slab bacon
1 pound lump or backfin crabmeat, picked over for shells
Mayonnaise, as needed
Salt, white pepper, and cayenne pepper to taste
2 tablespoons capers, drained
1 pound sharp Cheddar cheese, grated
1 jar (8 ounces) processed cheese spread
¾ cup flat beer or ale
1 teaspoon Dijon mustard
1 teaspoon Worcestershire sauce
2 egg yolks, beaten

Toast the crumpets whole, then split and butter. Keep warm.

Place bacon in freezer 20 minutes, then slice in thin strips. Fry in a skillet, stirring, until crisp. Remove bacon with a slotted utensil to paper towels to drain. (Reserve bacon grease for making corn bread sometime.)

Preheat oven to 400°F. Place the crab in a bowl and add just enough mayonnaise to bind it together. Mix the crab and mayonnaise very gently so as not to break up the lumps. Season very lightly with salt and white and cayenne peppers. Stir in capers.

To make the sauce melt the 1 tablespoon butter in a small heavy pan. Add the cheeses, beer, mustard, Worcestershire sauce. Season with salt and white and cayenne peppers. Stir and blend until cheese is melted. Stir in egg yolks.

Place toasted crumpets on a cookie sheet. Cover with a mound of the crab mixture and spoon sauce over crab just to cover it.

Bake about 10 minutes to heat through. Place under broiler, if needed, to brown cheese.

Crumble the reserved bacon, sprinkle it over the tops, and serve.

Bourbon-Apple Crisp with Vanilla Ice Cream

Serves 12 to 24, depending on size of portions

Mr. Taylor uses Rebel Yell bourbon whiskey for a true southern taste, but adds that Jack Daniels will do just fine.

8 to 10 tart apples, peeled, cored, and sliced
½ cup granulated sugar
Grated zest of 2 lemons
Ground nutmeg and butter, as needed for apples
A bottle of good bourbon whiskey, fitted with a pouring spout (see Note)
1 cup flour

1 teaspoon baking powder
¼ teaspoon salt
1 cup rolled oats
1 cup firmly packed brown sugar
½ cup (¼ pound) butter, softened
1 teaspoon ground nutmeg
1 teaspoon ground cinnamon
Heavy cream and French vanilla ice cream, for accompaniment

Preheat oven to 400°F.

Butter a 9- by 13- by 2-inch baking pan and fill with apples. Sprinkle with the granulated sugar, lemon zest, and a little nutmeg. Dot with butter. Drizzle some bourbon over all.

In a deep bowl combine flour, baking powder, salt, rolled oats, brown sugar, ½ cup butter, 1 teaspoon nutmeg, and cinnamon. Mix with your fingertips until crumbly. Pat down on top of apples.

Cover with aluminum foil and bake 30 minutes. Uncover and bake 20 minutes more to brown top. Remove from the oven.

Cut in squares while still warm and slip into dessert dishes. Pour a little heavy cream around, not over, each square. Top each square with a scoop of ice cream.

Serve immediately. In front of your guests, drizzle some bourbon over each portion.

• Chestertown •

A docked work boat rests at Tolchester Beach outside of Chester-town. The thousands of inlets along the Bay's 4,600 miles of shore-line provide natural harbor for pleasure and work craft.

Tucked away on the Chester River is the charming hamlet of Chestertown, Maryland. George Washington, having made numerous stops here during the Revolution, became familiar with the area's beauty and bounty, including the oysters and crabs served in the town's homes and taverns.

The countryside surrounding Chestertown is dotted with dairy farms and with fields of tomatoes, wheat, soybeans, corn, asparagus, potatoes, and the area's famous sweet summer peaches. The landscape is rich with waterfowl and deer, making the area a sportsman's paradise.

West of Chestertown is Rock Hall, Maryland, which is called the Oyster Capital of the Bay. There on the Bay, and along the mouth of the Chester River, are the homes and workplaces of many Chesapeake Bay watermen. On a breezy day you can sit on the shore and watch the Chesapeake Skipjacks moving majestically along under sailpower as they dredge oysters from the Bay bottom. Maryland law permits the dredging only under sail, no engines or motors allowed, making the Skipjacks the sole commercial sailing fleet in the country.

A refreshingly simple and honest local cuisine, the food of the region is dominated by the abundance of fresh seafood, game, and produce. The ingredients are showcased in the recipes of the people who work the Bay and the fields. This oyster center has originated such recipes as Scalloped Oysters and the Eastern Shore Oyster Roast, both of which have evolved in Chestertown over the centuries. The Amish settled in the area and with them brought recipes for Fasnachts, a wonderful risen doughnut, and molasses-rich Shoofly Pie. Corn is one of the primary farm crops around here and is highlighted in Kent County Sweet Corn Pudding. Once you've tried these superb dishes, it's easy to understand why George Washington kept coming back for more!

Catfish and Bacon Cakes

Serves 4

This is a south of the Mason-Dixon twist on codfish cakes. I realize my cholesterol level may go to pot, but I always fry these in bacon grease. Just no comparison!

Serve these cakes with eggs, scrambled or fried, and hot Sour Cream Biscuits (see page 171) or Hominy Muffins (see page 230).

1 cup chopped, cooked catfish fillets
1½ cups diced, cooked potatoes
¼ cup diced onion, sautéed in butter
1 egg, beaten
4 slices bacon, cooked and chopped
2 tablespoons bacon drippings or
   butter, melted
1 teaspoon salt
½ teaspoon black pepper
Vegetable oil and bacon drippings,
   for frying

In a bowl mix together fish pieces, potatoes, onion, egg, and bacon. Stir in bacon drippings, salt, and pepper.

Form fish mixture into little cakes. Heat oil and a touch of bacon drippings for flavor, in a skillet. Fry cakes on both sides until golden.

Julie's Dutch Babies

Serves 4

Gawd, these are good. An egg-enriched batter that bakes up light and fluffy and a perfect excuse to haul out the maple syrup. As for the name, I think you're all a bunch of sick tickets even to ask.

½ cup (¼ pound) butter, melted and
   cooled
6 eggs, beaten
1½ cups flour
½ teaspoon salt
1 tablespoon granulated sugar
1½ cups half-and-half
Softened butter, confectioners' sugar,
   and maple syrup, for accompaniment

Preheat oven to 425°F.

In a mixing bowl beat together the butter and eggs. Sift together the flour, salt, and sugar. Mix flour mixture into the butter mixture. Beat in the half-and-half.

Pour the mixture into a greased and floured 9-inch square baking pan. Bake 15 to 20 minutes.

Top with butter and confectioners' sugar. Serve with maple syrup.

Sausages and Hominy with Pan Gravy

Serves 4

This is a hearty, down-home, country breakfast dish that is great served with Buttermilk Biscuits (see page 99). Many grocers carry prepared hominy (puffed corn), which for some is an undiscovered treasure. Hominy has its own unique texture and flavor. It also goes well with meats and fowl as a starch for dinner entrées.

8 breakfast-sausage patties
3 tablespoons flour
2 cups milk
Salt to taste
Black pepper to taste, plus ½ teaspoon

1 can (1 pound, 13 ounces) hominy
½ teaspoon salt
1 teaspoon sugar
½ teaspoon black pepper
¼ cup (4 tablespoons) butter

In a skillet cook sausage patties until well browned. Remove the patties and keep warm; reserve 3 tablespoons of the fat in the skillet.

For the pan gravy, heat the fat and stir in the flour. Cook 1 to 2 minutes. Off the heat gradually whisk in 1 cup of the milk. Return to the heat and bring to a boil, stirring constantly. Season with salt and pepper to taste.

In a saucepan combine the hominy, the remaining 1 cup milk, salt, sugar, ½ teaspoon pepper, and butter. Heat to serving temperature.

Arrange the sausage patties and hominy on individual plates. Spoon the gravy over the top.

Crab and Ham Custards

Serves 6

A Bay version of a seafood flan, the sweet flavor of the crab and the fragrance of the cured ham combine to make a custard that is a sheer delight. If a sauce is desired, try Dill Shallot-Butter Sauce.

3 whole eggs, beaten
2 egg yolks
1 cup heavy cream
1½ cups milk
1 teaspoon salt
¼ teaspoon white pepper
⅛ teaspoon ground nutmeg
½ pound special crabmeat, picked over for shells
¼ pound country ham, ground
Hot water

Preheat oven to 300°F.

In a bowl mix together the eggs, egg yolks, cream, milk, salt, pepper, and nutmeg.

Butter six 6-ounce custard cups. In a small bowl mix together the crabmeat and ham and distribute evenly among the custard cups. Slowly pour egg mixture into cups, dividing it equally among them and being careful not to dislodge ham-crabmeat mixture from bottom.

Put the custard cups in a deep pan. Add hot water to pan to reach halfway up the sides. Bake about 50 to 60 minutes, or until a thin-bladed knife inserted in the center of the custard comes out clean. Serve warm.

Oyster Roast

Serves 3 or 4

Pure, honest, and straightforward is what I'd call this mouth-watering treat. When picking out oysters to be roasted, make sure they are good and heavy. A piping hot oven is a must, so be sure and preheat.

12 large oysters
2 slices bacon, lightly fried and cut in 12 pieces
Hot melted butter, for dipping
Lemon wedges, for accompaniment

Preheat oven to 450°F.

Scrub the oysters well in cold water. Lay them on a baking sheet and place in the hot oven about 10 minutes, or until oysters just begin to open.

Meanwhile, prepare the bacon and put the butter in a bowl. With a blunt edge of a knife, pry the oyster shells open and remove the top shell. Pour off the oyster liquor into the butter.

Place the oysters, topped with a piece of bacon, on a platter lined with a folded napkin. Serve with the warm liquor-enriched butter and lemon wedges.

Chicken and Corn Fritters

Serves 5 or 6

Fritters always make a welcome appetizer and these are no exception. Although not traditional, an apple chutney, served on the side, is ideal with these tasty morsels.

¾ cup flour
1½ teaspoons baking powder
¼ teaspoon salt
2 eggs, beaten
½ cup milk
1 tablespoon grated onion
2 tablespoons chopped fresh chives or parsley

Pinch ground nutmeg
¾ cup coarsely chopped cooked chicken meat (½-inch pieces)
½ cup corn kernels
3 to 4 cups vegetable oil, for deep frying
Ms. Jamie's Apple Chutney (see page 106), for accompaniment

In a large bowl sift together the flour, baking powder, and salt. Stir in the eggs. Beat in the milk, onion, chives, and nutmeg. Add the chicken and corn.

In a heavy skillet, heat the oil to 365°F. When hot, drop in batter by the tablespoonful, a few at a time, and fry until golden brown, about 2 to 3 minutes. Remove with a slotted utensil to paper towels to drain.

Serve with Ms. Jamie's Apple Chutney for dipping.

Eastern Shore Crab Soup

Serves 6 to 8

Almost every region and ethnic group on the Bay has its own version of crab soup. The additions of okra and rice set this one apart from all the others. Simply wonderful!

6 tablespoons butter
1 large onion, diced
1 green bell pepper, diced
4 cups sliced okra (about 1 pound)
1 tablespoon chopped garlic
2 quarts Fish Stock (see page 35)
4 large ripe tomatoes, diced, or 1 can (12-ounces) whole tomatoes, diced, with their juice

1 tablespoon Worcestershire sauce
1 teaspoon dried whole thyme
1 bay leaf
1 cup white rice
1 pound claw crabmeat, picked over for shells
Salt and black pepper to taste

In a large pot melt the butter. Add the onion, bell pepper, okra, and garlic. Cook over low heat, stirring occasionally, 15 minutes. Add the stock, tomatoes, Worcestershire, thyme, and bay leaf. Bring to a boil. Reduce the heat and simmer 20 minutes.

Add the rice and crabmeat and continue cooking 30 minutes. Season with salt and pepper.

Yam and Apple Soup

Serves 5 or 6

A fine Eastern Shore duo. It's thick and creamy, with the maple syrup adding just a hint of sweetness.

¼ cup (4 tablespoons) butter
1 medium onion, chopped
2 cups peeled, chopped yams
1 cup cored, peeled, and chopped apples
3 cups Chicken Stock (see page 33)

½ teaspoon dried whole thyme
¼ cup maple syrup
Salt and black pepper to taste
Lightly whipped cream flavored with maple syrup and freshly grated nutmeg, for garnish

In a pot, melt the butter. Sauté the onion 3 to 4 minutes. Add the yams, apples, stock, thyme, and maple syrup. Bring to a boil. Reduce the heat and simmer, uncovered, until the yams and apples are tender, 30 to 40 minutes.

In a blender or a food processor, purée the mixture. Return to the pot and reheat. Season with salt and pepper.

Serve in soup bowls. Garnish with whipped cream dusted with a bit of nutmeg.

Clam and Corn Chowder

Serves 10 to 12

An outstanding waterman's chowder. Make sure you don't add the clams until just before serving. An overcooked clam is a tough clam. And you may quote me on that.

Serve with crackers for crumbling into the chowder, and with hot corn bread on the side, to make a meal of it.

¼ pound salt pork, diced
¼ cup (4 tablespoons) butter
2 cups diced (⅛ inch) onion
½ cup diced (⅛ inch) green bell pepper
½ cup diced (⅛ inch) red bell pepper
½ cup diced celery
1 tablespoon chopped garlic
5 cups diced potatoes, peeled
2 cups fresh corn kernels (cut from about 5 ears)

2 quarts half-and-half
2 cups bottled clam juice or Fish Stock (see page 35)
1 teaspoon salt
1 teaspoon dried thyme
1 bay leaf
1 quart shucked clams, drained, juice reserved, and chopped
Black pepper to taste
Chopped fresh parsley and cayenne pepper, for garnish

In a pot render fat from the salt pork. With a slotted spoon, remove the bits of browned salt pork. Add the butter to the pot. When melted, sauté the onion, bell pepper, celery, and garlic 5 minutes. Add the potatoes, corn, half-and-half, bottled clam juice, salt, thyme, and bay leaf. Cook until the potatoes and corn are tender, about 30 minutes.

Add the chopped clams and their reserved juices. Cook over medium heat 10 to 15 minutes. Season with black pepper.

Garnish with parsley and a dash of cayenne.

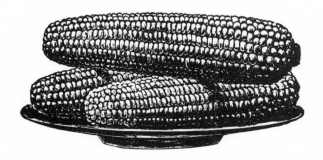

Deviled Crab

Serves 4

They love to give everything the devil around here and this crab is catching it, too. For this spicy creamed casserole in which the blue crab seems to revel, I prefer to use backfin crabmeat and fold it into the sauce at the last minute, so as not to disturb the lumps of meat.

2 tablespoons butter, plus melted butter for topping
2 tablespoons flour
1 cup milk
1 teaspoon salt
½ teaspoon black pepper
¼ teaspoon hot-pepper flakes

1 teaspoon Worcestershire sauce
1 teaspoon dry or prepared mustard
1 pound backfin or special crabmeat, picked over for shells
2 tablespoons chopped fresh parsley
Dried bread crumbs

Preheat oven to 350°F.

In a small saucepan melt the 2 tablespoons butter and stir in the flour. Cook 2 to 3 minutes, stirring constantly. Off heat, slowly whisk in the milk, salt, black pepper, pepper flakes, Worcestershire sauce, and mustard. Bring to a boil and cook, stirring, several minutes until thickened. Remove from the heat and cool slightly.

In a bowl gently mix the crabmeat, parsley, and cream sauce. Spoon the mixture into well-scrubbed crab shells or a buttered casserole dish. Sprinkle with bread crumbs and drip some melted butter over the tops. Bake 35 to 40 minutes, or until browned.

Pecan Scalloped Oysters

Serves 6

This Eastern Shore rendition of a traditional scalloped oyster casserole includes chopped pecans and bread crumbs. It is a simple recipe that follows the basic philosophy of preserving the natural flavor of the oysters.

1 quart shucked oysters, drained and liquor reserved
2 cups dried bread crumbs
½ cup coarsely chopped pecans
Salt and black pepper to taste

¾ cup (12 tablespoons) butter, cut in pieces
⅔ cup heavy cream
Paprika

Preheat oven to 350°F.

In a buttered shallow casserole, place a layer of bread crumbs and some pecans. Top with a layer of oysters. Season with salt and pepper. Dot with butter. Repeat until all oysters are used.

Mix together the cream and reserved oyster liquor and pour over all. Top with bread crumbs and dot with butter. Garnish with a little paprika and bake 30 to 35 minutes.

Steamed Soft-shell Clams

Serves 5 or 6

Here's a Chesapeake Bay–style clam feast. The soft-shell clams are steamed in an aromatic broth of wine and vegetables, then served piping hot in their shells with plenty of drawn butter and cooking broth for dipping.

To savor every bit of these wonderful bivalves, hold each clam by the snout, dip it into the hot broth, then dip it into the butter. After eating the body of the clam, peel the skin from the snout, dip it in the broth, then the butter, and eat it, too.

6 to 7 dozen soft-shell clams (manos)
½ cup (¼ pound) butter
1 small onion, finely chopped
¼ cup chopped celery
¼ cup chopped carrot
2 tablespoons chopped garlic

1½ cups dry white wine or water
½ teaspoon salt
¼ teaspoon black pepper
Bay leaf
Hot melted butter (optional) and lemon wedges, for accompaniment

Wash and scrub the clams.

In a large heavy-bottomed pot, melt the butter. Add the onion, celery, carrot, and garlic and cook several minutes. Add the wine, salt, pepper, and bay leaf. Bring to a rolling boil and add the clams. Cover tightly and steam just until clams open. Do not overcook!

Serve clams with steaming broth on the side, some hot melted butter, if desired, and lemon wedges.

Crab Imperial, Chestertown Style

Serves 4

Another version of the infamous crab imperial. Basically, there are two schools of thought on this dish. One holds with the mayonnaise-based type and the other with this, which has a cream sauce base. I find both styles delicious yet distinctly different. Try them and decide for yourself. (The mayonnaise version is on page 37.)

6 tablespoons butter
2 tablespoons flour
1 teaspoon dry mustard
1½ cups heavy cream
1 teaspoon Old Bay seasoning
¼ teaspoon black pepper
Dash hot-pepper flakes

½ teaspoon Worcestershire sauce
2 egg yolks
2 tablespoons chopped fresh parsley
¼ cup chopped pimiento (optional)
1 pound lump or backfin crabmeat, picked over for shells
Buttered dried bread crumbs

Preheat oven to 375°F.

In a saucepan melt the butter. Whisk in the flour and mustard. Cook 2 to 3 minutes, stirring frequently.

Off the heat stir in the cream, Old Bay, peppers, and Worcestershire. Return to the heat and boil, stirring often. Cook until thickened.

Off the heat beat in the egg yolks. Stir in the parsley and the pimiento, if using. Fold the crabmeat into the mixture. Spoon the mixture into well-scrubbed crab shells or individual casserole dishes. Sprinkle with bread crumbs and bake about 25 minutes, or until browned.

Bluefish Baked with Tomatoes and Capers

Serves 4

The meat of the bluefish is dark and rather oily. It's strong taste is complemented by this fragrant combination of tomatoes, capers, wine, and herbs. The addition of the waxed paper during baking enables the flavors to steam through the fillets while keeping them moist. Serve this sauce-rich dish with white rice. For more information on bluefish, for which I can offer no substitute, see page 11.

¼ cup olive oil
1 onion, diced
2 stalks celery, diced
2 tablespoons chopped garlic
¼ cup chopped green onions
1½ pounds tomatoes, peeled and chopped, with juice (about 3 cups)
1 cup dry white wine

3 tablespoons capers, drained and coarsely chopped
½ teaspoon dried whole thyme
1 bay leaf
Juice of 1 lemon
Salt and black pepper to taste
4 bluefish fillets (6 to 7 ounces each)

Preheat oven to 375°F.

In a heavy pot heat the oil and sauté the onion, celery, garlic, and onions until limp. Add the tomatoes, wine, capers, thyme, bay leaf, and lemon juice. Simmer 45 minutes. Season with salt and pepper.

In a baking dish make a layer of half of the hot tomato sauce. Arrange the fillets on top. Spoon the remaining sauce over the fish. Butter one side of a sheet of waxed paper large enough to cover the dish. Cover dish with paper, buttered side down. Bake 20 to 30 minutes, or until fish flakes at touch of a fork.

Remove fish fillets to a heated platter and spoon tomato sauce over them. Serve at once.

Roast Chicken with Sage Butter and Corn Bread Stuffing

Serves 4

In the early 1900s, when the hot, humid Baltimore air would take its toll on the population, hordes of breeze seekers would set sail on one of the many ferryboats crossing the Bay to the cool shores of Betterton. After a relaxing afternoon of lying on the beach at the mouth of the Sassafrass River, visitors returned to their Victorian hotels to change into evening wear and then enjoy a savory chicken dish just like this.

Corn Bread Stuffing (recipe follows)
1 roasting chicken (4 to 5 pounds)
3 tablespoons butter, softened
1 tablespoon finely chopped fresh sage or dried rubbed sage
Salt and freshly ground black pepper

Preheat oven to 400°F. Prepare the Corn Bread Stuffing.

Wash the cavity of the chicken with cold water and dry with paper towels. Sprinkle cavity with salt and pepper. Insert index finger between the skin and breast to separate.

In a small bowl mix together the butter, sage, salt, and pepper. Push the butter under the skin covering the breast.

Stuff the chicken with the Corn Bread Stuffing. Truss the chicken. Balance bird on a rack in a roasting pan. Place in the oven and immediately reduce the heat to 350°F. Bake 25 minutes per pound, basting occasionally.

If desired, make a pan gravy (see gravy Note, page 44)

Corn Bread Stuffing

6 tablespoons butter or bacon drippings
1 small onion, finely diced
3 stalks celery, finely diced
½ cup cooked corn kernels
3 cups corn bread pieces
1 egg, beaten
Milk, as needed
Salt and black pepper to taste

In a skillet melt the butter and sauté the onion and celery 5 minutes. In a bowl mix the sautéed vegetables with the remaining ingredients.

Brunswick Stew

Serves 3 or 4

Nowadays most recipes you find for Brunswick stew feature chicken as the main ingredient. It tastes fine, but it just ain't the case. This Brunswick Stew has been simmering squirrels since a lot longer back than any of the folks around here can remember. Of course you can chicken out. I won't tell.

Doug Turner, an avid squirrel hunter from outside Chestertown, says that squirrel fries up as nice or nicer than chicken, but he likes it best when his mother stews it this way.

2 squirrels, cut in serving pieces
Flour seasoned with salt and black pepper
2 tablespoons butter
2 tablespoons bacon drippings
2½ quarts boiling water (see Note)
1 large onion, coarsely chopped
4 large ripe tomatoes, chopped

1¼ cups fresh corn kernels (cut from about 3 ears)
4 potatoes, peeled and cut in quarters
1½ cups dried lima beans
1 teaspoon dried thyme
1 bay leaf
Salt and black pepper to taste

Lightly flour the squirrel pieces. In a heavy-bottomed pot, heat the butter and bacon drippings. Brown the squirrel well on all sides. Pour in the water and bring to a boil. Cover, reduce the heat, and simmer 1½ hours.

Add all the remaining ingredients. Cover and continue simmering another 1 to 1½ hours, or until squirrel is tender.

NOTE: For a richer stew, substitute Chicken Stock (see page 33) for the water.

Muskrat Braised in the Southern Manner

Serves 4

Most people on the Eastern Shore trap muskrat, or what they call "marsh rabbit." By whatever name one prefers, the animal makes for a wonderful taste experience. The meat, with its wild-ducklike flavor, is usually braised and is quite tender.

½ cup vegetable oil
2 muskrats, cut in serving pieces
Flour seasoned with salt and black pepper
1 large onion, chopped
1 bell pepper, diced
3 stalks celery, diced
2 tablespoons chopped garlic
2 cups coarsely chopped tomatoes

2 cups red wine
½ teaspoon cayenne pepper
½ teaspoon dried thyme
2 tablespoons Worcestershire sauce
1 tablespoon red wine vinegar
2 bay leaves
Salt and black pepper to taste

In a flameproof casserole or dutch oven, heat the oil. Dredge the muskrat pieces in the seasoned flour and brown in the hot oil on all sides. Remove from the pot and set aside.

Add the onion, bell pepper, celery, and garlic to the pot. Cook until soft. Return the muskrat to the pot. Add the tomatoes, wine, cayenne, thyme, Worcestershire sauce, vinegar, and bay leaves. Season with salt and pepper. Bring to a boil, cover, reduce the heat, and simmer 1½ to 2 hours, or until muskrat is tender.

Remove the muskrat to a heated platter. Reduce cooking liquids slightly by boiling over high heat. Spoon the braising liquid over the muskrat.

Pot Roast with Apple Cider

Serves 10

This family favorite produces a tender roast, with sweetly spiced braising juices. Serve it with boiled or mashed potatoes.

¼ cup vegetable oil or lard
1 beef rump roast or boneless chuck roast (4 to 5 pounds)
Flour seasoned with salt and black pepper
1 large onion, cut in ½-inch-thick slices
1¼ cups apple cider
2 tablespoons salt
1 teaspoon black pepper
½ teaspoon dried thyme
1 bay leaf
2 whole cloves
6 carrots, peeled and halved
4 tart apples, cored, peeled, and quartered

In a dutch oven heat the oil. Dredge the roast in the seasoned flour. Slowly brown roast on all sides. Remove the roast and set aside.

Pour off all but 3 tablespoons of the oil from the pot. Add the onion and cook until browned. Return the roast to the pot. Add the apple cider, salt, pepper, thyme, bay leaf, and cloves. Bring to a boil, cover, reduce the heat, and simmer about 2 hours. (Alternatively, put the covered pot in a preheated 325°F oven for 2 hours.)

When meat is almost tender (after about 1½ hours of cooking), add the carrots and apples. Cover and continue cooking until done.

Transfer the meat to a platter and surround with the carrots and apples. If desired, thicken the braising juices with flour to make a gravy (see gravy Note, page 44).

Pigs' Feet Any Whichaway

Serves 6 to 12

One finds pigs' feet in all sorts of places around here. Corner grocers have big jars of them pickled, jellied, or plain, ready to be fixed any way you please.

After the pigs' feet are cooked as described here, they are ready to be used however you like. They can be grilled, barbecued, or braised with sauerkraut . . . the list goes on and on.

Following this versatile recipe is my friend Mary Beth's pickling "solution," for your gastronomic gratification.

6 pigs' feet, split in half lengthwise
2 onions, sliced
4 stalks celery, chopped
2 bay leaves
1 tablespoon black peppercorns
1 tablespoon salt

In a large pot place the pigs' feet and generously cover with water. Add the onions, celery, bay leaves, peppercorns, and salt and bring to a boil. Reduce the heat and simmer until tender, 3½ to 4 hours.

Mary Beth's Pickling Solution for Pigs' Feet

Serves 6 to 12

Freshly cooked Pigs' Feet Any Which-away (see preceding recipe)
1 tablespoon whole cloves
1 bay leaf
Cider vinegar, as needed

To pickle the pigs' feet, place them in a large jar when they are still warm. Top them with the cooked onions from the pot.

In a saucepan, combine cloves, bay leaf, and enough cider vinegar to cover the pigs' feet. Bring to a boil and pour over the pigs' feet. Cover and refrigerate a few days before eating.

Get a bottle of beer, turn on the TV, put up your feet, and enjoy.

Smoked Neck and Cabbage

Serves 4

I'm sure there's a perfectly rational explanation why people from the Bay refer to this locally adored dish as "neck," when in fact it is a pig's butt. I haven't found the reason, however. What is rational is the combination of smoked pork and fresh cabbage. The pork ends up tender and the cabbage has a delightful smokiness. Serve with buttered boiled potatoes.

1 smoked pork butt (2 to 3 pounds)
2 bay leaves
1 onion, sliced
⅔ cup red wine vinegar

1 head cabbage
Prepared horseradish and mustard, for accompaniment

Place the pork butt in pot and add water to cover. Bring to a boil and add the bay leaves, onion, and vinegar. Return to a boil, cover, reduce the heat, and simmer about 20 minutes per pound.

Split the cabbage, remove the tough core, and cut in wedges. Add cabbage to the pot during the last 30 minutes of cooking.

Arrange the meat on a platter with the cabbage and potatoes. Serve horseradish and mustard on the side.

Sis's Sweet Potato Salad

Serves 6 to 8

Sis has been farming sweet pota-toes on the shores of the Chester River from the time she was able to stand on two feet. This is her recipe for a zesty, refreshing salad novelty to bring to a picnic in place of a conventional potato salad.

2 pounds sweet potatoes, scrubbed
3 tablespoons honey
1½ tablespoons red wine vinegar
1½ tablespoons fresh lemon juice

¾ teaspoon salt
¼ teaspoon black pepper
½ cup salad oil

Preheat oven to 400°F.

Prick the sweet potatoes with fork tines in a few places and bake until easily pierced, about 45 minutes. Cool and peel; cut in ½-inch cubes and place in a large bowl.

In a small bowl blend all the remaining ingredients together well and pour over the sweet potatoes. Marinate at least 1 hour before serving.

Kent County Sweet Corn Pudding

Serves 4 or 5

At the height of summer, the corn in Kent County is the sweetest imaginable. Visions of Sunday dinner on the farm, with a savory roast chicken accompanied with this corn pudding, fill my head even when I'm far from home.

2 cups fresh sweet corn kernels (cut from about 5 ears), coarsely chopped
2 eggs, beaten
1 tablespoon flour
1 tablespoon grated onion

2 tablespoons sugar
2 tablespoons butter, melted
1¼ cups milk
1 teaspoon salt
¼ teaspoon white pepper

Preheat oven to 325°F.

In a bowl combine all the ingredients and mix well. Pour the mixture into a well-buttered 1-quart baking dish. Bake about 1 hour, or until set.

Steamed Pattypan Squash

Serves 4

The scallop-rimmed pattypan squash, which is also known as cymling squash, is one of those most special treats of the summer months. I feel as though I could live on nothing but these squash and vine-ripe tomatoes from June to August. A simple preparation is best, so you don't mask their delicious flavor.

8 pattypan squash
Salted water
3 tablespoons butter

Salt, black pepper, and fresh lemon juice to taste

Wash the squash and cut in quarters. Barely cover the bottom of a heavy saucepan with salted water. Bring to a boil and drop in the squash. Cover and cook until tender.

Drain off liquid and add butter, salt, pepper, and lemon juice.

Baked Summer Squash Casserole

Serves 6

To dress up summer squash without overpowering their delicate flavor, try this creamy casserole accented with an aged Swiss cheese.

8 pattypan squash
3 tablespoons grated onion
¼ cup (4 tablespoons) butter, softened
2½ tablespoons flour
1½ cups heavy cream

Salt and black pepper to taste
⅛ teaspoon ground nutmeg
1 cup grated Swiss or Gruyère cheese
Buttered dried bread crumbs

Preheat oven to 350°F.

Cut and cook the squash in salted water as instructed in Steamed Pattypan Squash (see preceding recipe). Drain off the liquid.

Press the squash through the large holes of a colander. Add onion, butter, flour, cream, salt, pepper, and nutmeg. Mix well. Pour into a buttered 1½-quart casserole.

Top with grated cheese and bread crumbs. Bake about 20 minutes, or until browned.

Fasnachts

Makes about 4 dozen doughnuts

This recipe comes from Sharon Ventura, of Cecil County. It is an Amish potato doughnut that is traditionally made for Shrove Tuesday, or for what the Amish call Fasnacht.

3 medium potatoes, peeled
1 package active dry yeast
2¼ cups lukewarm water (105° to 115°)
About 7 cups flour
1 teaspoon salt

4 eggs, beaten
½ cup (¼ pound) butter, melted and cooled
1½ cups sugar
Vegetable oil, for deep-frying
1 teaspoon ground cinnamon

In the evening, just before supper, boil the potatoes in water to cover until tender, 30 to 40 minutes. Drain, reserve the water, and transfer the potatoes to a large bowl. Mash the potatoes.

When the potatoes have cooled, beat in 1 cup of the reserved water. Dissolve the yeast in ¼ cup of the lukewarm water and let stand until foamy, about 10 minutes. Add yeast mixture to the potato mixture. Cover with a towel and let stand in a warm place.

Around bedtime, mix together 2 cups of the flour, salt, and the remaining 2 cups lukewarm water. Add to the potato mixture. Cover, put back in the warm spot, and let rise overnight.

In the morning, mix together the eggs, melted butter, and 1 cup of the sugar. Beat in enough of the remaining 5 cups flour to form a stiff dough.

Turn out onto a floured board and knead dough until it is stiff enough to roll out, adding more flour as needed.

Place dough in a bowl, cover, and let rise again until doubled in bulk, about 1 to 1½ hours.

On a lightly floured board, roll dough out about ½ inch thick. Cut out doughnuts with a doughnut cutter. Cover the doughnuts with a towel and let rise again 15 to 20 minutes.

Heat vegetable oil to 375°F and deep-fry doughnuts, a few at a time, until golden brown, about 3 minutes per side (depending on size). Drain well on paper towels.

In a paper bag, mix together the cinnamon and the remaining ½ cup sugar. Shake doughnuts in the bag to coat.

Sticky Buns

Makes about 24 buns

Another sweet risen bread with Amish origins. I can't figure out how people lived before these sweet buns were invented. Incredible! The recipe appears complicated, but if you are familiar with making bread it is actually quite simple.

2 packages active dry yeast
½ cup sugar
1 cup lukewarm water (105° to 115°F)
¾ cup milk
1 teaspoon salt
½ cup (¼ pound) butter, melted

2 eggs, beaten
5 to 6 cups flour
Filling for Sticky Buns (recipe follows)
Topping for Sticky Buns (recipe follows)
Melted butter, for brushing on dough

Dissolve the yeast and 1 teaspoon of the sugar in lukewarm water and let stand until foamy, about 10 minutes. Meanwhile, combine the remaining sugar, milk, and salt in a saucepan and bring just to a boil, stirring to dissolve sugar. Remove from the heat, add the melted butter, and cool to lukewarm. Add the yeast mixture and eggs and beat well. Mix in the flour, 1 cup at a time, until a soft dough is formed.

Turn dough out onto a floured board. Cover with a towel and let rest 10 minutes. Knead the dough for 10 minutes, using more flour as needed to prevent stickiness.

Place in a well-oiled bowl, turning dough to coat all sides. Cover with a tea towel and let stand in a warm place to rise until doubled in bulk, about 1½ hours.

Prepare the filling and topping and set aside. Turn dough out onto a floured board and divide in half. Knead each half for 1 to 2 minutes, then roll each out into a rectangle 12 inches long, 8 inches wide, and ½ inch thick. Brush the dough with melted butter, leaving ½-inch borders around all 4 sides.

Sprinkle the rectangles with the filling mixture. Roll each up from a long side, jelly roll fashion. With a sharp knife, cut in slices about 1½ inches thick. Arrange slices in prepared pans strewn with topping. Cover with towels and let rise again about 30 to 45 minutes.

Meanwhile, preheat oven to 350°F. Bake buns about 30 minutes, or until brown. Remove from the oven and let sit 5 minutes. Invert onto a plate or platter and let the glaze run over the sides. Serve warm or cool.

Filling for Sticky Buns

½ cup granulated sugar
½ cup firmly packed dark brown sugar
½ cup raisins, plumped in hot water

½ cup chopped walnuts
2 teaspoons ground cinnamon
6 tablespoons butter, melted

In a bowl, mix together the sugars, raisins, walnuts, and cinnamon. Add butter and toss well.

Topping for Sticky Buns

1 cup (½ pound) butter, softened
2 cups firmly packed dark brown
  sugar
5 tablespoons dark cane syrup

¾ cup raisins, scalded in water
¾ cup walnut pieces

In a bowl mix together the butter, sugar, and syrup until very well blended. Butter four 8-inch cake pans and divide mixture among them. Sprinkle the raisins and nuts evenly over the sugar mixture.

Sour Cream Biscuits

Makes about one dozen biscuits

A wonderfully light biscuit that gets a slight zing from the addition of sour cream.

2 cups flour
½ teaspoon salt
1 tablespoon baking powder

¼ cup solid vegetable shortening
¾ cup milk
½ cup sour cream

Preheat oven to 400°F.

In a large bowl sift together the flour, salt, and baking powder.

Work in the shortening with fingertips or a pastry blender until mixture has the consistency of coarse meal. Beat in the milk and sour cream until smooth.

On a lightly floured board, roll out the dough ½ inch thick and cut out about 12 rounds. Place on a baking sheet and bake 8 to 10 minutes.

Hot Milk Cake

Makes one 10-inch cake, serves 8

From the Cecilton parish, Frances Dixon gives us her version of this classic American sponge cake. Serve plain or with ice cream or sweetened sliced strawberries.

2 cups granulated sugar
4 eggs, beaten
2 cups flour
1 tablespoon baking powder
½ cup (¼ pound) butter
1 cup milk
1 teaspoon vanilla extract
Confectioners' sugar, for dusting

Preheat oven to 325°F.

In a large bowl cream together the granulated sugar and eggs until fluffy. Sift together the flour and baking powder, then beat it into the sugar mixture.

In a saucepan combine the butter and milk and bring to a boil. Slowly pour hot milk mixture into the batter, mixing well. Mix in the vanilla.

Pour the batter into a greased and floured 10-inch tube pan. Bake 45 minutes to 1 hour, or until a toothpick inserted in cake comes out clean. Cool on a wire rack. Dust the top with confectioners' sugar.

Peach Cobbler

Makes one 8-inch-square cobbler, serves 6

This is the land of cobbler fanatics. Their voices reach a fevered pitch when touting the praises of a favorite cobbler or cobbler maker. In case you are unsure just exactly what a cobbler is, it's a deep-dish fruit pie with a rich biscuit-dough top. Try this one and you'll see how cobblers can inspire such fervent regional patriotism.

3 cups peeled, sliced ripe peaches (see page 215)
3 tablespoons plus 1 cup sugar
1½ tablespoons plus 1¼ cups flour
Pinch plus ¼ teaspoon salt
2 teaspoons baking powder
1 egg
¾ cup milk
¼ cup (4 tablespoons) butter, melted
Vanilla ice cream, for accompaniment

Preheat oven to 375°F.

Butter an 8-inch-square baking dish. In a bowl toss peaches with 3 tablespoons sugar, 1½ tablespoons flour, and pinch salt. Pour into the baking dish.

In a bowl sift together 1¼ cups flour, baking powder, and 1 teaspoon salt. Mix with the 1 cup sugar.

In a large bowl, beat together the egg, milk, and butter. Stir into the dry ingredients and mix well. Pour over the peaches and bake 40 minutes. Serve the cobbler warm, topped with vanilla ice cream.

Shoofly Pie

Makes one 9-inch pie,
serves 6 to 8

Molasses cookery at its finest. The Amish communities around Chestertown produce an outstanding molasses and this pie serves as a showcase. It has a wonderful caramellike texture and is a breeze to make. Be sure the screen windows are in place or the flies will be lighting on your pie. And I swear they're hell to pick out.

Pastry Dough for single-crust 9-inch pie (see page 31)
1 teaspoon baking soda
1 cup boiling water
1 cup molasses
1 cup flour
1 cup sugar
¼ teaspoon salt
¼ cup (4 tablespoons) solid vegetable shortening or butter
Molasses, for brushing on crust
Sweetened whipped cream and ground cinnamon, for garnish

Preheat oven to 350°F.

Prepare pastry dough and line a 9-inch pie pan.

Dissolve the baking soda in boiling water and add to molasses.

In a bowl mix together the flour, sugar, and salt. Work in shortening with your fingertips or a pastry blender until mixture has the consistency of coarse meal.

Brush the bottom of the pie crust with a little undiluted molasses. Pour in the molasses mixture and sprinkle the flour mixture on top. Bake 40 to 45 minutes, or until set.

Serve with whipped cream topped with a dash of cinnamon.

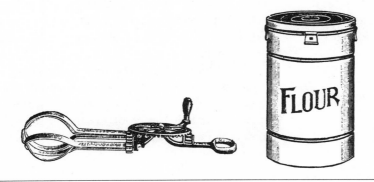

Strawberry Jam

Makes 5 half-pints

Make several batches of this un-cooked jam and you'll have the taste of summer with you the whole year through.

1 quart ripe strawberries
4 cups sugar

2 tablespoons fresh lemon juice
1 box (1¾ ounces) powdered pectin

Stem the strawberries, then crush or mash in a bowl. They should measure about 1¾ cups. Thoroughly mix the strawberries with sugar and let stand 10 minutes.

Combine the lemon juice with pectin and add to the fruit mixture. Stir 5 minutes.

Ladle into hot, sterilized jars and seal. Let stand at room temperature 24 hours to set.

Refrigerate what will be used soon (3 weeks) and freeze the remainder.

Brandied Peaches

Makes about 8 one pint jars

If you have this wonderful peach compote on hand, you can quickly turn a regular bowl of ice cream into a special treat. Or use it to fill a pie shell or turnover pastry. Let the peaches (and your imagi-nation) work their magic to perk up some old favorites.

5 pounds firm, ripe peaches
Boiling water
6 cups sugar
¾ cup cider vinegar

1 cup water
1 cinnamon stick
1 teaspoon whole cloves
1 cup brandy

Place the peaches in a large pot of boiling water. Let stand 2 to 3 minutes. Drain and remove skins and pits. Cut into sixths.

In a heavy pot combine the sugar, vinegar, and water. Tie the cinnamon stick and cloves in a square of cloth or cheesecloth. Add to the pot and bring to a boil.

Add the peaches and cook until tender, about 6 to 8 minutes. Remove the peaches with a slotted spoon and pack into hot, sterilized jars.

Add brandy to the liquid and boil until syrupy, about 10 to 15 minutes. Discard cheesecloth bag. Pour the hot liquid over the peaches and seal according to standard canning procedures (see Note on page 67).

Green Tomato Mincemeat

Makes about 8 pints

This mock-mincemeat preserve is a longtime favorite on the Eastern Shore. The firm green tomatoes hold up well, making a nicely textured, highly spiced blend. You can use a ratio of half diced apples and half mincemeat for a pie filling, or warm the mincemeat and serve it as a dessert topping on ice cream.

4 quarts green tomatoes, cut in chunks
3 cups granulated sugar
2 cups firmly packed brown sugar
3 cups raisins
2 teaspoons salt
½ cup chopped beef suet

1 cup cider vinegar
2 teaspoons ground cloves
½ teaspoon ground ginger
1½ tablespoons ground cinnamon
1 teaspoon ground nutmeg
½ teaspoon ground mace

In a large, heavy pot, place the tomatoes and add water to cover. Bring to a boil and drain. Repeat.

Add the sugars, raisins, salt, suet, and vinegar. Boil, stirring frequently, until mixture becomes about as thick as mincemeat. When almost finished cooking, add all the remaining ingredients.

Pour into hot, sterilized jars and process in a water bath according to standard canning procedures.

Eggnog

Serves a crowd

Fold plenty of beaten egg whites into this holiday tradition to make it as light as a feather. Vary the liquors as you will. Some folks prefer rye whiskey or different ratios of bourbon whiskey to rum. Half of the fun of this recipe is working on it until you get it right!

12 egg yolks
4 cups sugar
1 quart bourbon whiskey
2 cups dark rum
2 cups brandy

3 quarts heavy cream
1 quart (4 cups) milk
12 egg whites
Freshly grated nutmeg, for dusting

In a large bowl beat together the yolks and sugar until pale and ribbonlike.

Slowly whisk in the bourbon. Stir in the rum, brandy, cream, and milk.

Beat the egg whites until stiff, then gently stir into yolk mixture. Cover and refrigerate.

Serve chilled in a punch bowl. Ladle into glasses and dust with nutmeg.

· A Farmer's Feast
with Keith and Lee Dixon ·

The Dixon family at their Chestertown dairy farm.

When visiting with Keith Dixon and his wife Lee on their dairy farm outside Chestertown, the dinner conversation inevitably turns to cows. Lee touts the merits and virtues of Holsteins, while Keith, armed with facts and figures, swears by his Guernseys. I doubt if they will ever settle this long-standing family debate, but the one thing you'll never hear any argument about is their food. Judging from the way family and friends tear into the dishes made from the farm-produced vegetables, chicken, milk, and eggs, the Dixons' country-style Eastern Shore cooking is some of the finest to be found.

Dairy farming is no easy task. It's from sun up to sun down, seven days a week, the whole year around. Keith and Lee share all the farming duties with a goat, a dog, and the children at their heels. That policy of divvying up the daily chores carries over into the kitchen. They are both outstanding cooks and work together beautifully.

During deer-hunting season, Keith sets out with his brothers and his father, Frog, to bag their yearly allotment of this prized game. After the hunt they take to Frog's basement for a day devoted to the butchering ritual and to recounting the tales of the chase. The deer meat is then distributed among the family members, who fill their refrigerators and freezers for the season.

Deer, which fancy folk refer to as venison, is the featured item in the Dixons' menu. The rich Savory Deer Stew can be served in small portions as an appetizer, or by itself as the main dish at another meal. Slightly caramelized fried onions are a perfect topping for the full game flavor of the panfried deer steaks. The steaks are accompanied with farm-fresh Squash and Tomato Casserole and an innovative baked potato stuffed with cheese, country ham, and dill. Lee's Homemade Vanilla Ice Cream, an occasion in itself, can be further enhanced with the addition of sweet summer peaches. Put simply, down on the farm has never tasted so good!

Savory Deer Stew

Deer Steaks and Fried Onions

Potatoes Stuffed with Ham and Dill

Squash and Tomato Casserole

Homemade Vanilla Ice Cream

Savory Deer Stew

Makes a potful

Lard or vegetable oil for browning
2 pounds deer rump or round, cut in
   1½-inch cubes
Flour seasoned with salt and black
   pepper
2 large onions, sliced
1 quart boiling water
4 carrots, peeled and sliced
6 potatoes, peeled and cubed

1 teaspoon Old Bay seasoning
¼ teaspoon black pepper
1 bay leaf
Pinch dried thyme
2 cups fresh or frozen shelled peas
Hot rolls or biscuits, for accompaniment

In a dutch oven heat the lard. Dust the meat cubes in the seasoned flour and brown well on all sides in the hot fat.

Add the onions to the pot and cook a few minutes with the meat. Pour in the boiling water. Bring to a boil, cover, reduce the heat, and simmer 1½ hours.

Add all the remaining ingredients except the peas and simmer, uncovered, 1 hour.

Add the peas and continue simmering 20 to 30 minutes, or until meat is very tender. Adjust seasonings and serve with hot rolls. This stew is even better reheated the next day.

Deer Steaks with Fried Onions

Serves 4

4 deer steaks, 1 to 1½ inches thick
Flour seasoned with salt and black
  pepper
Butter and vegetable oil, for frying

2 onions, sliced in ¼-inch-thick rings
Salt and black pepper to taste

Dredge steaks in the seasoned flour. In a skillet heat equal amounts butter and oil. Fry the steaks about 7 minutes on each side, or a bit longer if you want them well done. Remove the steaks to a heated platter and keep warm.

If necessary, add additional butter to bring pan drippings to about 6 tablespoons. Heat the drippings, add the onions, salt, and pepper and cook over medium heat, stirring now and then, until the onions turn a darkish brown or caramel color.

Serve the onions on top of the steaks. Make a pan gravy from the cooking juices (see page 44) if you like. It makes a perfect topping for the rich stuffed potatoes, which follow.

Potatoes Stuffed with Ham and Dill

Serves 4 with good appetites

4 baking potatoes
½ cup finely diced country ham
½ cup minced green bell pepper,
  sautéed in butter
¼ cup (4 tablespoons) butter,
  softened

½ cup sour cream
2 tablespoons chopped fresh dill
Salt and black pepper to taste
½ cup grated sharp Cheddar cheese
  (optional)

Preheat oven to 400°F.

Bake the potatoes until tender when pricked with a fork, 40 to 50 minutes (depending upon size). Cut the warm baked potatoes in half lengthwise. Scoop out pulp, being careful not to break the skins. Set the skins aside.

Increase oven temperature to 450°F. In a large bowl mash the potatoes, then add the ham, bell pepper, butter, sour cream, and dill. Whip until the mixture is smooth. Season with salt and pepper.

Mound the potato mixture in the potato skins. Sprinkle with grated cheese, if desired. Place the potatoes on a baking sheet and bake 10 to 15 minutes, or until well browned.

Squash and Tomato Casserole

Serves 4

6 tablespoons butter
4 zucchini, thinly sliced
1 onion, diced
4 tomatoes, diced

Salt and black pepper to taste
Pinch Old Bay seasoning
¼ pound mozzarella or provolone
cheese, sliced

Preheat oven to 375°F.

Melt the butter in a skillet. Add the zucchini and onions and sauté a few minutes until half-cooked.

Remove from the heat and add tomatoes, salt, pepper, and Old Bay.

Pour into a buttered 4-cup casserole. Top with cheese and bake 10 minutes, or until cheese melts and begins to brown.

Homemade Vanilla Ice Cream

Makes about 3 quarts

1 quart (4 cups) half-and-half
1½ quarts (6 cups) milk
4 eggs
2½ cups sugar
2 tablespoons vanilla extract

½ teaspoon salt
Sliced fresh peaches, Brandied
Peaches (see page 174), or pitted
sweet cherries, for topping

Combine the half-and-half and milk in a saucepan and bring just to a boil.

Meanwhile, in a large bowl cream together the eggs and sugar until fluffy and pale in color. Beat in the vanilla and salt.

Gradually whisk in the hot milk mixture. Mix well. Pour the mixture into an ice cream freezer and freeze according to manufacturer's instructions.

Serve topped with fruit. This ice cream also makes outstanding shakes and hot fudge sundaes!

• Tilghman Peninsula •

*St. John's Methodist Church on Tilghman Island. Long known as
one of the major seafood industry centers on the Bay, Tilghman Island is located at the southernmost tip of the Tilghman peninsula
and is the home port to a large skipjack fleet.*

As its name suggests, Tilghman Peninsula has water everywhere. It is bordered by the Chesapeake, the Miles and Tred Avon rivers, and Harris and Broad creeks. Around here that translates into seafood.

And seafood abounds! The peninsula seafood philosophy, which comes from the now-defunct Tilghman Packing Plant, is "Eat seafood to insure your good health—avoid goiter, prevent anemia, help your stomach and keep a clear mind." It appears by the look of the rugged locals, the spring in their step and sparkle in their eyes, it must be true, for you'll be hard-pressed to find a dull-witted or iron-poor-blood one in the lot.

A majority of the folk around here work on the water or in a related business, such as the seafood packing houses. They work long, hard hours to provide seafood to the rest of the country so that everyone may enjoy fish-filled, goiter-free lives. This is no small task, but the residents of St. Michaels, Claiborne, Bozman, McDaniel, Sherwood, Neauitt, and Tilghman Island do their best.

The peninsula is named for Colonel Tench Tilghman, George Washington's confidential secretary and right-hand man, who made a desperate ride on horseback à la Paul Revere during the Revolution. It appears the colonel was rather prolific, considering the number of Tilghman descendants up and down the Eastern Shore of the Bay.

Owing to the wealth of fresh seafood, fowl, game, and produce on the peninsula, some of the finest examples of Chesapeake cookery are found in the recipes of the Tilghman community. Platters of Mrs. Harrison's Oyster Fritters, Green Tomato Fritters, and Miles River Crab Balls will be found gracing the tables of the region. The tidewater areas are home to all types of waterfowl that end up in such local recipes as Roast Wild Goose with Apple-Chestnut Stuffing. And the birds are not the only thing they stuff around here, as the recipe for stuffed bass deliciously attests.

Aunt Catherine's Gingersnap and Buckwheat Waffles

Makes 8 waffles

The ground gingersnaps give these waffles exactly that, a ginger snap. Catherine came up with this recipe as a treat for the children who came to visit her shore home during the summer.

1½ cups all-purpose flour
¼ cup buckwheat flour
3 tablespoons baking powder
1 tablespoon sugar
½ teaspoon salt
½ cup ground gingersnaps
3 eggs, separated

5 tablespoons butter, melted and cooled
2 cups milk
1 teaspoon vanilla extract
Warm maple syrup or sweetened whipped cream and fruit, for accompaniment

Preheat the waffle iron.

In a bowl sift together the flours, baking powder, sugar, and salt. Mix in the gingersnaps.

In a mixing bowl beat together the egg yolks, butter, milk, and vanilla. Stir in the dry ingredients. Do not overbeat.

Beat the egg whites until stiff peaks form. Fold into the batter; do not overmix.

Cook in the waffle iron, according to manufacturer's instructions, until golden brown. Serve with maple syrup.

Breakfast Sausage Pudding

Serves 6

A delightful change from the usual breakfast, this creamy casserole is actually a sausage-and-cheese bread pudding. If desired, country ham or cooked bacon can be substituted for the sausage.

4 slices bread, broken in pieces
1 pound sausage meat, cooked and drained
1 cup grated sharp Cheddar cheese

6 eggs, beaten
2 cups milk
Salt and black pepper to taste

Preheat oven to 350°F.

Place the bread in a well-buttered 10-inch-square baking dish. Top with the sausage and then with the cheese. In a bowl beat together the eggs and milk. Pour over all. Season with salt and pepper. Bake 1 hour.

Milk Toast for Aunt Minnie

Serves 2

This dish was added to our family's culinary archives by Aunt Minnie's sister Catherine (of waffle fame) during a medical crisis. It seems Minnie had come to the shore for a rest. While lounging on the screened porch she had a spell. The family thought it a case of the vapors, due to the high summer humidity, and the doctor was summoned. The diagnosis: "an upside down stomach." After ten days on this very same milk toast, Minnie was declared "cured."

¼ cup water
1½ tablespoons flour
2¼ cups milk
2 tablespoons butter

2 tablespoons sugar
Pinch salt
Pinch ground nutmeg
4 slices bread, toasted

In a small bowl mix together the flour and water until smooth. Pour the milk into a saucepan, add the flour mixture, and bring to a boil, stirring constantly.

Off the heat stir in the butter, sugar, salt, and nutmeg.

Place 2 toast slices in each bowl and cover with hot milk. Serve hot.

Mrs. Harrison's Oyster Fritters

Serves 6 to 8

Alice Harrison, matriarch of the ever-popular Harrison's Chesapeake House Restaurant on Tilghman Island, graciously provided this recipe for her light oyster fritters. Mrs. Harrison says that people on the Eastern Shore traditionally serve oyster fritters with chicken salad.

Alice Harrison presides over her kitchen staff at Tilghman Island's renowned Harrison's Chesapeake House Restaurant. Specialties here include their famous Eastern Shore fried chicken and crab cake platters.

1 cup flour
1½ teaspoons baking powder
½ teaspoon salt
¼ teaspoon black pepper
2 eggs, beaten

1 cup milk
1 quart shucked oysters with liquor
Vegetable oil, for frying
Tartar Sauce (see page 15)

In a large bowl mix together the flour, baking powder, salt, and pepper. In a small bowl mix together the eggs and milk. Beat the egg mixture into the dry ingredients until a smooth batter is formed. Stir in the oysters.

In a skillet pour in oil to a depth of 1 inch. Heat until hot, about 365°F. For each fritter, scoop out 4 oysters with batter. Fry until golden brown on both sides, about 5 to 7 minutes. Remove with a slotted utensil to paper towels to drain. Serve with Tartar Sauce.

Miles River Crab Balls

Serves 6

Jack Schnaitman, who's been fishing and crabbing this stretch of water all his life, claims the crabs from the Miles River are the best of the Bay. I informed him that a friend of mine had said the best crabs came from the Wye River. Jack responded, without missing a beat, "I guess he's never crabbed the Miles."

I don't know if it was the crabs or the recipe, but these crab balls are tasty and lighter than air.

2 egg whites
2 tablespoons mayonnaise
1 tablespoon dry mustard
Salt and black pepper to taste
2 slices stale bread, crusts discarded and bread crushed into crumbs
1 pound special or claw crabmeat, picked over for shells
Vegetable oil, for deep-frying
Tartar Sauce (see page 15)

In a bowl beat the egg whites until stiff. Gently mix in the mayonnaise, mustard, salt, pepper, and bread crumbs. Fold in the crabmeat, mixing only enough to blend evenly.

Shape into balls about 1½-inches in diameter. In a deep skillet or fryer, heat oil to 365°F. Deep-fry balls until golden brown, about 4 to 5 minutes. Serve with a bowl of Tartar Sauce for dipping.

Seafood Pâté

Serves 10 to 12

The ladies from the Methodist church on Tilghman Island have passed this recipe around. On formal occasions, it can be found on many a buffet table.

1 pound backfin or special crabmeat, picked over for shells
2 envelopes unflavored gelatin
⅓ cup cold water
½ pound shrimp, steamed (see page 29), peeled, and cut in pieces
½ cup finely diced red bell pepper
½ cup finely diced green bell pepper
½ cup finely diced celery
2 tablespoons fresh lemon juice
1 tablespoon grated onion
1 cup mayonnaise
1 cup sour cream
2 tablespoons tomato paste
Sliced almonds and olives, for garnish (optional)
Crackers or French bread, for accompaniment

In a small bowl sprinkle gelatin over water and let stand until soft. Set dish in a pan of hot water and stir to dissolve.

In a large bowl combine all the remaining ingredients, then add dissolved gelatin. Mix well and pour into an oiled 2-quart fish mold. Cover and chill overnight, or until firm.

To unmold, briefly dip the bottom of the mold into hot water and invert mold on plate. Garnish with sliced almonds for scales and olives for eyes. Serve with crackers.

Pot o'Greens, Ham, and White Bean Soup

Serves a crowd

A jazz festival of flavors all in one pot. The Jackson twins of Easton, Selma and Doretha, not only can turn out a mean pot of soup, but they nearly blow the roof off the church with one of their foot-tapping gospel hymns.

1 cup dried small white beans
2 quarts salted water
6 tablespoons bacon drippings
2 cups coarsely chopped onions
1 cup coarsely chopped celery
2 tablespoons chopped garlic
1 bay leaf
1 teaspoon dried thyme
1 teaspoon salt
½ teaspoon black pepper

½ teaspoon cayenne pepper
4 cups Chicken Stock (see page 33) or bouillon
2 pounds collard greens, coarsely chopped
1 pound cured ham, cut in chunks
3 to 4 tablespoons white vinegar
Cheese Biscuits (see page 230) or hot crusty bread, for accompaniment

Put the beans and salted water in a pot and bring to a boil. Remove from the heat, cover, and let stand about 1 hour.

In a skillet heat the bacon drippings and cook the onions, celery, and garlic several minutes. Return the beans to the stove and add the sautéed vegetables. Add the bay leaf, thyme, salt, and peppers. Pour in the stock and bring to a boil. Add the greens and ham. Simmer 2 to 2½ hours, or until the beans and greens are tender.

Season with vinegar, salt, and pepper. Serve with Cheese Biscuits.

Cantaloupe Soup

Serves 6 to 8

Maggie Haines, of St. Michaels, makes this soup every summer when the melons are at their sweetest. She says not to eat the soup too fast or you'll get dizzy. It also works well using ripe honeydew melons.

4 ripe cantaloupes
1 fifth dry champagne

¼ cup chopped fresh mint
Mint sprigs, for garnish

Peel and seed 3 of the cantaloupes and cut in pieces. In a blender purée the cantaloupe pieces in batches, adding champagne to each batch to thin to soup consistency.

Cut the remaining melon in half, discard the seeds, and scoop out the flesh with a melon baller. Add these balls to the soup along with the chopped mint.

Chill well and serve in chilled soup bowls. Garnish each serving with a sprig of fresh mint.

Waterman's Oyster Stew

Serves 6 to 8

Watermen are known for their skills in preparing seafood stews. This simple dish showcases the Chesapeake oyster at its finest. The oysters are not really cooked, but bathed in warm seasoned milk. The oysters do the talking in this dish.

3 tablespoons butter, plus butter for garnish
2 tablespoons finely chopped celery
2 tablespoons finely chopped onion
1 quart shucked oysters with liquor

4 cups milk, heated
2 teaspoons Worcestershire sauce
Dash salt, black pepper, and cayenne pepper
Paprika, for garnish

In a heavy-bottomed pot melt the butter. Sauté the celery and onion until limp. Add the oysters and their liquor to the pot. Cook only until edges of the oysters begin to curl slightly.

Add the milk and seasonings. Heat until the edges of the oysters have curled.

Serve at once. Garnish with a pat of butter and a dusting of paprika.

Panfried Oysters

Serves 5 or 6

Crisp, light, and melt-in-your-mouth are just a few of the ways to describe the absolutely joyous taste of one of the Chesapeake's finest oyster recipes. The gang around Tilghman fry up these plump oysters at restaurants, firehouse suppers, and in every kitchen that's got a stove for cooking.

20 to 24 oysters
2 cups flour seasoned with salt and
   black pepper
4 eggs, beaten
About 4 cups dried bread crumbs

Butter and vegetable oil, for frying
Lemon wedges and Tartar Sauce (see
   page 15) or Tangy Cocktail Sauce
   (see page 29)

Shuck the oysters. Dredge each oyster in flour, shake off excess, then dip in egg and roll in bread crumbs.

In a skillet heat equal amounts of the butter and oil to a depth of about ¼ inch. Fry oysters about 5 minutes or until golden brown. Remove with a slotted utensil to paper towels to drain well. While frying additional oysters, add more butter and oil as needed.

Serve hot with lemon wedges and Tartar Sauce.

Crab au Gratin

Serves 4 or 5

They say "thus and so" is "as American as apple pie." Well, I don't believe you can get much more American than the time-honored casserole. Around our way we've figured out how to make one out of just about anything that swims, trots, flies, or grows. So don't leave your pets unattended. This crab casserole is one outstanding Chesapeake classic.

½ cup (¼ pound) butter
¼ cup flour
½ teaspoon salt
2 cups milk
1 egg, beaten

1½ cups grated Cheddar cheese
1½ cups soft bread crumbs
1 pound backfin crabmeat, picked
   over for shells

Preheat oven to 350°F.

In a saucepan melt the butter. Whisk in the flour and salt and cook, stirring, 1 to 2 minutes. Do not brown the flour.

Off the heat whisk in the milk, egg, 1 cup of the cheese, and 1 cup of the bread crumbs. Fold in the crabmeat and mix gently.

Pour into a buttered 2-quart casserole. Top with the remaining cheese and bread crumbs. Bake 45 minutes.

Crab Supreme

Serves 6

One-pot meals and hearty casseroles are the order of the day in many Tilghman Island kitchens. This recipe, a cross between a casserole and a delicate pudding, has warmed the hearts and stomachs of many watermen.

8 slices bread, diced
1 pound crabmeat, picked over for shells
1 small onion, diced
½ cup mayonnaise
½ cup green pepper, diced

1 cup celery, diced
4 eggs, beaten
3 cups milk
1 cup heavy cream
1 cup grated sharp cheese
Paprika, for topping

Place half of the diced bread in the bottom of a buttered baking dish. In a bowl mix together the crabmeat, onion, mayonnaise, green pepper, and celery. Spread the mixture over the bread cubes in the baking dish. Place the remainder of the bread on top.

In a bowl beat the eggs and milk together. Pour over the crab and bread mixture. Cover the baking dish and refrigerate overnight.

The next day, preheat the oven to 325°F and bake the casserole 15 minutes. Remove from the oven and increase oven heat to 350°F. Pour cream evenly over the top of the casserole and sprinkle with cheese. Bake 1 hour, or until set.

Shrimp Creole

Serves 6

When Miss Helen of Tilghman wants to perk things up a bit on the island, she hauls out her heavy kettle and makes a batch of this Shrimp Creole. If your breathing's been heavy of late, you may want to go heavy on the Tabasco and throw in a pinch of cayenne. That should set the lungs to pumping free and clear.

½ cup (¼ pound) butter
1 cup finely chopped onion
¾ cup finely chopped green pepper
1 cup finely chopped celery
¼ cup flour
4 cups peeled, coarsely chopped tomatoes
2 teaspoons salt
¼ teaspoon black pepper
1 tablespoon brown sugar

3 bay leaves
6 whole cloves
1½ pounds shrimp, peeled and deveined
1 teaspoon Worcestershire sauce
½ tablespoon fresh lemon juice
½ teaspoon Tabasco sauce
Freshly cooked white rice, for accompaniment

In a heavy-bottomed pot, melt the butter and sauté the onion, green pepper, and celery until soft. Stir in the flour and cook, stirring constantly, 2 to 3 minutes.

Add the tomatoes, salt, black pepper, sugar, bay leaves, and cloves.

Bring to a boil. Reduce the heat and cook 1½ hours. Stir often, so that the tomatoes do not stick to the bottom of the pot.

During the last 10 minutes of cooking, add the shrimp, Worcestershire, lemon juice, and Tabasco. When the shrimp are done, serve over rice.

Stuffed Rockfish or Black Bass

Serves 5 or 6

These bass varieties lend themselves to being stuffed and baked. We generally bake bass whole, with just the head and tail removed. Two fillets with the skin still on also will do nicely if you prefer. The bacon imparts a wonderful flavor to the fish as it bakes.

3 tablespoons butter
¼ cup finely chopped celery
¼ cup finely chopped onion
2 eggs, beaten
½ teaspoon dry mustard
¼ teaspoon dried sage
½ teaspoon salt
¼ teaspoon black pepper

1 tablespoon chopped fresh parsley
6 slices stale bread, crusts discarded and bread cubed
Milk, as needed
1 whole rockfish or black bass (5 to 6 pounds), dressed, or 2 whole fillets with skin intact
3 slices hickory-smoked bacon

Preheat oven to 350°F.

In a small skillet melt the butter and sauté the celery and onion until soft; set aside.

In a mixing bowl combine the eggs, mustard, sage, salt, pepper, and parsley. Add the bread cubes and reserved celery mixture and toss well. If stuffing seems too dry, add milk to moisten.

Stuff the mixture into the cavity of the fish or between the 2 fillets. Secure opening closed with toothpicks or skewers.

Lay fish in a baking pan and arrange bacon slices on top. Bake 45 minutes, basting occasionally with milk.

Chicken Stewed with Tomatoes and Okra

Serves 5 to 6

Talk about country cooking! Honey, it don't get no more country than this. When those sweet summertime Eastern Shore tomatoes and okra get a hold of that chicken, it gets tasting so good it almost seems sinful. But don't worry, just get out your pot, put the chicken in, and I'm sure all will be forgiven.

6 tablespoons bacon drippings or butter
1 roasting chicken (4 to 4½ pounds)
1 large onion, chopped
3 stalks celery, diced
2 tablespoons chopped garlic
1 pound okra, cut in ½-inch pieces
2 cups chopped tomatoes with their juice
2½ to 3 cups Chicken Stock (see page 33) or water
1 teaspoon salt, plus salt to taste
2 teaspoons sugar
1 bay leaf
½ teaspoon dried marjoram
¼ teaspoon ground nutmeg
1½ cups corn kernels
Black pepper to taste
Freshly cooked white rice and Two O'Clock Club Corn Bread (see page 56), for accompaniment

In a heavy-bottomed pot or dutch oven, heat the bacon drippings and brown the chicken on all sides. Remove from the pot and set aside.

Add the onion, celery, and garlic to the pot and sauté 4 to 5 minutes. Add the okra, cover, and simmer 20 minutes.

Stir in the tomatoes and return the chicken to the pot. Pour in enough stock to reach three quarters of the way up the side of the chicken. Add 1 teaspoon salt, sugar, bay leaf, marjoram, and nutmeg. Cover and simmer about 1½ hours, or until chicken is tender.

Remove chicken from the pot. Add the corn to the pot and simmer, uncovered, 15 to 20 minutes. Pick the meat from the chicken and add it back to the pot. Heat chicken meat through and season with salt and pepper. Serve over rice with plenty of hot Corn Bread on the side.

Roast Mallards

Serves 2 to 4

Wild duck yields a delectable, full-flavored meat. Some city folk cringe at the notion of consuming these birds, claiming the meat to be tough and gamy. Of course this is only what they've heard, never having tried it themselves. Well, not true! Tender beyond belief, and an exquisite taste. So if you've been shy about waterfowl in the past, loosen up and give yourself a treat.

2 mallards
Salt and black pepper
2 stalks celery
1 small onion, halved
1 apple, cored and halved
1 cup hearty dry red wine
1½ cups Chicken Stock (see page 33) or bouillon, heated

2 whole cloves
4 black peppercorns
1 bay leaf
½ teaspoon dried thyme
¼ teaspoon dried sage
2 tablespoons flour
Salt and black pepper

Preheat oven to 500°F.

Wash the cavities of the ducks with cold water and dry with paper towels. Sprinkle cavities with salt and pepper. Stuff each with half of the celery, onion, and apple. Truss the ducks.

In the bottom of a shallow roasting pan, pour in the red wine and stock. Add the cloves, peppercorns, bay leaf, thyme, and sage. Set a rack in the pan and arrange the ducks on it. Place in oven and cook 10 minutes. Reduce heat to 350°F and continue cooking another 25 to 30 minutes, basting 2 or 3 times with pan juices.

Remove the birds to a heated platter and keep warm. Strain the pan juices and reserve. Defat the juices, reserving 3 tablespoons of the fat. In a saucepan heat the reserved fat and whisk in the flour. Cook, stirring, 2 to 3 minutes. Stir in the reserved juices and whisk over medium heat until thickened. Season with salt and pepper.

Split mallards lengthwise and discard stuffing. Serve with pan gravy.

Roast Wild Goose with Apple-Chestnut Stuffing

Serves 6 to 8

When approaching a goose with the intent of cooking it, it's a good idea to check its credentials. How old? If it weighs over eight pounds and was bagged in the fall, it is most likely an older bird. Senior birds are best prepared stewed or braised, while the younger ones are more appropriate for roasting.

This traditional shore stuffing is the perfect blend of chestnut and fruit to highlight the succulence of the goose.

Apple-Chestnut Stuffing (recipe follows)
1 young goose (4 to 5 pounds)

Salt and black pepper
1 onion, halved
About 3 tablespoons flour

Preheat oven to 400°F.

Prepare stuffing.

Wash the cavity of the bird with cold water and dry with paper towels. Sprinkle cavity with salt and pepper. Rub skin of goose with cut sides of the onion. Prick the skin all over with a fork. Fill the cavity with stuffing and truss closed. Place on a rack in a shallow roasting pan and put in oven. Reduce heat to 350°F and cook 2½ to 3 hours, basting frequently. Remove goose to a heated platter and keep warm. Pour the pan juices into a pitcher and defat, reserving about 3 tablespoons of the fat. In a saucepan heat the reserved fat and whisk in the flour. Cook stirring, 2 to 3 minutes. Stir in the reserved pan juices and whisk over medium heat until thickened (see gravy Note, page 44).

Carve goose and serve with stuffing and pan gravy.

Apple-Chestnut Stuffing

6 tablespoons butter
1 onion, diced
2 stalks celery, diced
2 cups sliced, peeled tart apples
2 cups bread cubes
1 cup chestnut pieces (see Note)

2 tablespoons dried sage
½ teaspoon dried thyme
1 egg, beaten
½ cup milk or water, or as needed
Salt and black pepper to taste

In a small skillet melt the butter and sauté the onion and celery until soft.

In a bowl mix together the apples, bread cubes, chestnuts, sage, and thyme. Add the sautéed vegetables and egg. Toss well. Sprinkle in milk to moisten. Season with salt and pepper.

NOTE: Jars of whole, peeled chestnuts may be found at many specialty food shops. If not, to shell chestnuts, cut an X on the flat side of each nut and place on a pan in a preheated 425°F oven for about 15 minutes. Remove from oven and, when cool enough to handle, peel away hard outer shell and fuzzy inner membrane.

Fried Frogs' Legs

Serves 3 or 4

You'll find lots of these hoppers making their homes in the ponds and marshes of the Eastern Shore. The legs, which have a delicate chickenlike flavor, are usually first given a good soaking in milk to sweeten them up a bit and then fried. I've included a variation that is reminiscent of a French Provençal preparation.

12 pair small frogs' legs
Milk to cover
5 tablespoons lemon juice
Flour seasoned with salt and black
  pepper

3 eggs, beaten
Dried bread crumbs
Vegetable oil, for frying

In a bowl place frogs' legs and add milk and 3 tablespoons of the lemon juice. Let stand several hours.

Drain and dry the frogs' legs and roll them in the seasoned flour. Shake off excess flour, dip them in the eggs, and then toss and coat well in bread crumbs.

In a skillet pour in oil to a depth of ¼ inch. Fry frogs' legs, turning, until golden brown. At the end of cooking, pour the remaining 2 tablespoons lemon juice over the legs and serve at once.

VARIATION: After browning the frogs' legs in oil, remove from the pan and pour off the oil. Deglaze the pan with ½ cup dry white wine. Return the frogs' legs to the pan and add 2 cups peeled and chopped tomatoes, 2 tablespoons chopped garlic, and the remaining 2 tablespoons lemon juice. Cover and simmer 10 to 15 minutes. Season with salt and black pepper.

Calf's Liver and Hickory-Smoked Bacon

Serves 4

The always popular pairing of liver and crisp bacon gets a wonderfully tasty sauce in this version. When preparing calf's liver, be sure not to overcook it or the delicate texture becomes grainy. It should be served on the pink side.

4 slices smoked bacon
3 tablespoons butter, or as needed
1 onion, thinly sliced
1 teaspoon chopped garlic
1 pound calf's liver, trimmed and sliced in serving pieces
Flour seasoned with salt and black pepper
¾ cup beef stock or bouillon
¼ cup Madeira wine
¼ teaspoon dried thyme
Salt and black pepper to taste
1 tablespoon flour

In a large skillet cook the bacon. Remove with a slotted utensil to paper towels to drain. Add the butter to the bacon drippings in the skillet. Add the onion and garlic and sauté until tender. Remove from pan with a slotted utensil and set aside.

Dust the liver slices in flour, shaking off the excess. If necessary, add additional butter to the skillet. Brown liver on both sides. Return reserved onion and garlic to the pan. Pour in the stock, wine, thyme, salt, and pepper. Cover and simmer about 20 minutes, or until done to your liking.

Remove liver with a slotted utensil to a platter. Dissolve flour in the pan juices; cook over medium heat, stirring, until thickened. Top the liver with bacon and pour on the gravy.

Miss Sara's Ham Loaf

Serves 8

This delightful variation on the standard meat loaf was created by Miss Sara Tyler from Easton. It is wonderfully spiced and the brown sugar topping turns it into a mealtime showstopper! Goes best with mashed potatoes and hot rolls.

1 pound country ham, ground
1 pound ground pork
2 eggs, beaten
1 onion, finely diced
½ cup finely diced green bell pepper
1 cup apple cider
Salt and black pepper
1 teaspoon dry mustard
¼ teaspoon ground thyme
¼ teaspoon ground nutmeg
2 tablespoons chopped fresh parsley
1 cup dried bread crumbs
½ cup firmly packed brown sugar
1 teaspoon dry mustard
2 tablespoons fresh lemon juice
2 tablespoons cider vinegar
2 tablespoons water

Preheat oven to 350°F.

In a bowl mix the ham and pork together with your hands. Work in the eggs. Add onion, bell pepper, cider, salt, black pepper, mustard, thyme, nutmeg, and parsley. Mix thoroughly. Add the bread crumbs and work into the mixture. Form into a loaf shape and place in a baking pan. Bake 1 hour.

While ham loaf is baking, prepare the topping. Combine all the remaining ingredients in a saucepan and simmer 15 minutes.

Remove the ham loaf from the oven and baste with baking pan juices. Spoon the sugar topping over the loaf and return to the oven 30 minutes.

Beef Stew

Serves 8 to 10

Miss Jackie Harris, from down Tred Avon River Way, has been turning out this stew for her family for years. She told me "some things you cook and others you brew, and this here stew requires brewing." So you can call it stew but don't forget to brew, and you'll wind up with one of the most robust potions to have passed your lips in years.

5 tablespoons rendered beef fat or butter
3 pounds lean beef, cut in 2-inch cubes
Flour
2 large onions, sliced ½ inch thick
1 large carrot, peeled and chopped in ½-inch pieces
1 leek, halved and chopped
2 whole cloves
¼ teaspoon ground allspice

1 teaspoon dried thyme
1 bay leaf
Beef stock or bouillon to cover
4 medium potatoes, peeled and cut in sixths
4 carrots, peeled and quartered
Salt and black pepper to taste
1 cup corn kernels
Sour cream, for garnish

In a heavy pot heat the fat. Dredge the beef cubes in flour and shake off excess. Brown cubes well on all sides in hot fat, then remove with a slotted spoon. Add the onions and cook 3 to 5 minutes.

Return the meat to the pot. Add the chopped carrot, leek, cloves, allspice, thyme, bay leaf, and enough stock to cover meat. Bring to a boil. Cover the pot, reduce the heat, and simmer 2 hours, or until meat is tender. Add the potatoes and quartered carrots during the last 45 minutes of cooking. Season with salt and pepper. Add the corn the last 15 minutes of cooking.

Serve in bowls with a dollop of sour cream.

Panfried Pepper Steak with Mustard Butter

Serves 4

A fine way to liven up an old favorite. When preparing the mustard butter, make some extra to freeze. You'll find it flatters fresh steamed vegetables or a grilled piece of fish.

Mustard Butter (recipe follows)
1½ pounds beef steak, ½ to ¾ inch thick
1 tablespoon paprika
1 teaspoon black pepper, plus black pepper to taste
2 tablespoons butter
2 tablespoons vegetable oil

1 large onion, sliced
2 green bell peppers, thinly sliced
1 tablespoon chopped garlic
2 large ripe tomatoes, chopped
2 cups beef stock or bouillon, heated
Salt to taste
2 to 3 tablespoons flour (optional)

Prepare Mustard Butter and chill well.

Rub the steaks with paprika and 1 teaspoon black pepper. In a skillet heat the butter and oil. Brown the steaks well on both sides and remove from pan. Add the onion, bell peppers, and garlic. Cook 5 minutes. Return the steaks to the skillet. Add the tomatoes and stock. Season with salt and pepper to taste.

Cover and simmer gently 20 to 30 minutes. Remove the meat and vegetables to a platter and keep warm. Boil the cooking juices to reduce them, or, if desired, stir flour into the juices and cook, stirring, until thickened. Pour over steaks.

Cut the Mustard Butter in rounds and arrange on top of the steaks.

Mustard Butter

½ cup (¼ pound) butter, softened
2 teaspoons minced fresh chives
1 tablespoon prepared mustard, preferably Dijon

¼ teaspoon salt
Black pepper to taste

In a bowl whip together the butter, thyme, mustard, salt, and pepper until fluffy. Form in a log on waxed paper, wrap, and chill.

Crab Salad

Serves 4 or 5

Perfect as the focal point of a summer salad plate or piled high on a sandwich, this item tickles the fancy of the true crab lover.

1 cup diced celery
½ cup mayonnaise
1 tablespoon fresh lemon juice
Dash Tabasco sauce

¼ teaspoon Worcestershire sauce
½ teaspoon salt
Dash white pepper
1 pound backfin crabmeat, picked
   over for shells

In a mixing bowl combine all the ingredients except crabmeat and mix well. Add crabmeat and mix gently.

Green Tomato Fritters

Serves 4

A slightly sweet spiced batter makes unbelievably good tomato fritters. This recipe uses two tomatoes, but from what I've seen at the supper table it's best to have more on hand.

2 large green tomatoes
Milk to cover
1 cup flour
2 teaspoons baking powder
½ teaspoon salt

2 eggs, separated
1 teaspoon sugar
⅔ cup milk
Pinch ground mace
Vegetable oil, for deep-frying

Core the tomatoes and cut in ¼-inch-thick slices. Place in a shallow bowl and add milk to cover. Let stand while making the fritter batter.

In a bowl sift together the flour, baking powder, and salt. Stir in the egg yolks, sugar, milk, and mace. Beat the egg whites until stiff peaks form, then gently fold into batter. Heat the oil in a deep skillet to about 365°F.

Remove the tomato slices from the milk, dip in batter, and fry, a few at a time, in hot oil until golden brown on both sides, about 5 minutes. Remove with a slotted utensil to paper towels to drain. Serve hot.

Fresh Green Beans in Mustard-Cream Vinaigrette

Serves 3 or 4

The mustardy cream vinaigrette provides a zesty marinade for fresh summer green beans. This dish can be served as a salad or as a vegetable course.

Salted water
1 pound green beans, trimmed
2 tablespoons red wine vinegar or sherry wine vinegar
1 teaspoon minced shallots
1½ teaspoons Dijon mustard

¼ teaspoon salt
7 tablespoons olive oil
2 tablespoons sour cream
½ cup diced pimientos

In a large pot bring a generous amount of salted water to a boil. Drop in the green beans and cook until tender yet still crisp, about 6 to 8 minutes. Remove the beans from the pot and immerse in ice water to cool quickly. Drain.

In a small mixing bowl combine the vinegar, shallots, mustard, and salt. Mix well. Pour in the olive oil in a slow, thin stream, whisking vigorously until emulsified. Fold in the sour cream and pimientos. Coat the green beans with vinaigrette and marinate several hours before serving.

Bayside Biscuits

Makes about 2 dozen biscuits

My family would make the trip over to Tilghman in the summer to visit Aunt Catherine. I still remember these tender biscuits and how wonderful they were dipped in her chicken gravy.

About 3 cups flour
4 teaspoons baking powder
1 teaspoon salt
1 teaspoon sugar
¼ teaspoon cream of tartar

½ cup solid vegetable shortening or lard
½ cup water
½ cup milk

Preheat oven to 450°F.

In a mixing bowl sift together the 3 cups flour, baking powder, salt, sugar, and cream of tartar.

Cut in shortening with fingertips or a pastry blender until mixture has the consistency of coarse meal. Mix together water and milk and add to flour mixture, stirring until a stiff batter forms. If the dough is too sticky, add a little more flour.

Wrap and chill the dough for at least 30 minutes. On a lightly floured board roll out dough ½ inch thick. Cut dough in about 24 rounds and arrange on a baking sheet. Bake 10 minutes, or until nicely browned.

Sally Lunn

Makes one 10-inch cake or about
2 dozen buns

*You'll find this sweet cake with its
bun-like texture on many tables
on the Eastern Shore. It's said
that the recipe was brought to the
region by early settlers from England, where it was originated by
Sally in the eighteenth century.
She sold her baked goods on the
streets of Bath to earn a living.
Sally's creation caught on and the
rest is history.*

1 package active dry yeast
*¼ cup lukewarm (105° to 115°F)
   water*
*¾ cup (12 tablespoons) butter,
   softened*
½ cup sugar
1 teaspoon salt
4 eggs, beaten
*1 cup heavy cream or evaporated
   milk*
4 cups flour

Dissolve the yeast in the warm water and let stand until foamy, about
10 minutes.

In a large mixing bowl, cream together the butter and sugar. Beat in
the salt and eggs. Mix well. Add the milk and yeast mixture. Beat in the
flour, 1 cup at a time, until a soft dough forms. Cover the bowl with a tea
towel and let rise in a warm place until doubled in bulk, 2½ to 3 hours.

Preheat oven to 375°F.

Punch down the dough and distribute evenly in a well-buttered
10-inch tube pan. Cover and let rise until double in bulk. Bake 45 to 50
minutes. Turn out of pan onto a rack to cool.

NOTE: Sally Lunn can be formed into small buns by filling buttered muffin
tins half full. Cover and let rise until double in size. Bake for 20 to 25
minutes.

Hush Puppies

Serves 4

*As soon as one crosses the
Mason-Dixon Line, hush puppies
abound. Perhaps the dogs in the
South were quite an unruly lot
and it was necessary to come up
with something to keep their
traps shut. Marge Clark, who
hails from outside of St. Michaels,
gave me her family recipe. She
doesn't have a puppy but her cat
Smoots loves them.*

1 cup white cornmeal
½ teaspoon baking powder
½ teaspoon salt
3 tablespoons grated onion
1 egg, beaten
*2 tablespoons lard or solid vegetable
   shortening, melted and cooled*
½ cup milk
Vegetable oil, for deep-frying

In a large bowl mix together the cornmeal, baking powder, and salt.
In a small bowl mix together the onion, egg, shortening, and milk.

Beat the wet ingredients into the dry ingredients. Form into little balls.
Heat oil in a deep skillet to 375°F. Deep-fry balls, a few at a time, until
golden brown on all sides. Remove with a slotted utensil to paper towels to
drain.

Peach Pie

Makes one 9-inch pie,
serves 6 to 8

The aroma of this robust pie made from sweet summer peaches is absolutely intoxicating. My cousin Doris has a farm where I helped with fruit picking as a child. Everyone was always reminded on their way to the field to pick an extra basket so she could make some pies for dinner. I never forgot!

Pastry Dough for double-crust 9-inch pie (see page 31)
6 to 7 cups peeled, pitted, and sliced peaches (see page 215)
½ cup granulated sugar
½ cup firmly packed brown sugar
3 tablespoons flour
1 teaspoon ground cinnamon
½ teaspoon ground nutmeg
¼ teaspoon salt
¼ cup heavy cream
1 egg, beaten with 1 tablespoon water (optional)

Prepare pastry dough and line a 9-inch pie pan with half of the dough. Preheat oven to 450°F.

Slice the peaches. In a large bowl mix together the sugars, flour, cinnamon, nutmeg, and salt. Add the peaches and mix gently. Sprinkle in the cream and toss. Pour peaches into pie shell. On a lightly floured board, roll out remaining pastry to form a top crust, transfer to pan, and flute the edges. Make a few vents in the top for steam to escape. If desired, brush the top with egg-water wash. Bake 10 minutes, then reduce heat to 375°F and continue baking 40 to 45 minutes.

Baked Apples

Serves 4

There's no finer sensation than coming out of the crisp fall air, hands still chilly from a southwesterly blowing off the Bay, and inhaling the aroma of baking apples touched with spice.

4 tart apples
3 tablespoons granulated sugar
2 tablespoons brown sugar
¼ cup (4 tablespoons) butter, softened
4 teaspoons raisins
½ teaspoon ground cinnamon
Pinch ground nutmeg
Boiling water
Heavy cream or soft vanilla ice cream, for accompaniment

Preheat oven to 375°F.

Core each apple, hollowing out the center to form a cavity about ¾ inch in diameter.

In a small bowl mix together the sugars, butter, raisins, cinnamon, and nutmeg. Evenly distribute the mixture among the apple cavities.

Pour a little boiling water into bottom of a baking dish. Put the apples in the dish. Bake about 40 to 45 minutes, or until soft. Baste the apples several times during cooking with pan juices. Serve warm with cream or ice cream.

Bread Pudding

Serves 6 to 8

A Mrs. Terrell, from round St. Michaels way, gave this rendition of the peninsula cooks' favorite method of ridding themselves of leftover bread. As with many country recipes, this is just a foundation from which one can vary the dish as desired. Add some nuts, fresh ripe fruit, or a splash of rum to lift the spirits.

4 cups milk
1 cup raisins
2 cups stale bread cubes or pieces
4 eggs
1 cup sugar

¼ cup (4 tablespoons) butter, melted and cooled
1 teaspoon vanilla extract
½ teaspoon ground cinnamon
Heavy cream, for accompaniment

Preheat oven to 350°F.

Combine the milk and raisins in a saucepan and bring just to a boil. Put the bread in a large bowl and pour the hot milk and raisins over the top.

In a mixing bowl beat together the eggs, sugar, butter, vanilla, and cinnamon. Add to the bread mixture and mix well. Pour into a buttered 2-quart casserole. Bake 35 to 40 minutes, or until set.

Serve warm with cream.

Bread and Butter Pickles

Makes about 6 quarts

An old-fashioned pickle that graces many a table and pantry on the Eastern Shore.

18 to 20 cucumbers
12 small onions
Salted ice water to cover
5 cups white or cider vinegar
5 cups water
2½ cups sugar

1 cup salt
4 teaspoons celery seed
4 teaspoons mustard seed
1 teaspoon ground turmeric
1 teaspoon whole cloves
2 teaspoons ground ginger

Thinly slice the cucumbers and onions. Place in a bowl with salted ice water and let stand 3 to 4 hours.

In a large pot bring all the remaining ingredients to a boil. Drain the cucumbers and onions, add to the pot, and bring to a boil again. Simmer 15 to 20 minutes.

Ladle into hot, sterilized jars, seal, and process in a water bath according to standard canning procedures.

Chow-Chow

Makes about 3 quarts

You've got me! I can't quite figure out where this one came from, but you'll find it up and down the Eastern Shore of the Bay. It's one outstanding pickled product.

4 quarts green tomatoes (about 8 pounds)
Salted water to cover
10 onions
6 green bell peppers
6 red bell peppers
1 bunch celery

1 head cabbage
2 quarts cider vinegar
6 cups sugar
2 tablespoons ground turmeric
1 tablespoon celery seed
3 tablespoons mustard seed

Coarsely chop the tomatoes, onions, peppers, celery, and cabbage. Place in a large bowl and soak in salted water overnight.

The next day, combine the vinegar, sugar, turmeric, celery seed, and mustard seed. Bring to a boil.

Drain and squeeze out the vegetables. Add to the pot with the vinegar mixture and bring to a boil again. Cook 2 minutes. Put into hot, sterilized jars, seal, and process in a water bath according to standard canning procedures.

Shade Sippin' Iced Tea

Serves 4 or 5

12 tea bags or 4 tablespoons tea leaves
½ lemon, cut in slices
1 sprig mint

4 cups boiling water
Ice cubes, lemon slices, and fresh mint leaves, for serving

In a bowl or glass jar place the tea, lemon slices, and mint sprig. Pour boiling water over all. Steep 5 to 6 minutes, then strain, cover, and let stand at least 2 hours before serving.

Serve in tall glasses with plenty of ice, lemon slices, and mint leaves.

Helen Cummings at her Tilghman Island home on Knapp's Narrows.

At the end of the scenic drive along the Tilghman Peninsula, a small drawbridge serves as the gateway to Tilghman Island. The island is home to Mrs. Helen Cummings, the wife of a Chesapeake Bay waterman. She has spent her entire life on these waters of the Eastern Shore.

No matter how a conversation with Mrs. Cummings begins, it always turns to the Bay, the life source for this community. This is true for most of the conversations with Tilghman folk. The water is their life and that's what they talk about.

After years of crabbing, fishing, and oystering, Helen's hands possess an astonishing dexterity for "picking" crabs and seeking out the delicate crabmeat, or for shucking the countless oysters harvested from the waters near her home.

Mrs. Cummings is typical of other Tilghman residents in her habits and methods of taking the precious products from the Bay and the surrounding fields and "putting them up"—canning, pickling, and freezing them—for future use. There's little waste around these parts.

When I asked Helen to plan a special summer menu that would be representative of Tilghman Island, there was no hesitation before she shot back with "crab cakes!" Tilghman Crab Cakes are the highlight of the summer season. Her version of this Chesapeake Bay staple is virtually all blue crab, lightly spiced and delicately bound with cracker crumbs. The accompanying dishes, the Eastern Shore's finest Sweet Summer Corn on the Cob and a fresh-tasting creamy Country Coleslaw, are summer personified. Plus, there is a dish of Stewed Tomatoes, which is about as Eastern Shore as you can get. And for an ending to this summer feast, you will probably ask, "Can she bake a cherry pie?" Well just try it and see for yourself!

Tilghman Crab Cakes

Sweet Summer Corn on the Cob

Country Coleslaw

Stewed Tomatoes

Cherry Pie

Tilghman Crab Cakes

Serves 4

1 egg, beaten
1 heaping tablespoon mayonnaise
1 heaping tablespoon dry mustard
3 whole club crackers (or Saltines),
   crushed into fine crumbs
1 teaspoon Worcestershire sauce
Juice of ½ lemon

1 pound lump or backfin crabmeat,
   picked over for shells
Butter or vegetable oil, for cooking
Crackers, Tartar Sauce (see page
   15), and lemon wedges, for accompaniment

Preheat the broiler.

In a small bowl mix together all the ingredients except the crabmeat. Beat until well blended.

Place the crabmeat in a bowl and pour the egg mixture over the top. Mix gently so as not to break up the crab lumps. Form into small round cakes with your hands, or use an ice-cream scoop, which does nicely.

Broil the cakes, brushed with a little butter. Alternatively, heat oil in a skillet and fry on both sides until browned. Serve with crackers, Tartar Sauce, and lemon wedges.

Sweet Summer Corn on the Cob

Serves 4

4 to 6 ears sweet corn
Salted water
½ cup milk
¼ cup sugar

2 tablespoons butter, plus melted
   butter for accompaniment
Salt and black pepper, for accompaniment

Husk the corn and set aside.

In a pot large enough to hold corn, combine ample salted water, milk, sugar and the 2 tablespoons butter. Bring to a boil and add the corn. Cook over medium heat 10 to 15 minutes, or until as tender as you like.

Serve with melted butter, salt, and pepper.

Country Coleslaw

Serves 4

1 medium head cabbage, coarsely
   grated
1 carrot, finely grated
1¼ cups mayonnaise
1½ teaspoons distilled white vinegar

¼ cup sugar
6 tablespoons evaporated milk or
   heavy cream
Salt and black pepper to taste

Toss the cabbage and carrot together in a bowl.

In a small bowl make a dressing by mixing together the mayonnaise, vinegar, sugar, and milk.

Dress the cabbage and carrot with the mixture. Season with salt and pepper.

Stewed Tomatoes

Serves 4

10 ripe tomatoes, peeled, or 2 cans (16 ounces each) peeled whole to-matoes

2 tablespoons butter
5 tablespoons sugar
Salt and black pepper

In a heavy pot combine the tomatoes and butter and cook, covered, over low heat 1½ hours.

Mash the tomatoes. Add the sugar, salt, and pepper. Cook 30 minutes, stirring often.

Cherry Pie

Makes one 9-inch pie, serves 6

Pastry for double-crust 9-inch pie (see page 31)
4 cups tart cherries, pitted
1¼ cups sugar
¼ cup flour
⅛ teaspoon salt

2 tablespoons butter
Vanilla ice cream, for accompani-ment (optional)

Prepare pastry dough and line a 9-inch pie pan with half of the dough. Preheat oven to 450°F.

In a bowl toss the cherries with the sugar, flour, and salt. Pour cherries into the pie shell and dot with butter.

On a lightly floured board, roll out remaining pastry to form a top crust, transfer to pan, and flute the edges. Make a few vents in the top for steam to escape.

Bake 10 minutes. Reduce heat to 350°F and bake 45 minutes, or until the crust is nicely browned.

Cool and serve as is, or better yet, with vanilla ice cream.

• Mouth of the Bay •

A lone bushel basket of blue crabs makes its way to the mainland aboard the Tangier Island mail boat. Accessible only by boat, Tangier Island has remained truly sheltered from the rest of the world for hundreds of years. The locals speak a unique language that is flavored with a distinctly Elizabethan dialect.

Here, where the waters of the Chesapeake Bay merge with the briny currents of the Atlantic Ocean, sits the city of Norfolk, Virginia, to the south, and Crisfield, Maryland, to the north. Situated in between are Tangier and Smith islands.

Norfolk, before World War II, was a small southern city whose primary commerce was its shipping port and a fishing industry. Now, as site of the world's largest naval base and home of the Atlantic headquarters of NATO, the city has become quite prosperous and cosmopolitan. Its history and old southern charm can still be experienced through the style and flavor of its cooking, however. The culinary world is more than familiar with the Norfolk tradition of pairing fresh shellfish with Smithfield ham, as exemplified in the elegant Norfolk Seafood Soufflé.

Tangier and Smith islands are both totally dependent on the Bay for their survival. These communities, until recently, were virtually cut off from the outside world. From these islands we get the true taste of a waterman's fifty clam chowder and other seafood prepared fresh from the Bay.

Crisfield, Maryland, labeled the Seafood Capital of the Country, was literally built on the shells of oysters. It is known worldwide as a mecca for soft-shell and blue crabs. Each summer Crisfield is home to the Miss Crustacean Beauty Pageant and to the Hard Crab Derby, the Chesapeake's version of the Indianapolis 500. Visit during derby time and you can sample delectable Crisfield Crab Cakes and the almost-still-kicking Fried Soft-shell Crabs. The soft-shell crab also shows itself off in the unique Crisfield Softshell Crab and Sweet Corn Chowder.

This region, in response to its sometimes harsh climate and environment, breeds a hale-and-hardy people with a partially learned, partially inherent respect for the Bay. The respect is evident in the honest preparation of their foods.

Salt Herring with Boiled Potatoes and Dill Cream

Serves 6 to 8

Salt herring was very popular with the old-timers. Miss Mary, a diehard salt-herring fan of Norfolk, gave me this recipe and explained that the herring was traditionally soaked on Saturday nights for serving on Sunday mornings. Salting fish is a venerable method of preservation that was common before adequate methods of refrigeration were developed. This dish makes a hearty, tasteful breakfast.

1 cup shredded salt herring
   or salt cod
Warm water
2 tablespoons butter
2 tablespoons flour
1 cup heavy cream
¼ teaspoon Tabasco sauce
Salt and black pepper to taste

Dash ground nutmeg
1 tablespoon chopped fresh dill
4 medium potatoes, peeled, boiled,
   and kept warm
Butter, for accompaniment
3 tablespoons chopped, cooked bacon,
   for garnish

Soak the salt herring in warm water 4 to 6 hours, to remove saltiness. Change water at least twice during the soaking. Drain and, with your fingertips, shred the flesh; it should measure about 1 cup.

In a pan melt the butter and stir in the flour. Cook a few minutes, stirring constantly. Do not brown the flour.

Off the heat whisk in the cream. Add the Tabasco, salt, pepper, and nutmeg. Bring to a boil, stirring continuously, and cook until slightly thickened. Stir in the dill.

Drain the cod and add to the sauce. Simmer briefly to heat cod through.

Quarter or slightly mash the potatoes and butter them. Spoon herring and sauce over potatoes and sprinkle with bacon.

Norfolk Red Flannel Hash

Serves 6

Miss Bobbie Gladding, a Norfolk seamstress, speaks with fond memory of her mother, who cre-ated this hash. She was of Boston heritage and grew up eating New England hash made with corned beef. She decided that the hams of her new home would do wonders for the dish. And they do just that. The "red flannel" refers to the color imparted by the beets.

½ cup (¼ pound) butter
1 onion, finely chopped
2 cups ground or finely chopped
   Smithfield ham
2 cups diced, peeled, boiled potatoes

1 cup diced, peeled, boiled beets
½ teaspoon black pepper
6 eggs, poached and kept warm
Hot sauce, for accompaniment

In a skillet melt ¼ cup of the butter and sauté the onion until soft. In a bowl combine the onion, ham, potatoes, beets, and pepper; mix well.

In a heavy skillet, melt the remaining ¼ cup butter and spread the hash mixture in the skillet. Cook until brown on the underside, making sure a nice crust has formed. Flip over and brown the other side.

Serve topped with poached eggs. Make sure to put a bottle of hot sauce out on the table for those who need a little something extra to get them going.

Lu-Lu's Peach and Pecan French Toast

Serves 4

Her real name is Lou Ann Barker and she hails from around Deal Island way, but to friends she's Lu-Lu. She has a favorite line when talking about people, places, or things: "Well [she, he, or it] is southern enough to drink out of Dixie cups!"

And that's how she refers to her famous French toast recipe.

6 eggs
¼ cup granulated sugar
2 cups heavy cream
1 teaspoon plus pinch ground cinnamon
2 pinches ground nutmeg
¼ cup (4 tablespoons) butter, plus
   butter for browning

¼ cup firmly packed brown sugar
½ cup water
3 ripe peaches, peeled, pitted, and
   sliced (see Note)
¼ cup coarsely chopped pecans
8 slices bread, preferably a bit stale

In a bowl beat together well the eggs and granulated sugar. Stir in the cream, 1 teaspoon cinnamon, and 1 pinch nutmeg.

To make the topping, melt the ¼ cup butter in a pan and beat in the brown sugar. Stir in the water and a pinch each cinnamon and nutmeg. Cook until mixture forms a light syrup. Put in the peaches and pecans. Simmer until peaches are tender.

Heat a skillet and lightly butter the bottom to prevent toast from stick-ing. Soak the bread slices in the egg mixture. Cook in skillet until browned on both sides, about 3 minutes per side. Top with the warm peach syrup.

NOTE: To peel peaches, drop them in boiling water and let stand 2 to 3 minutes. Remove from pan and slip off peels.

• *Mouth of the Bay Appetizers* •

Hot Crab Dip

Serves 10 to 12

Dips flourish all over these parts, in Crisfield, Deal Island, and over in Norfolk. I waded (literally) through tons of dip concoctions and this here "cracker topper" won the prize. If you prefer a bit more fire in your dip (as I do), double the amount of horseradish. Caution: It sets some people to sneezing.

8 ounces cream cheese, softened
2 tablespoons heavy cream
2 tablespoons grated onion
1 teaspoon prepared horseradish
1 teaspoon Old Bay seasoning
4 ounces sharp Cheddar cheese, grated
2 tablespoons chopped fresh parsley or chives
1 pound backfin or special crabmeat, picked over for shells
Crackers or French bread slices, for accompaniment

Preheat oven to 350°F.

In a bowl blend the cream cheese and cream until smooth. Mix in the onion, horseradish, Old Bay, cheese, and parsley. Gently fold in the crabmeat. Pour into a buttered 1½-quart casserole. Cover and bake 20 to 25 minutes.

Serve hot with crackers.

Tomato Pie

Serves 6 to 8

A fantastic appetizer or, as peculiar as it may sound, dessert. That's true, and I've seen it served both ways. It is perfect as a lunch dish with a tossed salad of dandelion greens and chopped hard-cooked eggs. The contrast of the bitter greens and sweetness of the pie is wonderful. For dessert, a dollop of whipped cream, slightly sweetened with maple syrup, works well. Now how's that for one pie!

Pastry dough for single-crust pie (see page 31)
6 ripe tomatoes, peeled and cut in ½-inch-thick slices
½ cup firmly packed brown sugar
Salt and black pepper to taste
Pinch ground mace
1 cup dried bread crumbs
1 tablespoon fresh lemon juice
¼ cup (4 tablespoons) butter
1 egg, beaten with 1 tablespoon water

Prepare pastry dough, wrap, and chill. Preheat oven to 350°F.

Butter the bottom of a 9-inch pie pan. Make a layer of tomato slices in pan and sprinkle with some of the sugar, salt, pepper, mace, and bread crumbs. Continue making layers as described, ending with bread crumbs. Sprinkle on lemon juice and dot with butter.

On a lightly floured board, roll out pastry to form a top crust, transfer to pan, and flute edges. Brush the top with egg-water. Bake 30 to 35 minutes, or until nicely browned.

Crisfield Fried Manos

Serves 4 to 6

The soft-shell clams from the Chesapeake are known as manninose, or manos for short (see page 10 for more information). Clam-feast groupies rate these critters as some of the best to be had. They eat them like peanuts, so keep the cooking fat hot and be ready to fry some more.

4 eggs, beaten
1 cup milk
1 teaspoon salt
1 cup flour
1 cup yellow cornmeal
Vegetable oil, for deep-frying

Tangy Cocktail Sauce (see page 29) or Tartar Sauce (see page 15) and lemon wedges, for accompaniment
4 cups shucked soft-shell clams (manos)

In a bowl mix the eggs, milk, and salt together. In another bowl mix the flour and cornmeal together.

In a deep skillet heat the oil to 375°F. Dip the clams into the egg mixture, then toss them in the cornmeal mixture and shake off the excess. Fry in the hot deep fat, a few at a time, 1 to 1½ minutes, or until golden brown. Do not overcook because it toughens the clams. Remove with a slotted utensil to paper towels to drain.

Serve with Tangy Cocktail Sauce and plenty of lemon wedges.

Soft-Shell Crab and Sweet Corn Chowder

Serves 4

The most superbly decadent chowder one could ever imagine. I think this recipe could have only been conceived of around this part of the Bay, with its easy access to low-cost soft-shells. In most metropolitan areas the softs are a pricy item, making this a decidedly upscale down-home chowder.

1 cube (2 inches) salt pork, cut in small pieces
1 large onion, thinly sliced
3 stalks celery, diced
3 cups half-and-half
1 cup Fish Stock (see page 35)
1 teaspoon salt
½ teaspoon black pepper
½ teaspoon dried thyme
1 bay leaf
4 cups peeled, diced potatoes
3 cups corn kernels
6 soft-shell crabs, cleaned and quartered (see page 7)
¼ cup (4 tablespoons) butter
Crackers, for accompaniment

In a pot render fat from the salt pork. Add the onion and celery to the pot and sauté several minutes. Pour in the half-and-half and stock. Add salt, pepper, thyme, and bay leaf and bring to a boil. Add the potatoes and simmer until barely tender. Stir in the corn and cook 10 minutes.

Add the soft-shell crabs and simmer 15 to 20 minutes. Off the heat stir in the butter, then serve with crackers.

Deal Island Summer Tomato Soup

Serves 8 to 10

A light soup with the flavor of ripe summer tomatoes bursting through. I suggest serving it with freshly made garlic croutons.

1 cup (½ pound) butter
2 cups diced onions
2 cups diced celery
3 green bell peppers, diced
2 tablespoons chopped garlic (optional)
3 cups water
4 pounds tomatoes, peeled and quartered
4 teaspoons sugar
2 teaspoons salt
2 bay leaves
1 teaspoon dried thyme or 6 fresh basil leaves, chopped
¼ teaspoon ground nutmeg
Freshly ground black pepper and garlic croutons, for garnish

In a soup pot melt the butter. Add the onions, celery, bell peppers, and garlic, if using. Cook, stirring, 10 minutes, being careful not to burn the vegetables. Add the water, bring to a boil, and simmer 30 to 40 minutes.

Add the tomatoes, sugar, salt, bay leaves, thyme, and nutmeg. Simmer 45 minutes.

Pass the soup through a sieve. Return to the pot and reheat to serving temperature. Adjust seasonings.

Serve in soup bowls topped with freshly ground pepper and croutons.

Norfolk Seafood Stew

Serves 6

The epitome of summer shore living and dining. The finest ingredients are brought together from the waters of the Bay, the smokehouse, and the fields.

6 tablespoons butter
1 cup diced onions
1 leek, quartered, and chopped
1 clove garlic, chopped
¼ cup (4 tablespoons) flour
⅔ cup diced Smithfield ham
4 cups Fish Stock (see page 35)
1 cup dry white wine
2 cups peeled, quartered tomatoes
1 cup peeled, diced potatoes
1 teaspoon salt

4 threads saffron, ground or finely minced
1 bay leaf
½ pound bass, cod, or other firm-fleshed fish fillets, cut in chunks
1 pound soft-shell clams (manos), well washed
½ pound special crabmeat, picked over for shells
Tabasco sauce and hot crusty bread, for accompaniment

In a heavy-bottomed soup pot, melt the butter and sauté the onions, leek, and garlic until soft. Stir in the flour and cook, stirring constantly, 3 minutes.

Add the ham, stock, wine, tomatoes, potatoes, salt, saffron, and bay leaf. Bring to a boil, reduce the heat, and simmer for 40 minutes.

Stir in the fish, clams, and crabmeat. Cover and cook until the clams open.

Serve in bowls with Tabasco on the side and lots of crusty bread.

Norfolk Seafood Soufflé

Serves 4

The distinctive invention of the Norfolk cooking style is the pairing of Smithfield ham and seafood. The refinement of the Old South comes across in this truly impressive soufflé.

1 cup backfin or lump crabmeat, picked over for shells
½ cup finely diced Smithfield ham
½ cup peeled, chopped steamed shrimp
3 tablespoons butter
3 tablespoons flour
1 cup milk

2 tablespoons dry sherry
4 egg yolks
Salt, black pepper, and ground nutmeg to taste
¼ teaspoon Tabasco sauce
⅔ cup grated Swiss cheese
6 egg whites

Preheat oven to 375°F.

In a bowl toss together the crabmeat, ham, and shrimp. Set aside.

In an enamel pan melt the butter and whisk in the flour. Cook 2 minutes, stirring constantly. Do not brown the flour.

Off the heat gradually whisk in the milk and sherry. Return to the heat and bring almost to a boil, stirring all the while. Beat in the egg yolks, one at a time. Season well with salt, pepper, and nutmeg. Stir in the Tabasco and all but 3 tablespoons of the cheese. Gently fold in crabmeat mixture. Beat the egg whites until stiff peaks form and gently fold into soufflé mixture.

Butter a 2-quart soufflé dish and sprinkle the reserved cheese on the bottom. Pour in the soufflé mixture and bake about 30 minutes, or until nicely browned and firm. Serve at once.

Baked Stuffed Fish

Serves 4

A typical Eastern Shore dinner special. Not much fussing goes on with the stuffing, and after sampling you'll see why. It stands out all by itself and sings a beautiful song of seafood taste.

1 pound backfin crabmeat, picked over for shells
6 tablespoons butter, melted and cooled
Salt and ground pepper to taste

2 tablespoons chopped fresh parsley
1 whole rockfish, black bass, bluefish, or flounder (3 to 3½ pounds), dressed
Milk, as needed

Preheat oven to 350°F.

In a bowl place the crabmeat, pour the melted butter over the top, and toss. Season with salt and pepper. Mix in the parsley. Stuff the crab mixture inside of the fish and secure with skewers or sew together.

Cover the bottom of a baking dish with milk about ¼ inch deep. Place fish in the dish. Sprinkle lightly with salt and pepper.

Bake 50 minutes to 1 hour, or until fish flakes at the touch of a fork. Baste occasionally during baking with the milk from the dish.

Crisfield Crab Cakes

Serves 4

Yet another illustration of the multistyled crab cake. I was virtually raised on crab cakes, but had never tried this preparation, a simple approach that brings forth the pure essence of the precious blue crabmeat.

Down in this part of the Bay, life is not always easy, but it is pleasantly simple. And the locals can't see taking a delicious commodity like crabmeat and covering it up with a lot of heavy sauces. What you get with these crab cakes is a mouthful of pure crustacean ecstasy.

1 egg, beaten
½ cup (¼ pound) butter, melted
1 tablespoon fresh lemon juice
1 tablespoon Worcestershire sauce
2 tablespoons chopped fresh parsley
1 pound backfin crabmeat, picked over for shells

1 cup dried bread crumbs
Vegetable oil, for frying
Tartar Sauce (see page 15) and lemon wedges, for accompaniment

In a small bowl mix together well egg, butter, lemon juice, Worcestershire, and parsley. Place crabmeat in a bowl and pour egg mixture over the top. Mix gently, then sprinkle with bread crumbs and toss. Form mixture into 8 cakes.

In a heavy skillet pour in oil to a depth of about ½ inch. Fry crab cakes in hot oil on both sides until golden brown, about 3 minutes per side. Remove with a slotted utensil to paper towels to drain. (These crab cakes are also wonderful broiled.)

Serve with Tartar Sauce and lemon wedges.

Fried Soft-shell Crabs—Crisfield Style

Serves 4

Crisfield is soft-shell crab country. The townspeople live them, breathe them, catch them, and cook them better than anyone anywhere else in the world. The softs are fresher than fresh here, and cooks don't horse around with lots of fancy ways of preparing them.

Make sure that when you purchase soft-shells they are alive and kicking. Fry them as described here, and enjoy one of the real treasures of the Chesapeake Bay.

8 prime soft-shell crabs, cleaned (see page 159)
1 cup flour
1 teaspoon salt
¼ teaspoon black pepper
¼ teaspoon cayenne pepper
½ cup (¼ pound) clarified butter
Tartar Sauce (see page 15) and lemon wedges, for accompaniment

Dry the crabs well. Mix the flour, salt, and peppers together. Dust soft-shells with the seasoned flour.

In a skillet, heat the butter and fry the soft-shells until nicely browned. This doesn't take long, just a couple minutes on each side, so don't overcook. Drain well on paper towels and serve with Tartar Sauce and lemon wedges.

SOFT-SHELL SANDWICH VARIATION: On every Chesapeake menu you will find soft-shells served in a sandwich. They use white bread slathered with mayonnaise and put in a leaf of iceberg lettuce. This may sound like a waste of soft-shells, but people love it, and the crab claws sticking out from between the bread slices are nice and crunchy.

Miss Tootsie's Bourbon and Pecan Soft-shell Crabs

Serves 4

Now, to be sure, Crisfield is the capital of soft-shells, but Miss Tootsie of the Virginia shore doesn't believe they have a monopoly on them. Miss Tootsie still dons her white gloves and her hat with a wispy lace veil before marketing. She believes in "proper" manners when entertaining, and she believes this soft-shell technique to be the best in Norfolk.

This is a bit more complex than the Crisfield version (see preceding recipe), but it produces a marvelous taste sensation when you bite into the crabs and encounter the wonderfully crisp, nutty coating.

8 prime soft-shell crabs, cleaned (see page 159)
½ cup flour seasoned with salt and black pepper
3 eggs, beaten
1 cup pecans, toasted and finely ground, plus 16 pecan halves

12 tablespoons clarified butter
¼ cup bourbon whiskey
Juice of 1 lemon
1 tablespoon chopped fresh parsley
Salt and black pepper to taste

Dry the crabs. Dust them in the seasoned flour, then dip them in the eggs. Coat lightly with ground pecans.

In a skillet heat 9 tablespoons of the butter and sauté the soft-shells for 3 minutes on each side, until golden brown. Take care during the cooking so that the pecans don't burn. Remove soft-shells from the pan and drain on paper towels.

Turn up the heat to high and deglaze the pan with the whiskey. Add the remaining 3 tablespoons butter and briefly sauté the pecan halves. Squeeze in the lemon juice and add the parsley. Season with salt and pepper.

Arrange the soft-shells on a platter and pour pan sauce over them.

Waterman's Chicken

Serves 4

The watermen are a good solid lot who turn out a mean pot of fish or fowl. Seems that back in the 1800s, maybe due to the great oyster demand, the watermen developed a taste for carbonated beverages made from cola nut and coco leaves. These drinks delivered a somewhat "natural" stimulant and those oysters were soon flying out of the bay.

Things have since settled down. And this chicken dish is a good way to settle down for a fine dinner and evening of good conversation with friends.

1 frying chicken (2½ to 3 pounds), cut in serving pieces
3 tablespoons butter
3 tablespoons vegetable oil
1 onion, chopped
1 leek, halved lengthwise and chopped
½ pound fresh mushrooms, quartered
3 tablespoons flour
4 cups peeled, seeded, and coarsely chopped tomatoes

2 cups Chicken Stock (see page 33) or bouillon
1 tablespoon Worcestershire sauce
½ teaspoon Tabasco sauce
½ teaspoon dried thyme
1 bay leaf
Salt and black pepper to taste
Boiled potatoes, for accompaniment

Dry chicken pieces well. In a dutch oven or flameproof casserole, heat the butter and oil. Brown the chicken well on all sides. Remove from the casserole and set aside. Add onion, leek, and mushrooms to the pot and sauté 5 minutes. Stir in flour and cook 2 minutes, stirring all the while.

Add all the remaining ingredients, mix well, and return chicken pieces to pot. Bring to a boil, cover, and simmer over low heat about 40 minutes.

Serve with boiled potatoes.

Deer Loaf

Serves 6 to 8

This sure is a change from a midweek meat loaf. It is actually an occasion. Ground veal and beef are added to the deer meat to mellow the gamy flavor. Try it and increase or decrease the deer meat to your liking. This loaf is wonderfully robust.

3 biscuits Shredded Wheat
Milk, as needed
2 eggs, beaten
1 pound deer meat, ground
½ pound ground veal
½ pound ground beef
1 small onion, finely diced
2 stalks celery, finely diced

¼ green bell pepper, finely diced
1 cup chopped tomatoes
1 tablespoon Worcestershire sauce
2 teaspoons dried oregano
Salt and black pepper to taste
Peeled, quartered potatoes and carrots (optional)

Preheat oven to 375°F.

In a bowl soak the biscuits in just enough milk to soften. When soft, mash with a fork and blend with the eggs.

Put the ground meats in a large bowl and mix together well. Add the biscuit mixture, onion, celery, bell pepper, tomatoes, Worcestershire sauce, oregano, salt, and ground pepper. Work the mixture with your hands until everything is combined.

Shape into a loaf and put in a baking pan. Pour hot water into the bottom of the baking pan to reach about ¼ inch up the side of the loaf. Bake about 1 hour.

If desired, place potatoes and carrots around loaf during the last 40 minutes of cooking.

Jill's Potted Pheasant

Serves 2

You're probably thinking that this bird's got a drinking problem. Not so. "Potted" simply refers to a stewing or braising method. Jill, from Pocomoke City, says that young birds need to be hung a day or two before cooking, to bring up their flavor. Serve the pheasant with buttered noodles or roasted potatoes.

1 pheasant (about 2½ pounds), cut in serving pieces
Flour seasoned with salt and black pepper
½ cup solid vegetable shortening or lard
2 onions, thinly sliced
2 leeks, quartered lengthwise and finely chopped

1½ cups heavy cream
Juice of 1 lemon
1 bay leaf
Pinch ground mace
Salt and freshly ground black pepper to taste

Dredge the pheasant pieces in the seasoned flour. In a dutch oven or flameproof casserole, heat the shortening. Brown the pheasant well on all sides.

Arrange the onions and leeks on top and around pheasant. Add all the remaining ingredients. Bring to a boil, cover, reduce the heat, and simmer about 1 hour, or until pheasant is tender.

Tangy Peach Short Ribs of Beef

Serves 3 to 4

These ribs are so tender the meat falls from the bone. The spiced peaches make for a sweet and tasty rib that's finger-licking good.

3 pounds beef short ribs, cut in 3-inch pieces
Flour seasoned with salt, black pepper, and cayenne pepper
¼ cup vegetable oil or rendered beef fat
1 onion, finely diced

2 cloves garlic, minced
¾ cup beef stock or bouillon
2 cups peeled, sliced peaches
3 tablespoons dark brown sugar
3 tablespoons cider vinegar
½ teaspoon ground cinnamon
¼ teaspoon ground cloves

Preheat oven to 325°F.

Dust the ribs in the seasoned flour. In a dutch oven heat the oil and brown the ribs well on all sides. Remove the ribs and set aside. Pour off all but 3 tablespoons of the fat from the pot. Add the onion and garlic to the pot and sauté briefly.

Return the ribs to the pot and add all the remaining ingredients. Mix well, bring to a boil, and cover pot.

Place pot in the oven and bake 1½ to 2 hours, basting the ribs often.

Lamb Fricassee

Serves 5 or 6

A fragrant lamb and vegetable stew. Lots of hot crusty bread and a tossed garden salad will round out the meal.

3 tablespoons butter
3 tablespoons vegetable oil or rendered lamb fat
2½ pounds lamb shoulder, cut in 1-inch cubes
Flour, for dusting, plus ¼ cup flour
2 leeks, quartered lengthwise and chopped
1 large onion, coarsely chopped
1 tablespoon chopped garlic

4 carrots, peeled and quartered
4 small potatoes, peeled and quartered
Salt and black pepper to taste
1 sprig rosemary
1 bay leaf
½ pound green beans, trimmed
1 cup corn kernels
⅔ cup heavy cream

Dust the lamb cubes in flour. In a heavy pot heat the butter and oil and brown the lamb cubes well. Remove lamb from the pot. Add the leeks, onion, and garlic to the pot and sauté 3 to 4 minutes. Add the ¼ cup flour and stir several minutes.

Return lamb to the pot. Add just enough water to cover the meat. Bring to a boil, reduce the heat, and simmer, uncovered, 1 hour.

Add the carrots, potatoes, salt, pepper, rosemary, and bay leaf. Cook until the vegetables are almost tender. At this time add the green beans, corn, and heavy cream. Cook until vegetables and meat are tender.

Adjust seasonings and serve.

Braised Beef Tongue

Serves 6 to 8

Country cooking has always been known for its use of every part of the animal, and beef tongue is well liked by many around the Bay. Tongue is a versatile meat and lends itself especially well to braising recipes. I find this preparation particularly fine-tasting. If you have been leery of eating tongue, this is a perfect starting point.

1 beef tongue (2½ to 3 pounds)
½ pound smoked bacon, sliced
4 thin slices Smithfield ham
2 large onions, finely diced
2 carrots, finely diced
2 stalks celery, finely diced
1½ cups beef stock or bouillon, heated

1 cup dry white wine
2 cups peeled, seeded, and chopped tomatoes
½ teaspoon salt
¼ teaspoon black pepper
1 bay leaf
½ teaspoon dried thyme

Soak the tongue in water to cover 4 to 5 hours. Change the water 2 or 3 times.

Bring a saucepan filled with water to a boil and blanch the bacon several minutes; drain.

Place the tongue in a dutch oven or flameproof casserole. Cover with about half of the slices of bacon. Put the remaining bacon, ham, onions, carrots, and celery in the pot around the tongue. Pour in the stock, wine, tomatoes, salt, pepper, bay leaf, and thyme. Bring to a boil, cover, reduce the heat, and simmer about 2 hours.

Remove the tongue from the pot and cut off gristle and bones at broad end. Starting at the broad end, peel off the skin. Slice tongue and serve on a deep platter topped with bacon and ham slices. Strain the juices and serve over the sliced tongue.

• *Mouth of the Bay Vegetables* •

Country Asparagus

Serves 4 to 6

The asparagus season doesn't last long around the Bay, but while it does the locals just can't get enough of the spears. Around these parts asparagus is topped with a Hollandaise Sauce (see page 26) for special occasions. But even without the Hollandaise, the fresh spears are something to celebrate.

2 pounds asparagus
Salt to taste
6 tablespoons butter

Salt and black pepper to taste
Juice of 1 lemon

Cut off the tough ends of the asparagus. Tie spears into about 4 bundles with string.

Select a pot that is tall enough to accommodate the asparagus standing upright. Fill half full with water and add salt to taste. Bring to a boil. Place the asparagus bundles stem ends down, in the boiling water. Cover and boil about 8 to 10 minutes, or until tender but still somewhat crisp. Remove bundles from the pot and cut off strings.

In a large skillet melt the butter. Gently toss the asparagus in the butter, then season with salt, pepper, and lemon juice.

Stuffed Eggplant

Serves 5 to 6

Add some cooked crabmeat, shrimp, or chicken to this stuffing and you will have turned a vege-table dish into a complete meal.

2 small eggplants
6 tablespoons butter, plus butter for topping
1 onion, finely chopped
2 tablespoons chopped garlic
4 tomatoes, peeled, seeded, and chopped

2 tablespoons fresh lemon juice
2 tablespoons chopped fresh parsley
2 cups dried bread crumbs, plus bread crumbs for topping
Salt and black pepper to taste
1 cup hot water

Preheat oven to 350°F.

Cut the eggplants in half lengthwise and scoop out the pulp, forming walls about ¼ inch thick so that the eggplant shells will hold together. Chop the pulp.

Melt the 6 tablespoons butter in a skillet and sauté the onion and garlic 2 to 3 minutes. Add the chopped eggplant, tomatoes, and lemon juice. Cook

5 minutes. Add the parsley and 2 cups bread crumbs. Season with salt and pepper.

Stuff pulp mixture into the eggplant shells. Place them in a buttered baking dish and pour the water in the bottom. Sprinkle bread crumbs on top and dot with butter. Bake about 40 minutes.

Hot Slaw

Serves 4 to 6

A fantastic change of pace from mayonnaise-dressed slaws. Perfect on a luncheon buffet or as a vegetable side dish to accompany pork or beef.

⅓ cup red wine vinegar
1 teaspoon prepared mustard
½ teaspoon celery seed
3 tablespoons sugar
1 teaspoon salt

¼ cup vegetable oil
¼ cup bacon drippings
½ teaspoon black pepper
1 small head cabbage, chopped

In a pot combine all the ingredients except the cabbage. Heat, stirring to dissolve the sugar. Add the cabbage and stir to coat. Cover and cook 8 to 10 minutes. Serve hot, of course.

• Mouth of the Bay Breads •

Cheese Biscuits

Makes 8 to 10 biscuits

Cheese breads, turnovers, and all manner of other cheese and wheat teams abound in Chesapeake cookery. I prefer making my cheese biscuits with a good-quality sharp Cheddar, but they can be made with any sharp cheese of your liking.

1 cup flour
1½ teaspoons baking powder
¼ teaspoon salt

2 tablespoons lard or solid vegetable shortening
¼ cup milk
⅔ cup grated sharp Cheddar cheese

Preheat oven to 400°F.

Sift together the flour, baking powder, and salt. Work in the lard with fingertips or a pastry blender until mixture is the consistency of coarse meal. Mix in the milk and cheese.

Turn dough out onto a floured board and knead about 1 minute. Roll out the dough ½ inch thick and cut out 8 to 10 rounds with a biscuit cutter.

Arrange on a baking sheet and bake about 15 minutes, or until golden. Serve hot or at room temperature.

Hominy Muffins

Makes about 2 dozen muffins

These yeasted country muffins have the mellow flavor of hominy. They make fabulous breads to offer your breakfast guests.

1 cup milk
1 cup canned hominy, drained
¼ cup (4 tablespoons) butter, melted
¼ cup sugar
1 teaspoon salt

2 tablespoons grated orange rind
½ package active dry yeast
¼ cup lukewarm (105° to 115°F) water
3½ cups flour

In a saucepan bring the milk just to a boil, then pour into a bowl. Add the hominy, butter, sugar, salt, and orange rind and mix well. Stir until lukewarm.

Sprinkle the yeast in warm water and let stand until foamy, about 10 minutes. Mix yeast mixture into milk mixture.

Beat in flour, 1 cup at a time. Cover the bowl with a tea towel and let stand in a warm place overnight.

In the morning, punch down the dough and divide it among about 24 buttered muffin-tin wells, filling each about two thirds full. Cover and let rise in a warm place 1 hour.

Preheat oven to 400°F and bake muffins 15 to 20 minutes, or until golden. Serve hot.

Rhubarb Bread

Makes 2 loaves

Mouth of the Bay folklore has it that rhubarb is to be used as a spring tonic. After being cooped up during a blustery winter, one's blood needs freshening. I've never been keen on chewing on rhubarb stalks, so I tried perking up my weary blood with this bread. I felt better right away, plus it's one of the most delicious health remedies to be found.

1 cup (½ pound) butter, melted
1½ cups firmly packed brown sugar
2 eggs
1 cup milk
1 teaspoon vanilla extract
2½ cups flour

1 teaspoon salt
1½ teaspoons baking soda
1½ cups finely diced, peeled rhubarb (see Note)
⅔ cup chopped pecans

Preheat oven to 350°F.

In a large bowl cream together the butter, sugar, and eggs. Beat in the milk and vanilla.

In another bowl sift together the flour, salt, and baking soda. Add to the creamed mixture and stir until smooth.

Fold in the rhubarb and pecans. Pour into 2 greased and floured, 9-by 5-inch loaf pans. Bake 50 minutes, or until a toothpick inserted into the center of the loaves comes out clean.

NOTE: To peel rhubarb, use a paring knife and cut almost all the way through, toward the rounded smooth side. Pull the skin down the sides of the stalks and the fibrous strings will come right off.

Squash Pie

Makes one 9-inch pie,
serves 6 to 8

A local standard that takes this
fine summer vegetable and blends
it into the smoothest savory custard pie imaginable.

Pastry for single-crust 9-inch pie (see
   page 31)
2½ cups steamed and strained yellow
   or pattypan squash
⅔ cup sugar
3 eggs, beaten

1 teaspoon salt
½ teaspoon ground cinnamon
¼ teaspoon ground nutmeg
¼ teaspoon ground mace
2 cups heavy cream

Prepare pastry dough and line a 9-inch pie pan. Preheat oven to 450°F.
   Steam the squash until very tender and force through a sieve or colander;
you should have 2½ cups sieved pulp.
   In a bowl beat together the sugar and eggs until fluffy. Mix in the salt,
spices, and cream. Add the squash to the bowl and mix well. Pour mixture
into the pie crust.
   Bake 15 minutes. Reduce heat to 325°F and bake 30 minutes more, or
until set. Best served while still a bit warm.

Old-fashioned Chess Pie

Makes one 9-inch pie,
serves 6 to 8

Now you're talking "old timey"
and southern to boot. Serve
warm, topped with lightly
whipped cream.

Pastry for single-crust 9-inch pie (see
   page 31), partially baked
½ cup (¼ pound) butter, softened
½ cup granulated sugar
½ cup firmly packed dark brown
   sugar

3 eggs
1 tablespoon yellow cornmeal
2 tablespoons fresh lemon juice
1 teaspoon vanilla extract

Prepare pastry dough and line a 9-inch pie pan. Preheat oven to 350°F.
   In a bowl cream together the butter and sugars. Beat in the eggs,
cornmeal, fresh lemon juice, and vanilla. Mix well.
   Pour into pie shell and bake 45 minutes, or until browned and set.

Strawberry-Rhubarb Pie

Makes one 9-inch pie,
serves 6 to 8

A more perfect match could not have been made in heaven. Rhubarb is very popular on the Eastern Shore. It has quite the sour edge, but when paired with ripe strawberries its unique flavor shines through.

Pastry for single-crust 9-inch pie (see page 31), fully baked
1½ pints strawberries, stemmed
2 cups diced, peeled rhubarb (see Note on page 231)
1 cup sugar

3 tablespoons cornstarch
½ cup water
1 tablespoon fresh lemon juice
¼ teaspoon salt
1¼ cups heavy cream
Sugar to taste, for whipped cream

Prepare pastry dough and line a 9-inch pie pan; fully bake as directed.

In a pot place half of the strawberries. Mash with a fork or potato masher. Add the rhubarb and 1 cup sugar. In a small bowl combine the cornstarch, water, lemon juice, and stir to dissolve cornstarch. Add to the pot. Cook over medium heat until mixture is thick and rhubarb is tender.

Halve the remaining strawberries and arrange in the baked pie shell. Pour the rhubarb-strawberry mixture into the shell, cover, and chill.

When ready to serve, sweeten the cream with sugar, taste, whip lightly, and top the pie.

Blackberry Flummery

Serves 6

In Europe a flummery is an old-fashioned pudding thickened with grain. Americans translated this dessert into a fruit pudding thickened with cornstarch. There are numerous types of flummeries found in this area. Here's one that's "just the berries"!

2 pints blackberries
1 cup sugar
1 cup heavy cream, heated
¼ cup cornstarch

¼ cup milk
¼ teaspoon salt
Sweetened whipped cream, for accompaniment

In a heavy pot combine the blackberries and sugar and cook over medium-low heat until the sugar dissolves, about 15 minutes. Stir in the hot cream and simmer 10 minutes.

In a small bowl stir together the cornstarch, milk, and salt until smooth. Stir cornstarch mixture into the berry mixture and cook over low heat, stirring constantly, until thickened, about 10 minutes.

Pour into oiled individual molds or one large mold. Cover and chill thoroughly.

To unmold dip base of mold(s) briefly in hot water and invert onto serving plate(s). Serve topped with whipped cream.

Mouth of the Bay Preserves, Pickles, and Beverages •

Nora's Applesauce

Serves 8

You sometimes forget how easy applesauce is to make, and how far superior homemade is to store-bought. Nora Harris, who is from Salisbury, provided me with this delicious recipe for her home-made applesauce.

10 medium-sized tart apples, peeled, cored, and cut in pieces
1 cup apple cider

1 teaspoon ground cinnamon
½ teaspoon freshly grated nutmeg
Maple syrup to taste

Place the apples in a heavy-bottomed pot. Add the cider, cinnamon, and nutmeg. Cover the pot and cook over medium-low heat until the apples are soft, about 20 to 25 minutes.

Stir in maple syrup. Serve warm or cold.

Pickled Watermelon Rind

This is watermelon country and this is one of the oldest methods of "conserving" these sweet, crispy snacks. The yield on this recipe varies according to the size of your watermelon

1 medium size watermelon
1 tablespoon pickling lime
7 cups sugar
3 cups white vinegar

1 tablespoon whole cloves
1 tablespoon whole mace
2 sticks cinnamon, broken up
Juice of 2 lemons

Cut the rind off the watermelon by removing all the green skin and red pulp. Cut the rind into 2-inch squares. Place in a large bowl and add water to cover and the pickling lime. Let stand overnight.

The next day, pour off the water and rinse rind pieces well. Place rind in a heavy-bottomed pot, add water to cover, and cook about 2 hours. Drain and rinse again in cold water, set aside.

Combine the remaining ingredients in the same pot. Bring to a boil, stirring to dissolve sugar. Put the rind into the syrup and simmer until rind is transparent, about 2 hours. Skim foam from surface often.

Ladle rind and syrup into hot, sterilized jars, and process in a water bath according to standard canning procedures.

Ginger Beer Fruit Punch

Serves a crowd

An effervescent fruity punch with a zesty ginger bite.

2 cups cranberry juice
2 cups pineapple juice
2 cups grapefuit juice

Sugar, if desired
Ice cubes
3 bottles (12 ounces each) ginger
  beer

Mix the juices together in a pitcher. Check to see if the mixture is too tart for your taste. If so, sweeten with a bit of sugar. Pour into a punch bowl over ice. Add the ginger beer just as the company's coming in the door.

· *A Dockside Feed with Alva Crockett* ·

Alva Crockett at his Tangier Island home.

Virginia's Tangier Island is, to put it mildly, a hard-to-get-to kind of place. It breeds a hardy citizenry and one of the finest examples of Tangier stock is Alva Crockett, whose great uncle was Davey Crockett. Now how's that for hardy? A three-term former mayor of Tangier Island, Alva was born and raised here, and he is an outspoken champion of the attributes of Chesapeake Bay cooking, waterman's style.

After having Alva recite the dishes on his Tangier menu, I had him describe the recipe preparations and techniques in his own words, as he does best. Alva possesses a gift for calling things as he sees them. He believes in simplicity: the simplicity of cooking and the simplicity of nature. Why mess up nature by loading the cooking process with lots of spices? Makes no sense to him and, after sampling his recipes, I get his drift.

For a true taste of the cooking of a Chesapeake Bay waterman, try the Tangier Island Fifty Clam Chowder. It contains no milk or cream to mask the superb flavor of these Chesapeake Bay mollusks. Alva makes no bones about not dressing up his Fried Soft-shell Crabs. When you have fresh-from-the-Bay, alive-and-kicking soft-shells to put in the skillet, the simplest preparation is best. The salty-smoky taste of the Kale and Country Ham makes it the perfect vegetable dish to accompany the soft-shells. Alva loves puddings for dessert. His great old-fashioned recipe for a creamy banana-walnut pudding is just the right finish to this Mouth of the Bay meal.

Tangier Island Fifty Clam Chowder

Fried Soft-shell Crabs

Kale and Country Ham

Old-fashioned Banana and Walnut Pudding

Tangier Island Fifty Clam Chowder

Serves about 12

4 onions
½ pound salt pork, cut in ¼-inch
  squares
8 large potatoes
50 hard clams, well washed,
  shucked, and liquor reserved

Salt
Black pepper
Crackers, for accompaniment

"Cut the onions into little diced pieces, real fine like. The finer the better.

"Fry out the salt pork in your frying pan. Add the onions and cook 'em for a few minutes.

"Use good-size potatoes and cut 'em in little squares, no more than an inch in diameter.

"In a pot, mix your cooked onions and diced potatoes together. Cover with the clam liquor you saved and enough water to cover it all. Milk is good for babies and on cereal. That's about it, not in this chowder. Simmer until potatoes are tender.

"Cut each clam into 6 to 8 pieces. Add to the chowder and cook for about 10 minutes. Don't cook too long cause you can overcook clams so they're as tough as wood on a bar.

"Season with salt and pepper. Serve with crackers."

Fried Soft-shell Crabs

Serves 4

8 prime or jumbo soft-shell crabs
Flour seasoned with salt and black
  pepper

Crisco (solid vegetable shortening) for
  frying

"Take the soft-shells and you clean 'em yourself. Take the eyes, the 'dead men' (all them little fingers on the sides, some call it the 'devil') and cut them out.

"Roll 'em over in flour. Fry 'em on a medium heat in a little Crisco for 8 minutes on each side. Drain on paper towels.

"I ain't one of these kind for spices, so I like 'em as is, just served with plenty of french fries, but you all might like a little Tartar Sauce (see page 15) and lemon with yours."

Kale and Country Ham

Serves 4

1½ pounds kale
Salt to taste
½ pound country ham

Black pepper to taste
White or red wine vinegar to taste

"In a pot just big enough for your kale, fill it up 'bout halfway with cold water. Pour in a little salt and round about ½ pound of some smoky country ham cut up into inch squares.

"Bring all that to the boil and add the kale. Don't forget to wash your kale first or it'll be gritty as the devil. Cook on a medium heat 'bout 45 minutes to an hour.

"Pour off some of the water and season with salt and pepper. You might wanna sprinkle on a little vinegar for some bite."

Old-fashioned Banana and Walnut Pudding

Serves 4

½ cup sugar
3 tablespoons cornstarch
¼ teaspoon salt
2 cups milk
1 teaspoon vanilla extract

½ cup mashed ripe banana
½ cup chopped walnuts
Banana slices and heavy cream, for
    accompaniment (optional)

"Get yourself a saucepan. Mix the sugar, cornstarch, and salt all together.

"Mix in a little cold milk and stir it around good so it don't get lumpy. Stir in the rest of the milk. Bring to the boil over a medium heat, stirring it all the while. When it comes to the boil, keep stirring and cooking it for 1 more minute.

"Take it off the heat and beat in the vanilla.

"Now, cool pudding for a while and then stir in the bananas and nuts. Chill till good and set.

"When serving, put some sliced banana atop the pudding and a bit of cream if you like."

· Index ·